THE MARKET, COMPETITION AND DEMOCRACY

To Δ for the way she struggled

The Market, Competition and Democracy

A Critique of Neo-Austrian Economics

Stavros Ioannides

Lecturer
Department of Political Science and International Studies
Pantion University of Social and Political Sciences
Athens, Greece

Edward Elgar

Published by
Edward Elgar Publishing Limited
Gower House
Croft Road
Aldershot
Hants GU11 3HR
England

Edward Elgar Publishing Company
Old Post Road
Brookfield
Vermont 05036
USA

A CIP catalogue record for this book is available from the British Library

Library of Congress Cataloging-in-Publication Data
Ioannides, Stavros.
The market, competition, and democracy: a critique of neo -Austrian economics/Stavros Ioannides.
p. cm.
Includes bibliographical references.
1. Austrian school of economists. 2. Neoclassical school of economics. I. Title. II. Title: Neo-Austrian economics.
HB98.I63 1992
33015'7–dc20 91–40668
CIP

ISBN 1 85278 531 4

Printed and bound in Great Britain by
Billing and Sons Ltd, Worcester

Contents

Preface

Research for this book began in 1985 aiming, initially, at producing a survey of the social theories which lay at the basis of the New Right phenomenon of the last decade. For someone reared in the Keynesian reappraisal school and Marxist economics, taught at London's Birkbeck College in the 1970s, the domination of the political agenda by neoliberal ideas in the 1980s seemed to reverse all I had been trained to think as the inevitable development of the post-war capitalist economies.

By the mid-1980s the literature on the positive features of free markets was already vast, and I attacked it conscientiously. At the beginning it all seemed like a muddle of Adam Smith repetitions which did not bother to reflect on the differences separating the end of the 18th from the end of the 20th century. All in all, I felt I was dealing with a political fashion which was not worth a scientific theory name and which could easily be dismissed as 'apologetic' of the policies of neoliberal governments already in power. That is, until I encountered a stumbling block in the form of an individual called Hayek. It is not just the sheer scope and size of the man's work that is bound to intimidate anyone who approaches it critically (John Gray has aptly referred to Hayek in a private conversation with the author as the last of the political economists), but it is the fact that someone with my intellectual and academic background cannot help but form a love–hate relationship with him.

To begin with, Hayek offers one of the most powerful, and thus difficult to confront, arguments for the linkage between economic and political freedom put forward in our century. But it is his epistemological outlook that accounts for the love–hate relationship. On the one hand, we find in Hayek one of the most forceful critiques of neoclassical general equilibrium theory while, on the other, his insistence on the uncritical acceptance of tradition cannot but upset one who sees modern society as inherently unequal and unjust. Let me elucidate this further. My intellectual vantage point of democratic socialism can accommodate Hayek's view that a regime of comprehensive central planning will inevitably lead to economic collapse and political totalitarianism. However, it was precisely the same intellectual vantage point which could not but revolt against his philosophical conviction that modern man has no other choice but to 'submit to the anonymous and seemingly irrational forces of society'.

The effort to come to grips with Hayek's thought led in two directions. The first concerned the origins and extentions of his work, a line of enquiry that points to the works of Mises and Carl Menger before him, but also to the contemporary followers of their tradition. Thus a 'school' of thought began to appear, the neo-Austrian school of economics. Although serious differences between the various members of the school indeed exist, it is precisely Hayek's influence which can, I believe, be seen as providing the unifying thread that allows them to be seen as a single school of thought.

The second direction of enquiry concerned the essence of neo-Austrian theory. A critical analysis of this school has to address two issues. First, it has to assess the differences that separate it from the orthodox neoclassical theory, in order to establish whether these differences are indeed as radical as neo-Austrians themselves claim them to be. Second, it is evident that a critique has to confront the fundamental element of Hayek's – and more generally of neo-Austrian – thought, the conviction that society cannot be rationally evaluated and, thus, improved upon.

The book addresses these two questions. Concerning the first question, I will claim that the differences between the neoclassical and the neo-Austrian views are not as significant as the supporters of the latter school believe them to be. However, it is on the second question on which my critique will mainly focus. I will try to show that, contrary to what neo-Austrians believe, scientific and, thus, 'objective' understanding of social processes is indeed possible. It is precisely this possibility that provides the basis for the evaluation of modern society and for political action aiming at redesigning it. On these grounds, I will argue that the idea of democracy must not be seen merely as a technique for the election of the administrators of public affairs but, most importantly, as an absolute value which has the character of a prerequisite for human freedom. It is, therefore, the neo-Austrians' mistrust of the democratic ideal which, in the final analysis, undermines their plea for liberty.

This book is an abridged version of a PhD thesis submitted to the Pantion University of Social and Political Sciences in Athens, Greece, in 1989. There are three people who deserve special thanks for their help during the conception of my ideas and the actual writing of the thesis. Nikos Petralias has proved a patient supervisor and a tireless discussant, even when he was not given a written text to comment upon, and that was most of the time. Simon Clarke has always been ready to offer stimulating ideas on New Right politics and ideology. In many ways this book is owed to him, as he deserved at least to read the outcome of our discussions in his own language. Finally, Michalis Psalidopoulos has provided both friendship and endless encouragement, especially at times when they were both badly needed. Of course, their invaluable assistance does not imply full agreement with the final formulation of my ideas.

I wish to thank the Department of Sociology of the University of Warwick where I spent the most productive six months of the writing of the thesis as a visiting academic. Special thanks are also due to Haris Ioannidou for her help with the translation. Finally, I wish to thank Demetra Katis. As she well knows, she has been the force behind it all.

Stavros Ioannides
Athens

1 Introduction

The 'crisis of economics' theme keeps coming to the forefront of academic discussions on economic theory, increasingly so since the mid 1970s. Regardless of one's opinion about the nature of the crisis, what is nowadays obvious is that economists lack a commonly-accepted theoretical framework. This realization transcends the small circle of academics who occupy themselves with matters of theory and, as a consequence, the public's confidence in economics as a science has sharply declined. In a series of articles in *The Guardian*, Milne (1987) described precisely this aspect of the crisis when he said that 'though ever active behind the scenes, economists now barely rate above despised politicians in public esteem...'.

The collapse of the old orthodoxy

In order to understand the nature and the implications of this crisis, we have to focus upon what is above termed as the lack of a commonly-accepted theoretical framework. The question immediately raised is whether a consensus ever really existed among economists. In a social science such as economics, this question takes on a different meaning from that raised in relation to natural sciences. If Kuhn's (1967) epistemological ideas are accepted, the coexistence of more than one paradigm can, in the natural sciences, only occur during periods of transition between paradigms, thus marking what he described as a scientific revolution. In the social sciences, by contrast, the coexistence of rival paradigms seems to be the norm.

Since the domination of a paradigm in economics does not imply universal acceptance, we propose as more appropriate the use of the looser term 'orthodoxy'. An orthodox theory is one espoused not by all, but by a majority in the academic community. At different historical periods, different schools of economic thought have come to command the status of theoretical orthodoxy. Therefore, if the crisis of economic theory is taken to mean that there is not a single school of thought presently commanding this status, the first question to ask is what was the orthodoxy preceding the present crisis.

The period from the end of the war to the beginning of the 1970s was one of the rare periods of relative theoretical consensus. Keynesian macroeconomics, on the one hand, and Walrasian micro theory, on the other, constituted the theoretical edifice of academic curriculae in economics around the world. Although the articulation of the two approaches has never been entirely frictionless, the 'neoclassical synthesis' appeared to have convinced the majority of economists. Once the problem of articulation could be assumed convincingly settled, this theoretical dualism seemed to offer some research advantages. At a high level of abstraction, micro theory could investigate the principles of coherence of the market system, while macroeconomic analysis could focus on the overall movement of the economy on the basis of more realistic assumptions, in other words by setting aside the various 'perfections' of micro theory.

The picture changed dramatically, however, around the beginning of the 1970s. Stagflation, the fiscal crisis of the state and the crisis of the welfare state are often cited riddles that confronted the previous economic orthodoxy. As the decade progressed, the effectiveness of Keynesian prescriptions for the attainment of full employment was rapidly diminishing. The debate between those who consider this ineffectiveness as proof of the failure of Keynesianism as a whole, and those who see it as signifying only the failure of a particular version of Keynesianism, still continues. What no one doubts, however, is that fewer and fewer economists continued to believe that the orthodox theory could offer convincing answers to the problems confronting western societies. The crisis of economic theory had therefore surfaced and the orthodoxy had collapsed.

It was, of course, inevitable that this crisis would have profound implications on the level of politics as well. Economics is, after all, the most political of social sciences, as its propositions have a direct effect upon social conditions. It was, therefore, to be expected that the crisis of Keynesian orthodoxy would negatively affect the credibility of that part of the political spectrum – social democracy – which had, in the post-war era, made Keynesianism the cornerstone of its political philosophy.

The political and moral commitment to full employment and income redistribution, which were the pivots of the social democratic political project, seemed in the 1970s to be increasingly incompatible with the need to fight inflation and depression. This explains why the new theories which appeared in this period seemed to share two fundamental elements. The first can be termed an 'either-or' element: economic policy can either aim at curbing inflation or at maintaining full employment, but it cannot achieve both goals at the same time. And since the ineffectiveness of Keynesian policies in maintaining full employment was evident, it was inevitable that the latter goal would be given priority. The second element concerns the political origin of the new theories. The impasse of a political project perceived as originating in the left, made it inevitable that the new theories would be inspired by the political philosophy of the conservative part of the political spectrum.

This conservative political orientation of the new theories explains why they are often described by a single label, whether this is 'neoliberalism' or 'economic theories of the New Right'.[1] Their common political origin should not, however, conceal some fundamental differences among them. It is precisely these differences that account for the fact that none of these theories has convincingly managed to claim for itself the status of a new orthodoxy, in spite of their vehement attack upon Keynesianism. It is indicative that while in the mid-1970s monetarism seemed the school of thought capable of raising such a claim, the early 1980s witnessed a steep decline in its appeal to the academic community. The theory of New Classical Economics had instead caught the interest of the majority of economists, particularly in the US. Since the mid-1970s there has also been increasing interest in the revival of the neo-Austrian school, which takes a critical stance both toward Keynesianism and the new theories mentioned above.

How can one account for the phenomenon of schools of thought rising and declining within such short periods of time? Any appeal to notions like analytical superiority or predictive ability do not seem to offer satisfactory explanations of such changes. In the social sciences, theories are, after all, notoriously non-testable. A more plausible explanation can instead be achieved if we seek the factors which explain their appeal to the economic community in the methodological, ideological, and political content of each theory.

Let us note, for instance, some general characteristics of the three neoliberal theories mentioned above. First, they all see the restriction of the state's role in the economy as a major precondition of economic revival in today's world. Second, and more important for our purposes, is the fact that all three theories came to the forefront of academic attention in recent years, but their basic principles had been put forward some decades ago. Monetarism is based on a modified version of the quantity theory of money expounded by Milton Friedman in the 1950s, while the basic premise of the New Classical School – the 'rational expectations' hypothesis – was introduced by Muth in 1961.[2] As for the neo-Austrian school, its principles were put forward in the inter-war period by Ludwig von Mises and Friedrich Hayek, although its supporters claim that its origins are to be found further back in the thought of Carl Menger. The reasons for these theories returning to the forefront after years of relative oblivion, are certainly not to be sought within any developments in academic discussions but, rather, in wider changes in the overall intellectual, ideological and political climate of the last decades.

The common elements of these three theories should not, of course, blur their important differences. We will here stress one basic difference that reveals two diverse positions toward the Keynesian orthodoxy. Although both monetarism and the New Classical school are critical of Keynesianism, their principles do not question the Walrasian orthodoxy of micro theory. In effect, their macroeconomics can be perceived as an extension of the Walrasian principles to the level of macro theory. When Friedman introduced the 'permanent income hypothesis' or when Lucas incorporated the 'rational expectations hypothesis' into his theory, what they were actually trying to achieve was the introduction of the perfect knowledge assumption of micro theory in macroeconomics. By contrast, the theorists of the neo-Austrian school aim their critique both against Keynesian as well as against Walrasian orthodoxy. For them, the very distinction between micro and macro theory is methodologically unacceptable. It is precisely this character of a general alternative to the orthodoxy of the past that makes the study of neo-Austrian theory especially interesting.

The radicalism of the neo-Austrian school

The fact that neo-Austrian theory stands critically toward the dualism of the previous orthodoxy, allows its supporters to claim for it the status of the only general theory in economics. It is this supposed generality that ascribes to neo-Austrian theory a *radical* character, in the sense that it challenges fundamental and hitherto unquestioned premises of economic thought.[3] A survey of the points of disagreement between the neo-Austrian and orthodox theories will reveal a range of differences that can only be compared with the large differences separating Marxian from orthodox theory. We will, of course, return in length upon all these differences in the coming chapters. We wish, however, to briefly present here the main features of the neo-Austrian school which reflect its radicalism.

A forgotten offspring of the marginal revolution

According to the orthodox view on the development of economic doctrines, all modern schools of thought have their origins in the 'marginal revolution' of the 1870s. Jevons, Menger and Walras are supposed to have introduced a homogeneous paradigm based on the subjectivism of the concept of marginal utility as well as on the mathematical expression of economic relations through the use of marginal analysis. Neo-Austrians reject this homogeneity on the grounds that what is today perceived as the paradigm introduced by the marginal revolution, stems exclusively from the work of Walras.[4] Claiming that their theory revives the specifically Mengerian tradition of the marginal revolution, neo-Austrians can thus argue that they propose a much deeper reconstruction of the foundations of economic thought than any other of the new theories.

It is indeed interesting to consider the relation of the other new theories to the previous orthodoxy. Monetarism is merely a version of the Keynesian model with two important modifications: the quantity theory of money replaces Keynes's 'liquidity preference', and the 'permanent income' hypothesis replaces the Keynesian assumptions about the marginal propensity to consume. The New Classical theory, on the other hand, introduces a macroeconomic model in which individuals are in a position to foresee correctly all possible effects of changes in the money supply. Compared to these essentially minor revisions of Keynesianism, neo-Austrians seem justified in arguing that a truly general theory must necessarily involve a much deeper revision of economic principles.

The rejection of the distinction between micro and macro theory
As already pointed out, the methodological distinction between micro and macroeconomics is rejected by neo-Austrians. It has been seen, however, that both monetarism and the New Classical school try to bridge the gap between the two levels of analysis, by transferring assumptions from the micro to the macro level. Could one then argue that the transcendence of this methodological dualism is not an exclusive feature of neo-Austrian theory, but that it characterizes all new theories? In fact, neo-Austrians are not just seeking ways to bridge this dualism, but actually to deny its methodological legitimacy. More specifically, they consider the level of macro theory methodologically unacceptable. Believing that economic aggregates do not interact or relate to each other, they find a theory which presumes to explain such interactions and interrelations a mere absurdity. In contrast with the other new theories, therefore, the neo-Austrian school is not seeking to replace Keynesianism with an alternative macroeconomics but is, rather, arguing for the total abandonment of the macroeconomic level of analysis.

The rejection of the concept of equilibrium
The centrality of the concept of equilibrium for the theoretical orthodoxy which developed out of the marginal revolution is undoubted. This does not mean, however, that the limitations of this concept have not been acknowledged. In fact, its static nature, in the sense that it presents the economy as a motionless system that only changes as a result of exogenous disturbances, has been repeatedly pointed out. All efforts, however, to construct a disequilibrium theory have not managed to displace the equilibrium concept from the toolbox of theoretical economics. Thus, the outright rejection of this concept by neo-Austrians, coupled with their insistence that their approach constitutes the only truly dynamic theory, seems indeed a radical claim.

This neo-Austrian position is analysed in depth in Chapter 6. Some of its implications are, however, pointed out here. An objective understanding of economic processes presupposes that the economy can be described by a representative moment of its functioning – the state of equilibrium. By rejecting the equilibrium concept, one, therefore, rejects the possibility of an objective knowledge of economic phenomena. This means that the outcomes of the operation of the market system cannot be objectively known and, consequently, improved upon by any sort of exogenous intervention. Thus, any intervention in the functioning of the system must be seen as hindering its own dynamics. The political implications of this approach are of course obvious: state interventionism leads to stagnation rather than development.

The economy and institutions

According to the predominant view on the development of economic thought, the marginal revolution armed economic theory with the tools with which it could tackle concrete questions with the rigour of the natural sciences. However, the significance of the marginal revolution actually goes much further than the achievement of analytical rigour. The central concern of classical political economy was the problem of order in capitalist society, along with the more specific question of the institutions that helped maintain this order. In contrast, the marginal revolution established the study of exchange as the only legitimate object of economic science. Thus, the problem of institutions was taken to lie beyond the scope of economics and to be the object of another science.[5]

Neo-Austrian theory reinstates this problem as a legitimate object of economic enquiry. Actually, neo-Austrians consider the question of the compatibility of institutions with the requirements of market society to be the central object of enquiry. The role of the institutions which are considered to be products of the market order is seen as positive, since they are, by definition, compatible with it. Institutions, on the other hand, which are the result of the political process, are supposed to affect market society in a negative manner, as their functioning may hinder the market's evolution. Thus, the radical element of neo-Austrian theory lies in the fact that it presumes to be in a position to evaluate institutions.

An alternative methodology

The most radical element of neo-Austrian theory stems, however, from the fact that it is based on a methodology significantly different from that of orthodox theory. Stated briefly, the principle of methodological individualism replaces the positivist outlook shared by both neoclassical and Keynesian economics. What is particularly interesting about neo-Austrian methodology, is the fact that its principles stem from the field of the philosophy of knowledge – an area of philosophical enquiry much wider than that of economic methodology. This is especially apparent in the work of Hayek, who deals with issues as diverse as jurisprudence, political science, epistemology and psychology.[6] Neo-Austrians may indeed be right in claiming that their economic methodology is only part of a much more comprehensive philosophical outlook, which critically differentiates itself from the whole edifice of the orthodox epistemology of the social sciences.

The appeal of neo-Austrian theory, and its political implications

The current revival of interest in neo-Austrian ideas is indeed remarkable, considering that the school was thought of as having been irreversibly defeated, after its blooming in the 1920s and 1930s. It was the alleged defeat of neo-Austrians in two of the major debates of the 1930s – trade cycle theory and the socialist calculation debate – that led to the eclipse of the school. The awarding of the Nobel prize to Hayek in 1974, jointly with G. Myrdal, marks, therefore, the revival of the school and, at the same time, the reversal of an academic verdict that remained unchallenged for more than three decades. Although the circle of economists who consider themselves supporters of the neo-Austrian paradigm is still small, their influence seems to be slowly growing. An explanation of this growing appeal stems, as we will argue, from the fact that neo-Austrian theory seems to drive a political position to its logical limits.

In order to clarify this assertion, we need to compare the central position of neo-Austrian theory with those of the other new schools. Monetarists are strong critics of state interventionism, but they do not deny the importance of the state's role in the economy. In fact, they assign to the state the vital function of controlling the money supply. A similar position is clear in the work of the New Classical theorists. The rational expectations assumption implies that state interventionism is ineffective, as all state actions will be correctly anticipated by individuals. However, even within this framework, state action *can* be effective, provided that it comes as a big unanticipated shock. By contrast, neo-Austrian theory does not merely aim to restrict the state's involvement in the economy but, rather, to deny the effectiveness of any such involvement. The radical political conclusion of this position is a demand for such institutional reforms which will render any intervention impossible.

Three major questions

The range of differences between neo-Austrian and orthodox theories is so wide that the mere task of singling out the central issues on which our critique must focus is a problem on its own. Let us address this problem by posing the following question: What theoretical view of the functioning of a market system can be conceptually compatible with the main political conclusion of neo-Austrian theory, which is the rejection of any state role in the economy?

It seems that this conclusion can only be based on a conception of economic phenomena as being fundamentally indeterminate. This claim can become apparent when the implications of the converse conception are considered. If the workings of the economy are understood as determinate phenomena, then the state can always intervene in order to correct economic outcomes. If, on the other hand, the state can never objectively perceive the functioning of the market system, as neo-Austrians believe, this possibility of intervention ceases to exist. In economic theory, therefore, the 'fundamental indeterminateness' assumption means that the observer of economic phenomena can never predict the outcomes of market processes and, consequently, the results of his/her intervention upon them.

If the indeterminateness assumption is brought under closer scrutiny, it is noticed that it is made up of two distinct elements. The first is the denial of the possibility of any objective knowledge of economic phenomena. According to neo-Austrians, the observers of economic activity can only notice and study the actions of individuals, and it is only upon such observations that they can construct theories about the operation of the system as a whole. Aggregate phenomena, on the other hand, can never be observed empirically and cannot, consequently, serve as a basis for scientific knowledge. As products of the interaction among countless individual activities, they are bound to be only transitory, since they are sensitive to changes in individual behaviour. Thus, from the point of view of the observer of economic phenomena, the operation of the market system constitutes an aggregate phenomenon which must be considered as indeterminate, in the sense that it lacks any objectively perceivable regularities.

The second element of indeterminateness concerns what neo-Austrians claim to be the dynamic nature of their theory. Unlike orthodox neoclassical theory, which perceives the individual as passively reacting to price signals, the individual of neo-Austrian theory forms and follows strategies for the attainment of his/her goals. Changes in the individuals' behaviour cannot thus be considered as changes in the data of analysis but, rather, as the heart of the problem economic theory is trying to explain. And since the interaction between individual strategies never subsides, the economic process must be conceived as being in ceaseless motion. Economic dynamics is, therefore, an entirely indeterminate phenomenon, since changes in individuals' strategies are entirely subjectively determined and thus unpredictable in principle.

As the rejection of any objective understanding of economic processes as well as the dynamic conception of the market economy as a system in ceaseless motion, seem to be the two sides of the indeterminateness assumption, a critical analysis of neo-Austrian theory must set these two issues at the centre of its attention.

The objectivity of economic processes

As already mentioned, the neo-Austrian rejection of any objective understanding of economic phenomena is intended as a critical argument against the positivist outlook of the neoclassical school. Thus, the critical analysis of this position must immediately deal with an important methodological problem. Is it possible to reaffirm an objective perspective of the economy without, at the same time, having to revert to a typically neoclassical analytical framework?

Such a reversion can indeed be avoided, if the analysis retains one of the basic concepts of neo-Austrian theory, that of process.[7] As an analytical tool, the concept of process consists of two distinct elements. The first is the principle of endogeneity, the view of all economic processes as being endogenously mobilized. This principle is, in essence, entirely incompatible with any static understanding of economic activity, that is, any idea that the market system can be concisely and objectively represented by one of its moments – a view which would a priori exclude any endogenous interaction in the system.

The second element, that of time, stems from the acceptance of the endogeneity principle. If it is assumed, as neoclassical theory does, that individuals only react to price changes, then the lapse of time between the initial stimulus and the individual's response is theoretically insignificant. In the behaviourist framework, what counts is the certainty of the response, and not the time that it takes to reveal itself. What counts even less is the sequence of events which will follow, as the stimulus–response framework describes a closed system which does not allow any feedback effects. On the basis of this reasoning, the neoclassical school rids itself of the necessity to consider the element of time in its theorizing. The acceptance of the endogeneity principle, however, changes dramatically our understanding of the functioning of the economy. The series of events kept in perpetual motion by the interaction among the individuals' strategies cannot be compressed to a single moment, but it must be understood as unfolding in real time. Moreover, the sequence of events becomes an issue of fundamental importance, as each event really constitutes the cause of the one succeeding it.

As employed by neo-Austrians, the concept of process seems a major weapon against the objective perception of economic activity of the neoclassical school. Interestingly, however, neo-Austrians are not the first to discover the potential of this concept, as it has always been a standard theoretical tool of Marxian theory. But whereas neo-Austrians use the concept of process to establish the fundamental indeterminateness of economic activity, Marxists have always employed it both in their critique of neoclassicism as well as in their effort to establish the objective tendencies of economic development. Therefore, it is Marxian theory which seems to us to offer the desired analytical framework, as it transcends the positivist outlook of the neoclassical school while allowing, at the same time, an objective understanding of economic phenomena. Our aim is not, of course, to juxtapose

Marxian and neo-Austrian theory, but to show that some of the most questionable elements in the assumptions of the latter can only be overcome within the alternative analytical framework of Marxian theory.

On this basis, we will try to establish two points. The first is that, contrary to what neo-Austrians believe, the concept of process enables us to objectively identify patterns and tendencies of economic activity. Therefore, the fact that economic phenomena emerge as products of innumerable individual actions does not mean that they are not characterized by objectively-definable properties. Our second point concerns the objectivity of theoretical categories. It will be argued that some of the central concepts of neo-Austrian theory, like those of entrepreneurship or capital goods, are not entirely subjective, as claimed by neo-Austrians, but that they take an objective character, that of capital. Of course, this is a kind of objectivity radically different from that of the neoclassical school, since it is not based on the empirically observed properties of these categories but, rather, on the objectivity of their function in the market system. If convincingly argued, these two points constitute a major blow to the neo-Austrian position on the question of economic objectivity.

The dynamic character of neo-Austrian theory

The concept of process is also seen by neo-Austrians as justifying their claim about the dynamic character of their theory. We have already seen, however, that they consider a dynamic theory to be a major prerequisite for the establishment of the fundamental indeterminateness assumption. We are thus faced with a paradox. We have pointed out that the concept of process consists of two elements, the principle of endogeneity and the element of time. Evidently, the concept of process introduces a causal understanding of the sequences of economic events. Therefore, in neo-Austrian theory, causality paradoxically coexists with indeterminateness.

The question now raised is whether a theory based on such reasoning can be considered to be genuinely dynamic. First, it will be argued that a necessary feature of any genuinely dynamic theory must be its ability to determine the direction of economic change. We will show that while neo-Austrians can account for the perpetual motion within the market system, they cannot exclude the possibility that the overall characteristics of the system may remain unaltered through time. We will discover that the direction of change of these characteristics is, within neo-Austrian theory, a matter of accident. The incorporation of dynamics in economic theory seems, therefore, to be as difficult for neo-Austrians as it is for the neoclassical school.

To challenge our argument, neo-Austrians could, of course, argue that their theory can establish the mechanism that sets economic change in motion, even though it cannot determine its direction. This mechanism is in fact described by their theory of capital. In their account, it is the independent decisions of individuals to consume less today in order to consume more in the future, which account for the phenomenon of economic change.

The second point we will try to establish is that the entirely subjective category of capital of neo-Austrian theory is incompatible with the concept of the cyclical reproduction of the economy, which is based, in its turn, on the concept of the reproduction of capital. We will argue that, without the idea of 'reproduction', capital cannot fulfill the role which economic theory has always assigned to it – the role, that is, of linking the present with the future. Thus, since neo-Austrian theory cannot accommodate the idea of 'reproduction', its dynamic character is put into question.

From economics to politics

The rejection of the neo-Austrian position on the issues of objectivity and dynamics leads, as has been seen, to the rejection of the fundamental indeterminateness assumption. Our position must not, of course, be interpreted as a reaffirmation of a positivist determinism, of the kind that characterizes neoclassical theory. In our view, what the economist-observer can perceive is not every minute detail of economic activity, but only the general patterns and tendencies which the market system produces. However, the rejection of the indeterminateness assumption also sheds doubt on the central political conclusion of neo-Austrian theory, which sees the role of the state in the economy as a priori negative as well as coercive.

Let us briefly describe the reasoning behind the neo-Austrians' political position. The indeterminateness assumption implies that the market system constitutes an entirely self-regulating 'order'. Thus, its functioning does not require any supra-economic regulation, except for the institutional arrangements of the liberal state – freedom of property and contract. On these grounds, neo-Austrians consider state interventionism not as a requirement of market activity itself but, rather, as a product of the invasion of politics in the sphere of the economy. The steadily-increasing role of the state in the economies of all capitalist countries since the end of the 19th century is, therefore, explained as the result of the gradual extension of suffrage, which is seen as turning governments to electoral hostages of organized interest groups. In order to reverse this tendency, modern society must, according to neo-Austrians, accept the restriction of the democratic principle in the administration of public affairs.

The first point to try and establish concerns the neo-Austrian account of the development of state interventionism. The rejection of the indeterminateness assumption and the reaffirmation of the concept of reproduction shed doubt on any perception of the market system which stresses its self-regulating nature. It will be argued that the process of the reproduction of capital creates the obstacles to its own expansion. Capital accumulation can, therefore, continue only if assisted by a supra-economic institution like the state, the operation of which is not bound by these obstacles in the same way that the accumulation of private capital is. This reasoning leads, of course, to a complete reversal of the neo-Austrian account of the state's role in the economy. The extension of this role is not a product of the sphere of politics but of the economic process itself. The neo-Austrian insistence on the total abolition of any such role seems, therefore, as an entirely Utopian aim.

A second point which will be argued concerns the social control of the process of reproduction. Since state interventionism is a requirement of the sphere of the economy, the restriction of democratic politics cannot abolish the state's involvement in economic affairs. Instead, what it can actually achieve is the abolition of any social control on the activities of the state. The latter would, therefore, still play a decisive role in shaping the social outcomes of the reproduction process. The performance of each member of society in the market process would still depend not only on his/her individual efforts but also on the operation of a supra-economic institution over which he/she has absolutely no control. Therefore, the restriction of the sphere of democratic politics would actually lead to a situation where each individual's ability to shape the framework of social activity would be determined exclusively by his/her ownership of capital. In the last chapter of the book it will indeed be argued that, instead of promoting freedom as neo-Austrians believe, their theory necessarily leads to an authoritarian political project.

Our methodology

Neo-Austrians claim that their theory constitutes a general critique of economic orthodoxy. Thus, although this analysis aims to establish some specific critical points, it is this claim of generality that is really at issue. The exposition of the theory must, therefore, be structured in a way that brings out both the range of theoretical issues that neo-Austrians deal with and the articulation of their specific arguments into a coherent analytical framework. The presentation of each issue of neo-Austrian theory will begin by identifying the points of difference from the previous orthodoxy. In questions related to the institution of the market, its differences will be traced from orthodox micro-theory. In questions related to the overall functioning of the economy, the focus will be on the differences from the orthodox version of Keynesianism.

We will carry out our critique in what could be described as three consecutive stages. During the first stage, the analysis will operate within the logical framework of each neo-Austrian argument. We will, therefore, begin by accepting this framework, and will then proceed to pose two questions.

The first is whether each argument really constitutes a radical break with the previous orthodoxy, and the second whether it seems to support the neo-Austrian positions on economic objectivity and dynamics.

The second stage of the analysis concerns the common elements between neo-Austrian and Marxian theories. We will observe that in matters where the differences between neo-Austrian and orthodox theories seem to be deeper, the former also appears to come very close to the Marxian analytical framework. This should not be surprising if one bears in mind some important similarities between the two approaches. We have, initially, a common starting point for both schools: their critical stance toward the positivist methodology of orthodox theory. Second, both theories reject the empirical objectivity of economic phenomena, as they are trying to locate their causes in the interaction of forces not immediately perceivable by the economist-observer. Finally, they both investigate the dynamics of this interaction, by rejecting from the outset an understanding of the economy as a system at rest and by employing the concept of process.

The third stage of the analysis will attempt to reveal the limits of neo-Austrian theory as a critique of orthodox economics. If it is shown that neo-Austrian theory does not succeed in its effort to deny any objective understanding of economic processes, and if it is also shown that the economic model it proposes does not differ significantly from the static model of the orthodox neoclassical school, then the assertion that neo-Austrian theory constitutes a radical critique of economic orthodoxy will be undermined. We will claim such a critique to be indeed possible, but only if based on an analytical framework that transcends the rigidly subjectivist neo-Austrian outlook and tends toward a Marxian framework of analysis.

An outline of the book

Chapter 2 will deal with the historical origins and the central methodological premises of the neo-Austrian school. The emergence of the Austrian school in the work of Carl Menger will be examined, and the question of Menger's relation to Jevons and Walras – the other protagonists of the marginal revolution will be addressed. It will be shown that some of the distinguishing principles of Menger's unique methodology were abandoned by his immediate disciples Wieser and Böhm Bawerk, and were only revived some decades later by Mises and Hayek, thus marking the emergence of the neo-Austrian school. Finally, the methodological principles of neo-Austrian theory, as put forward by Mises and Hayek, will be presented.

The next four chapters deal with the different aspects of the concept of the market process, and examine its relevance for the neo-Austrian positions on the questions of objectivity and dynamics. If the orthodox terminology could be accepted here, this part of the book could be said to deal with neo-

Austrian micro theory. Chapter 3 is devoted to the presentation and analysis of the neo-Austrian theories of competition and knowledge. Chapter 4 deals with the neo-Austrian critique of the theory of monopoly. Chapter 5 analyses the theory of entrepreneurship. Finally, in Chapter 6, the neo-Austrian rejection of the equilibrium concept is examined.

Chapters 7 to 10 can also be considered as dealing with one integral part of neo-Austrian theory, in the sense that they present and analyse the different aspects of the neo-Austrian understanding of the overall movement of the economy. Chapter 7 examines the theory of capital, and Chapter 8 the theory of money. Chapter 9 deals with the neo-Austrian theory of the trade cycle. Finally, in chapter 10, the neo-Austrian critique of macroeconomic policy is examined, with special emphasis on the most recent and radical neo-Austrian proposal, that is, the denationalization of money.

Chapters 11 and 12 deal mainly with the political implications of neo-Austrian theory. In Chapter 11, the positions of the two camps during the 'socialist calculation' debate are analysed, and on this basis a criticism of the neo-Austrian understanding of the state's role in the economy is attempted. In the last chapter, after a brief review of the conclusions on the questions of objectivity and dynamics, the social content of neo-Austrian political ideas as well as the relation between politics and economics which they imply are examined.

Notes

1. For a concise presentation of these theories see Gamble (1986).
2. See Friedman (1956) and Muth (1961).
3. For an account of the radical element in neo-Austrian theory see Addleson (1986), who compares the 'radical subjectivism' of the neo-Austrian school to 'neoclassical subjectivism'.
4. See Kirzner (1981, p. 111).
5. As Clarke (1982) claims, this science is sociology.
6. See Hayek (1952a), which is his major work in theoretical psychology.
7. On the fundamental character of the concept of process for neo-Austrian theory see Lachmann (1976).

2 Origins and methodological principles of neo-Austrian theory

Contemporary neo-Austrians see the foundations of their theory as stemming from the thought of Carl Menger. It is for this reason that the discussion of neo-Austrian methodology must begin with a brief assessment of Menger's contribution to economics. However, before proceeding to establish the links between Menger and his 20th-century followers, it is necessary to examine the uniqueness of his contribution to the marginal revolution – a uniqueness which sets his thought apart from the theories of the other protagonists of the 1870s.

According to the dominant account of the history of economic doctrines, Menger, Jevons and Walras introduced in the 1870s – independently of each other – the principle of marginal utility. Though differences among the three economists are acknowledged, they are thought of as being of minor importance and are usually taken as convenient criteria for assessing the methodological competence of the three protagonists. Taking the rigour of modern neoclassical theory as the norm, it is, of course, no wonder that Walras is closest to modern standards of rigour.[1] We will begin our reference to Menger's thought by examining the differences between Menger's formal analysis and that of orthodox neoclassical theory, and then proceed to investigate the methodological principles that account for these differences.

Menger and neoclassical formalism

The subjectivist theory of value which is implicit in the principle of marginal utility, is usually supposed to constitute the fundamental innovation of the marginal revolution. Instead of being conceived as a function of costs of production – as it was seen by classical economists – the value of commodities was now thought to be determined by the subjective valuations of consumers. Though it is certainly true that subjectivism is a common element in the theories of Menger, Jevons and Walras, there seem to be differences concerning the degree of their subjectivism. Walras maintained that the principle of competition rests on the individual consumer's valuations of utility. He stressed (1984, p. 84), however, that the task of the economist is not to study individual behaviour but to discover the laws to which individual exchanges tend to conform 'automatically'. The subjectivist element seems to be stronger in Jevons, since his principle of marginal utility is constructed on the basis of the evaluating behaviour of a single individual.

However, even Jevons (1970, p. 86) finally admitted that the object of theory is not the investigation of individual behaviour but the study of 'an aggregate of individuals'.

Menger's unique subjectivism is quickly revealed in the first pages of his *Principles of Economics* (1981), in his attempt to provide a definition of the economic 'good'. In order for a thing to be considered a good, more is necessary than the physical property of its being capable to satisfy a human need. What is also essential is human knowledge of this capability.[2] This link between subjectivism and knowledge shows that the subjectivist element in Menger's thought is not merely a methodological step toward the study of economic aggregates, but is itself an object of study. The introduction of human knowledge in economic theory poses the question of how individuals form their views of the world or how they acquire knowledge. At the core of Menger's theory we find, therefore, a conception of human action as information-seeking behaviour in a world characterised by uncertainty.[3] Thus, nothing seems more distant from Menger's subjectivism than the perfect knowledge and perfect certainty assumptions of the neoclassical school.

Menger's aversion to mathematics is a second distinguishing characteristic of his theory. In the literature on the marginal revolution, the views are divided on whether this aversion is a result of Menger's lack of mathematical training or is an a priori methodological stance.[4] However, bearing in mind Hutchison's remark that in the marginal revolution the adjective is more important than the noun,[5] Menger's anti-mathematical stance poses the question of how truly marginalist his theory is.

If we consider the use of differential calculus as the essence of the marginalist method, Menger's economics will certainly not qualify as marginalist. If we take notice, however, of the way in which he (1981, p. 127) described, through an arithmetical example, the process by which commodity values are derived from individual valuations, the marginalist element of his approach seems beyond doubt. In this example, Menger showed that consumers try to equalize the utility they attain from the last unit of each commodity they acquire. He stressed himself, however, that he aimed not at the mathematical formulation of a utility function but, rather, at illustrating that the process by which goods acquire value is a manifestation of the subjective character of economic behaviour. We will later see that it is precisely the subjectivist element of Menger's thought which precludes the mathematical formulation of economic relations.

A third, often cited, distinguishing feature of Menger's theory is its lack of a concept of equilibrium as well as of the related notions of perfect market or perfect competition. In Menger's price theory, the analysis follows exactly the reverse direction from the one followed by orthodox neoclassical microeconomics. He began by studying the exchange between two individuals isolated from the rest of the community and then proceeded to study exchange under monopolistic conditions, in order to finally address the case of 'bilateral competition'. What is remarkable is that, even in this final case, Menger (1981, p. 224) believed that sellers are in a position to set prices as if they were monopolists. The difference from the 'price-taking' assumption – under perfect competition – of neoclassical theory is, of course, striking.

The absence of an equilibrium concept from Menger's thought raises some critical questions regarding his theory. The first is whether it affects his ability to explain the formation of prices. As Jaffé (1976, p. 519–20) points out, however, Menger did not intend to explain prices but to show the process of interaction among the deeper forces at work during market exchange. A second question is whether Menger recognized at all the existence of forces which lead markets toward some kind of equilibrium. Streissler answers affirmatively stressing, however, at the same time, the importance of time in Menger's thought.[6] What was theoretically important for Menger was not the analysis of the equilibrium state but of the process of exchange. It is this 'process analysis' which Hayek (1973, p. 279) considers to be one of the most important methodological cleavages between Menger's theory and the static general equilibrium approach of Walras, and which lies behind the concept of the market process of neo-Austrians.

Philosophical origins and extensions of Menger's theory

The publication of Menger's *Principles of Economics* in 1871 marked the birth of the Austrian school. Since Austria did not have any indigenous economic tradition, one must ask what were the intellectual influences Menger received. Following the literature on Menger, we could separate those influences into negative and positive ones. The former include classical political economy as well as the Historical school of economics, which, at the time, commanded the position of theoretical orthodoxy in Germany.[7] The positive influences include, on the one hand, the Aristotelian philosophical tradition which was particularly strong in Austrian 19th century culture and, on the other hand, the subjectivist philosophical and psychological conceptions of value, which were later to find their fullest expression in the theories of Brentano and his followers.[8]

It is this latter subjectivist approach that explains Menger's reaction towards classical political economy. The latter understood value as determined by production costs, in contrast to the theory proposed by Menger which saw value as a function of the subjectivist concept of utility. His reaction now against the Historical school concerned the latter's methodological principles. According to the Historical school, the only epistemologically legitimate understanding of economic phenomena is one based on the actual historical facts. Thus, the proper method of approaching economic phenomena is inductive, in the sense that it must not attempt to analyse them in terms of universally applicable laws but in terms of the particular characteristics the economist can actually observe.[9]

Menger's methodology is, by contrast, entirely deductive, as he sees the study of economic phenomena grounded on the observer's ability of 'understanding'.[10] What is it, however, that the observer can really understand? It is certainly not every minute detail that his/her senses register. As a result of sharing the same social experiences with his/her fellow human-beings, the observer is able to abstract from concrete details and understand the 'essence' of economic phenomena.[11] In contrast, therefore, with the Historical school which treated all aspects of reality as scientific data, the Aristotelian Menger concentrated on the essence, the deeper reality that lies beneath the concrete appearance of a phenomenon. It is this methodological premise that really explains Menger's aversion to mathematical formulations. As he explained himself in a letter to Walras (1965, p. 3), quantitative analysis can never reveal the 'nature' of economic phenomena.

The notions of understanding and essence lie at the heart of Menger's deductive – or 'a priorist' as it is often described – method. Both notions are constituted on a theoretical level which lies beyond any empirical testing. Consequently, a theory based on them will necessarily be itself non-testable.[12] Such a theory is, according to Menger, 'exact', not in the sense that it fits the exact historical facts but in the sense that it can explain the exact essence of economic phenomena.

In such a view, the economist must first decide which phenomena he/she is in a position to understand. If he/she chooses to concentrate on phenomena which appear at the level of the economic system as a whole – the 'national economy' in Menger's terminology – the analysis is bound to fail. As in physics, one cannot know the outcome of a system of forces unless one knows the individual forces that constitute it. The economist, therefore, cannot understand the phenomena of the national economy prior to understanding the economic actions of individuals. It is only at this level that he/she can understand the motivation that lies behind these actions and, therefore, capture their essence. It is, thus, only at the level of individual action that the economist can single out, from the numberless human activities that appear in reality, those types of behaviour which constitute the most elementary form of the phenomenon he/she is trying to analyse.

Having established the essence of economic phenomena at the level of individual action, economists can then proceed to compose a theory capable of explaining the phenomena which appear at the level of the national economy. It is on these grounds that Menger described his method as 'atomistic' or 'compositive'. In essence, we have here the approach of what would later be termed methodological individualism – a stance which lies at the foundation of neo-Austrian methodology.[13]

One of the most difficult problems facing Menger's method can now be addressed. Menger acknowledged phenomena which do not seem, at least at first glance, to be explainable on the basis of the principle of methodological individualism. The analysis of institutions, such as the market and money, or even language and the system of justice, seems to require a transcendence of this principle, since their emergence cannot be attributed to an individual's actions. Menger's problem was, therefore, to prove that the origins of such institutions could still be traced back to the actions of individuals, while, at the same time, avoiding a 'social contract' understanding of them as products of some collective will. His solution (1985, p. 155) was to consider these phenomena as products of human action but not of human design, in other words, as unintended results of human action, in the sense that their emergence was not planned by any single or collective will.[14] With this approach, the individualist basis for the analysis of these phenomena is reaffirmed, as will be seen in Chapter 8, in the analysis of Menger's account of the historical emergence of money.

Menger and the Austrian school of economics

Though it is true that Menger's thought was not the product of an indigenous economic tradition, it is also true that during the 50 years that followed the publication of his *Principles*, Vienna came to be accepted as the most important centre of economic theory outside the Anglo-Saxon world. Menger's work certainly initiated an Austrian tradition in economics, though the question is whether the initiation of a tradition is equivalent to the establishment of a school. In order to show that this is a valid question, we need merely list some names of young Austrian economists who were prominent in the debates of the 1920s and 1930s and who emigrated shortly before Austria's annexation to Germany. There is Haberler, Hayek, Machlup, Mises, Morgenstern, Rosenstein-Rodan, Schumpeter, and so on – to mention only those who were to attain international recognition in the next few decades.[15] To what extent can these economists be seen as constituting a single theoretical school?

Interestingly, this difficulty in precisely describing the Austrian school does not arise only for the Austrians of the third generation mentioned above but also for Menger's immediate disciples, Wieser and Böhm Bawerk. The differences between their theories and the thought of their mentor – especially in matters of method – are indeed striking. Wieser constructed his theory on the assumptions of perfect competition and price-taking behaviour of individuals.[16] In contrast to Menger, he also expressed a moderate reformist tendency, aiming at the satisfaction of the 'general' interest of society.[17]

Böhm Bawerk, on the other hand, based his theory of capital on a view which treated capital as an objective category, entirely independent of the level of individual action.[18] Menger himself was to write that Böhm Bawerk's theory 'is one of the greatest errors ever committed'.[19]

It is easily seen, therefore, that the main methodological cleavage between Wieser and Böhm Bawerk, on the one hand, and Menger himself, on the other, is the abandonment by the former of Menger's individualist methodology. It is the reaffirmation of the principle of methodological individualism in the 20th century by Mises and Hayek which marks the appearance of the neo-Austrian school.[20]

Ludwig von Mises: the science of praxeology

At the heart of Mises's methodological stance, a unique view about the consequences of the subjectivist theory of value is found. He believed that the element of subjectivism does not only allow a more comprehensive theory of exchange than the one espoused by classical political economy, but it also creates the possibility of a more comprehensive understanding of all social, and not only economic, phenomena as products of 'human action'. The subjectivist theory of value treats choice, as expressed through action, as the cause of all market phenomena. This view constitutes the methodological basis for the understanding of all social outcomes. On these grounds, Mises (1949, p. 3) claimed that economics is only a part, though perhaps the most elaborated, of a more universal social science, that of praxeology.

Mises defined human action as springing from the individual's attempt to change those aspects of his/her condition which he/she finds disagreeable. If the individual were content with these aspects, there would, obviously, be no reason to act. Therefore, human action is, by definition, purposeful behaviour, as it aims at an end. Each individual's ends are entirely subjective and they are, thus, seen by Mises a lying outside the scope of science. The only legitimate object of the science of praxeology is, therefore, the study of the ways in which individual choices are translated into actions – the study of the use of means for the attainment of subjective ends. The distinction between means and ends allows some initial remarks concerning the epistemological nature of praxeology. First, the object of praxeology is, according to Mises (1949, p. 11), entirely different from that of psychology, because it studies the actual use of means rather than the mental processes through which individuals choose their ends. Second, Mises (1949, p. 20) considers the object of praxeology to be rational behaviour. This does not mean that individuals are infallible – in the sense that they always choose the right means for the attainment of the desired ends – but, rather, that action itself is an expression of human reason.

The element of rationality allowed Mises to establish some further implications of the category of action. Since the individual acts rationally, the category of action implies 'causality' or the individual's ability to discover causal relationships between the available means and the desired ends. In its turn, the notion of causality implies that human action must necessarily be understood as unfolding in time, since the use of means, the cause, cannot be conceptualized as occurring simultaneously with the appearance of the results.[21]

It is now clear that the category of action is, for Mises, the ultimate given, the most elementary category to which any social phenomenon can be analysed. On this basis, he attacked the impermissible, in his view, adoption by social scientists of the methodology of the physical sciences. Positivism and behaviourism are seen as constituting examples of such a methodological adoption, as they try to explain social phenomena in terms of a stimulus–response framework. Mises pointed out that the concept of stimulus cannot be analysed with the methods of the physical sciences, since the response is not determined by the physical properties of the stimulus but by the entirely subjective way in which the individual perceives it. The understanding of the essence of human action is, therefore, the only methodologically sound basis for scientific knowledge.[22]

Thus, human action is the fundamental a priori category on which social theory should be constructed. On these grounds, Mises (1949, p. 39) considers praxeology an entirely deductive science. As all its theorems are derived from the fundamental axiom of human action, their character is perfectly certain and incontestable. As a special branch of the science of praxeology, economics is itself a deductive science. This means that the only valid theorems of economics are the ones deduced logically from the a priori category of human action. In this context, and taking into consideration that social collectives do not act, Mises (1949, p. 42) maintains that any theory presuming to explain the behaviour of economic aggregates is methodologically unsound. Finally, since the category of action is independent of any normative content, all theorems derived from it are necessarily also normatively neutral.[23]

Friedrich Hayek: complex phenomena and spontaneous orders

The development of Hayek's views on the methodology of the social sciences lies at the core of any discussion about the homogeneity of neo-Austrian theory and methodology. Taking into account Hayek's views on the deductive nature of economics as well as on the relation between the methodologies of the physical and the social sciences, Hutchison (1981a), among others, distinguishes two different phases in this development. During the first phase, Hayek is supposed to follow Mises with regard to both the a priorist nature of economic theory as well as the sharp distinction in the methodology of the physical and the social sciences. In the second phase, under the influence of Karl Popper, Hayek supposedly distanced himself from Mises, as he introduced the criterion of 'falsifiability' for the validity of social theories and, at the same time, accepted a fundamental affinity between the methodologies of the two groups of sciences. Our presentation of Hayek's ideas on methodology will reveal that his thought has indeed evolved through time. Contrary to Hutchison, however, it will be argued that Hayek never entirely abandoned Misesian a priorism. It is indeed the co-existence of these two epistemological paradigms in his work that explains the homogeneity of the neo-Austrian school.

According to Hayek's writings in 1943, the understanding of human action presupposes a classification of the elements of human environment – of the 'objects' of man's activity. This classification cannot, of course, be based on the physical properties of those objects. A thing is classified in a category such as weapon or money or tool, not because it bears a physical resemblance to every object in the same category but because people believe that it belongs to this category. According to Hayek (1943, pp. 59–61), only on the basis of this classification can the researcher impute action to the 'intention' of the actor and thus approach human action as intelligible behaviour.

However, if the understanding of the actor's intentions requires the knowledge of the classification of the outside world which exists in his/her mind, the question arises of how the researcher can obtain this knowledge. Mere empirical observation of human behaviour is certainly not sufficient, because any such observation can only be based on a pre-existing system of classification of sensory data. Against this empiricist or inductive approach, Hayek claimed that the researcher can obtain the classification present in the actor's mind, only because he/she shares this classification with the actor as they both share the same social experience.

As Hayek does not see the classification of objects of action realized through direct empirical observation, he bestows it with the epistemological status of an a priori given. The methodology of the social sciences becomes, thus, entirely deductive. Based on the classes of human behaviour which we know a priori, we construct hypothetical models which simulate the functioning of social collectives. These collectives are not, therefore, objectively given data but only constructs of the imagination of the social scientist. Any science attempting to establish systematic relationships between them is, thus, based on the methodological illusion that social phenomena can be studied with the methodological principles of the physical sciences.[24] On the other hand, the deductive character of the methodology of the social sciences makes their conclusions unverifiable and unfalsifiable. According to

Hayek, therefore, the only criterion of their validity is the consistency of their derivation from the a priori principles.

At first glance, Hayek seems to agree with Mises on the central importance of the category of human action, although his insistence on the intelligibility of action as well as the importance of imputing action to the individual's intention, reveals that, in his view, the ultimate given in the social sciences is not action by itself but action inexorably linked with consciousness. Beginning with the works of the 1950s, however, we observe Hayek's gradual departure from Mises's rigidly a priorist methodology. The understanding of human behaviour is still fundamental for the analysis of any social phenomenon, but Hayek now admits that theories of social collectives are, at least to some degree, empirically testable.[25]

The decisive turning point in Hayek's views on methodology must be placed in the middle of the 1950s. In 1952, Hayek (1952/1979, Part One) attacked 'scientism' (the uncritical adoption of the methodology of the physical sciences by social scientists), but by 1955 he appeared to have revised this stance, as he was now under the influence of Popper.[26] He now saw the dividing line on questions of methodology as not between physical and social sciences, but between sciences which study simple phenomena and those which study complex phenomena – where the complexity of a phenomenon is related to the number of variables that determine it.[27]

The number of variables involved, determines the 'predictive ability' of a science. The greater this number is, the more difficult it is to predict the actual form a specific phenomenon will assume. However, whereas in some physical sciences this is merely a practical difficulty – which might be overcome with improved techniques of data collecting and processing – in the social sciences the difficulty is, as Gray (1986, p. 40) observes, of a deeper epistemological nature. The researcher aims to understand human action, but individuals act on the basis of the knowledge they possess at any particular moment. Therefore, in order to really be able to understand action, the researcher must first obtain the knowledge which the individual possesses. According to Hayek (1963, p. 61), however, this is impossible because knowledge is a supra-conscious category – a kind of possession that the individual is not aware of.

The core of Hayek's philosophy of knowledge has now been reached. Hayek (1963, p. 43) believes that human action follows rules of conduct which lie beyond the actor's consciousness – for example, a child becoming grammatically competent in order to use the complex code of language; an athlete performing in a particular sport; or someone trying to mimic the grimaces of another person. In all these instances, an individual displays the possession of a skill without being able to articulate the exact rules that constitute this behaviour. The fact that the knowledge of these rules lies beyond the consciousness of individuals means that it cannot be alienated from them, or even consciously transmitted.

Thus, the complexity of social phenomena does not arise only as a result of the great number of variables involved but, mainly, as a result of the researcher's inability to obtain the knowledge which is supra-consciously held by individuals. This claim raises, of course, the important question whether the social sciences have any predictive ability at all. Hayek, however, did not believe that social theory aims to predict the exact form a social phenomenon will take. He stressed (1964, p. 35), instead, that its aim is to investigate whether the multiplicity of individual actions leads to the establishment of a pattern or order. In the social sciences, therefore, the discovery that the multiplicity of individual actions tends to establish a type of order is a valuable conclusion, even though it can never lead to the prediction of the exact form this order will actually take.

We can now take up directly the question of the relation of Hayek's methodological views to those of Mises and Popper. Hayek sees the social scientist building hypothetical models which reveal the patterns or orders that emerge as outcomes of countless individual actions. Described in this form, Hayek's approach seems to be very similar to Popper's hypothetico-deductive method. Popper, however, has also introduced the 'empirical content' and the 'falsifiability' criteria for testing the validity of social theories, where a theory can be falsified if its conclusions contradict empirical observation.

In his Popperian phase, Hayek (1964, p. 32) seemed to accept the principle of falsifiability. At the same time, however, he claimed that the empirical testing of social theories is complicated further: the empirical data on the basis of which we must verify or falsify the existence of the social orders we have deductively constructed, are themselves complex phenomena. Moreover, since empirical data stem from reality itself, their degree of complexity is greater than that of the theories we are trying to test. Thus, according to Hayek (1964, pp. 28–9), in the social sciences, we have to accept the validity of deductively constructed theories, even if their empirical content is very small. Therefore, the social scientist must rely on a central core of hypotheses which are empirically non-testable.

On the basis of the above, the distinction proposed by Hutchison between an a priorist and a Popperian phase in Hayek's thought appears rather superficial. The same can be said of Gray's account (1986, pp. 16–21), which sees little change in Hayek's methodological position through the years, and considers this position as having remained consistently closer to Popper rather than to Mises. It has been shown that Hayek's views have indeed evolved, with the Misesian influence giving way to the Popperian one, but at no time does Hayek's thought coincide precisely with the epistemological views of either of the two thinkers. Thus, Barry's conclusion that Hayek tries throughout his whole work to combine two different philosophies of social sciences, seems more to the point.[28] It is precisely the fact that Hayek never distanced himself decisively from Mises's methodology that allows contemporary neo-Austrians (for example, Kirzner, 1976) to declare the homogeneity of their philosophical tradition.

Spontaneous orders and natural selection of rules of conduct

In order to stress the fact that social orders are products of human action but not of a single or collective will, Hayek describes them as 'spontaneous'.[29] Since, however, a spontaneous order is a product of human action, its particular form must be determined by the mode of acting, which is itself determined by the compliance of all actors with a system of rules of conduct. Different systems of rules will thus lead to the spontaneous emergence of different orders.[30]

As has been seen, Hayek believes that the greatest part of these rules of conduct constitute a knowledge that lies beyond consciousness. This view poses a number of questions regarding the emergence of these rules, their transmission from generation to generation, and the mutations they can undergo. According to Hayek (1988, p. 25), all these questions can be answered within the framework of a theory of evolution, which he borrows from biology in order to apply to the evolution of systems of rules. He claims (1983, p. 30) that the first systems of rules arose out of the self-preservation instincts of prehistoric man. As the preservation of small prehistoric societies depended heavily on co-operation among its members, the rules of conduct that evolved spontaneously relied on the sentiments of solidarity and altruism.

The transmission of rules from generation to generation can, equally well, be explained by such a theory. This transmission is, of course, of a cultural instead of a genetic nature, but its mechanism is thought by Hayek to be exactly the same with that of biology. As in the latter, rules are transmitted from individual to individual, independently of the population – the overall social order. The institution of the family is seen as an example of the transmission of the rules that constitute the 'market order' of contemporary society. In pre-industrial societies, the family was for the individual the only sphere of social and productive life. It was, therefore, natural, according to Hayek (1982, vol. II, pp. 134–5), for heads of families to conceive of society as a network of family units linked through markets. It was this understanding, and the system of rules compatible with it, which formed the tradition that the family transmitted to its new members.

Finally, Hayek believes that the theory of evolution can also explain the mutations of systems of rules. As in biology, the mechanism that describes this process is the mechanism of natural selection. In contrast, however, with the process of transmission which operates between individuals, natural selection operates at the level of the population as a whole.[31] In Hayek's account, the moment a member of prehistoric society decided to withhold some resource of the community as his/her private property, this individual began to introduce a new culture. Whether, however, this new culture and the system of rules that it initiated would finally replace the old system depended on the level of prosperity achieved by those groups who first adopted it. The establishment of the market culture is, therefore, explained, according to Hayek (1988, p. 16), by the prosperity and the population growth achieved by the societies that adjusted to it. It was this prosperity that prompted other backward societies to imitate the new culture, thus leading to its proliferation through the whole of contemporary society.

This line of reasoning leads Hayek to the view, shared by all neo-Austrians, that theoretical knowledge of social phenomena is impossible. The key element here is the concept of accident, which Hayek introduces into social theory as one of the conceptual tools borrowed from biology. The mutations of systems of rules are thought of as accidental phenomena,[32] which are, thus, theoretically unpredictable. Therefore, the evolution of human society is seen as a series of accidental events. The principle of natural selection can, according to Hayek (1983, pp. 46–7), only explain the domination of one system of rules out of the multitude that emerged in the past at every point of mutation. Therefore, if, at every such point, the initial set of systems were different, a different system of rules might have dominated.

The market culture

The market culture is the system of rules which has, through the process of natural selection, emerged as the major determinant of individual behaviour in market society. As for any such system, knowledge of the rules that constitute it is impossible, since this knowledge is considered supra-conscious. Its acceptance by modern man, however, should, according to Hayek, be independent of the possibility of knowledge. Since it is a system of rules which has ensured prosperity more than any other, its advantageous nature for human society is beyond doubt. On this basis, Hayek calls for the uncritical acceptance of tradition,[33] as tradition is nothing but the system of rules which has come to dominate a society's culture. This conclusion explains Hayek's aversion to psychoanalysis.[34] If, as the latter claims, social rules unconsciously oppress man's inner world, then Hayek's insistence on the uncritical acceptance of tradition would only further reinforce this oppression.

In spite of his differences with Freud, Hayek seems to share with him a crucial insight. The domination of the market culture does not imply that primitive systems of rules have totally vanished. The sentiments of solidarity and altruism, which characterized small prehistoric societies, continue to survive in modern man as primordial instincts. However, these sentiments are not only incompatible with the market order, but they actually tend to subvert it. On the basis of these sentiments, a member of society may raise claims to entitlements just because of the fact that he/she is a member. By contrast, on the basis of the market culture, a person's claim is only determined by his/her contribution to society, as this contribution is evaluated by the impersonal institution of the market.[35] The survival of the market society will, thus, depend on its ability to suppress modern man's primordial instincts.

The fact that these instincts are supposed to survive in contemporary society poses, however, a problem for a theory which attempts to explain social development on the basis of the theory of evolution. This survival implies that, unlike the irreversible nature of biological evolution, a social order is always in danger of regression. Systems of rules which the process of natural selection has set aside, not only never disappear completely but, instead, continue to constitute part of the supra-conscious knowledge of individuals. Thus, the possibility of a clash between the primordial instincts, on the one hand, and the market culture, on the other – a culture which has, after all, only recently been adopted – is ever-present.

Hayek expresses the optimistic view that the complete disappearance of man's primordial instincts is only a matter of time. They survive only because they have been part of culture for thousands of years. Thus, as the market culture becomes more consolidated, their influence and their subversive potential will diminish. This optimistic prospect, however, is plausible only if one supposes that in modern society there are no forces which tend to revive those instincts. This is where Hayek's optimism expires, as he believes that such forces not only exist, but are constantly gaining momentum. He sees the dramatic development of big private and public organizations which isolate modern man from direct contact with the market, as one such force. Another such force is the intellectual tradition that Hayek terms 'rational constructivism', which starts with Descartes and includes thinkers like Hegel, Bentham and Marx.

The development, since the end of the last century, of large organizations such as corporations and the state bureaucracy, has moulded whole generations of individuals who have lost any direct contact with the market. Thus, instead of understanding participation in society as a contribution evaluated through the market, modern man has gradually built a way of thinking that conceives of participation as belonging to a hierarchical structure. In such a framework, according to Hayek (1982, vol. II, pp. 134–5), the idea of contribution to society is distorted and becomes translated to obedience to the organization's superior organs. For Hayek, nothing is more distant from the market culture than this development.

Hayek views rational constructivism, the other major threat to market society, as a product of the Enlightenment. Descartes's rationalism attributes all social phenomena to human reason. If, however, social phenomena can be explained rationally, then they must be understood themselves as products of human reason, or purposeful constructs. And if all social institutions are constructs of an individual or a collective will, then their appropriateness for human prosperity as well as the possibility of social intervention for their improvement, become legitimate objects of scientific enquiry. Evidently, this line of reasoning comes in direct opposition to Hayek's insistence on the uncritical acceptance of tradition.[36] It is, therefore, easily understood why Hayek considers the tradition of rational constructivism as the common cradle of all theories – from utilitarianism to socialism – aiming at the rational reconstruction of society.

To conclude this chapter it is important to stress an important difference between Hayek and Mises. The latter (1922/1981, p. 258) claimed that 'the development of human reason and the development of human society are one and the same process'. Mises's rigid rationalism lies at the basis of his utilitarian philosophical outlook, apparent in his conviction that in an economy which functions freely each individual's reward is the maximum possible. Hayek's critical stance toward rational constructivism implies, by contrast, that, since we cannot use reason to understand the system of rules that governs the functioning of contemporary society, we have no other choice but to submit 'to the anonymous and seemingly irrational forces of society'.[37] Evidently, this is a position which is incompatible with utilitarianism, as it implies a theoretical justification of market society which is independent of the rational evaluation of its outcomes. However, it is important to note that, as far as the theory of social evolution is concerned, contemporary neo-Austrians seem to be inspired by Hayek rather than by Mises.

Notes

1. See Schumpeter (1954, p. 919) and Arrow and Hahn (1971, p. 3).
2. See Menger (1981, p. 52). Smith (1986, p. 3) stresses exactly this point saying that 'an economy presupposes consciousness'.
3. See Streissler (1973, p. 161) and Jaffé (1976, p. 522).
4. For the first view, see Schumpeter (1954, p. 918) and Stigler (1941, p. 147). For the second, see Hayek (1934, p. 15) and Jaffé (1976, p. 521).
5. It is cited by Blaug (1968, p. 299).
6. See Streissler (1973, p. 174): 'Walras's tatonnement takes a minute; Menger's tatonnement takes a century!'.
7. See Hayek (1934).
8. See Fabian and Simons (1986) and Chisholm (1986).
9. For a description of the methodology of the historical school, see Hayek (1933).
10. See Hayek (1973, p. 277).
11. See Smith (1986, p. 3).
12. See Menger (1985, pp. 69–70) who stressed exactly this point by comparing economics to mathematics: 'To want to test the pure theory of economy by experience in its full

reality is a process analogous to that of the mathematician who wants to correct the principles of geometry by measuring real objects'.

13. See Hayek (1973, p. 276) and Hutchison (1981b, p. 184). The principle of methodological individualism explains, from yet another point of view, Menger's aversion to mathematical formulations. The description of an exchange economy as a system of simultaneous equations, is grounded on the premise of interdependence, the idea that every economic magnitude is affecting all others and is, at the same time, being affected by them. If, however, one tries to understand the essence of economic phenomena on the basis of the actions of individuals, then this essence must be considered to be the primary cause of the series of events that follows every action. As Kauder (1965, p. 98) points out, Menger replaced the principle of interdependence with that of 'genetic causality'. Methodological individualism seems, therefore, incompatible with the principle of interdependence.
14. Let us note the political implications of this position. If we agree with Menger that social institutions are organic phenomena, in the sense that their functioning is essential for the existence and prosperity of human society, while, at the same time, they are unintended outcomes of social activity, it follows that any political proposal aiming at the reconstruction of institutions must be treated with extreme caution and even suspicion. It is on these grounds that Menger praised the work of Burke and Savigny, although he was less adamant than they in denying any possibility of improving institutions. See Menger (1985, p. 233).
15. See Craver (1986) for an account of the situation facing Austrian economists in the 1920s and 1930s, and of the reasons that led each one of them to emigrate.
16. See Streissler (1973, pp. 170, 167).
17. Hayek (1983, p. 17), who was Wieser's student, says that Wieser showed sympathy for a mild Fabian socialism.
18. See Streissler (1973, p. 169).
19. See Schumpeter (1954, p. 847).
20. The term 'neo-Austrian' school is also used by Shand (1984) and Hutchison (1981a, p. 203).
21. For the same conclusion, see Rothbard (1976, p. 20).
22. The affinity with Menger's thought is now obvious. Let us, however, also point out a difference of emphasis between Mises and Menger. For the latter, methodological individualism is the most fundamental methodological principle. For Mises, by contrast, this principle is merely a theorem derived from the a priori category of human action.
23. Let us present two characteristic examples of deductive reasoning. The first concerns the epistemological nature of the equilibrium concept. According to Mises, the tendency toward equilibrium is not an economic law derived from empirical observation but is, instead, a corollary of the a priori category of human action. As action always aims at the improvement of the individual's position, it follows that the state of rest is the situation where action has achieved its ends and the individual has no further inducement to act. Thus, on the basis of the a priori category of human action, Mises has reached a conclusion about the behaviour of the economic system as a whole. The second example comes from the major political conclusion of his theory. Mises claimed that liberalism is the only social system that ensures social progress. As this conclusion was reached through the elaboration of the fundamental category of action, it must, in his view (1976, p. 39), necessarily be considered normatively neutral. Therefore, whoever disagrees with the principles of liberalism, cannot be seen as simply holding a different set of principles for the organization of society, but rather, as committing a serious scientific error.
24. See Hayek (1943, pp. 67–9). It is on these grounds that neo-Austrians reject the methodological validity of macroeconomic theory. In their account, the problem with the latter is that it takes aggregate magnitudes such as consumption, investment and so on, as objectively given data, whereas, for neo-Austrians, these are merely constructs of the economist's imagination.
25. This shift is actually evident even in Hayek (1937, p. 44) where he claimed that the state

of equilibrium can be assumed to hold a priori only in the context of an agent's plan, whereas, in the context of the market as a whole, the concept of equilibrium is derived from empirical observation.

26. See Hayek (1955) and the Preface in Hayek (1967).
27. In this framework, the science of mechanics must be understood as dealing with simple phenomena – usually described by a mathematical function relating a dependent variable to one or a few independent variables. On the other hand, social sciences, and even some physical sciences such as meteorology and geology, study complex phenomena, because the dependent variable is determined by the simultaneous functioning of a large number of independent variables. See Hayek (1964).
28. See Barry (1979, pp. 40–41), but see also his revised position in Barry (1981).
29. The close relationship between Hayek's concept of the spontaneous order and Menger's unintended results is, of course, obvious.
30. This does not mean that a system of rules will necessarily lead to the establishment of an order, as it is possible that it may lead to disorder; see Hayek (1967a, p. 67).
31. See Hayek (1967a, p. 67).
32. See Gray (1986, p. 32) and Hayek (1988, p. 20).
33. See Gray (1986, p. 42). The political implications of the uncritical acceptance of tradition will be dealt with in Chapter 12.
34. Hayek (1982, vol. III, p. 174) considers Freud to be the greatest 'destroyer of civilisation'. Hayek's effort to distance himself from Freud probably explains why he uses the term supra-conscious knowledge instead of the simpler term unconscious.
35. The sentiments of solidarity and altruism can only be expressed toward a very small circle of individuals around each person. It is for this reason that Hayek (1976, p. 59) claims that they can never form the basis of a culture that tends to spread through the whole of human society.
36. According to Hayek (1988, pp. 21–2), tradition is 'that which lies between instinct and reason'.
37. See Hayek (1946, p. 24).

3 Competition and knowledge

The centrality of the concept of competition for all schools of economic thought could not have been more forcefully stressed than by J.S. Mill (1864, vol. I, p. 306), who claimed that 'only through the principle of competition has political economy any pretension to the character of a science'. The universal acceptance of this concept does not mean, however, that its meaning has remained unchanged throughout the development of economic doctrines. The views on this subject could be divided into two camps. First, according to the orthodox neoclassical school, the analytical rigour of the concept of competition has been steadily sharpened, as evidenced by the transition from the concept of 'free' competition of classical political economy, to that of 'perfect' competition of modern micro theory.[1] The second camp includes all the views which are critical toward the concept of perfect competition, either because of its distance from reality or because of its static nature.[2] Neo-Austrian theory clearly belongs to the second camp. However, before proceeding to analyse the neo-Austrian critique of perfect competition, it is necessary to briefly sketch the meaning of this concept and demonstrate its central role in neoclassical theory.

In orthodox literature, the concept of perfect competition is usually defined as a state determined by the simultaneous fulfilment of a set of assumptions. The following are the most commonly cited such assumptions:

1. Individuals must be assumed to act rationally.
2. The number of both buyers and sellers must be so large that no individual can determine the market's price through his/her actions.
3. There must be no collusion between dealers, either on the supply side or on the demand side of the market.
4. All consequences of exchange appear within the market so that there are no external effects.
5. There must be perfect freedom in the mobility of resources across industries.
6. Every individual must have perfect knowledge of market conditions.

The concept of perfect competition is useful to neoclassical theory because it provides the foundation for the establishment of two crucial notions. The first is equilibrium, which is defined as the state that emerges after all actions and interactions amongst market participants have ceased.[3] The second is a theoretical criterion for the classification of markets according to the intensity of competition. When actual market conditions approach the ideal described by the assumptions of perfect competition – especially in terms of the second of the assumptions listed above – the market is supposed to be competitive. On the other hand, when actual conditions diverge from this ideal, competition is supposed to be imperfect and the market itself is described as monopolistic or oligopolistic.

Competition as a process

The neo-Austrian reaction against the concept of perfect competition was first voiced by Hayek in 1946. He claimed that, if it were ever possible for all the assumptions of perfect competition to actually hold simultaneously, then all activities commonly associated with the verb 'to compete' would become virtually impossible. According to Hayek, perfect competition is an abstraction which misses the most important aspect of competition, its dynamic nature. Any economist, Hayek (1946a, p. 93) concluded, who believes that the concept of perfect competition explains not only the general characteristics of the state of equilibrium, but also the process leading to the emergence of that state, is merely deceiving him/herself.

Kirzner examines the nature of this deception through the use of the standard analytical tools of neoclassical microeconomics. He argues that in drawing the demand and supply curves of the Marshallian scissors, we implicitly assume that there is a strong force pushing the price toward the point of intersection and, thus, that the equilibrium price is the only possible market outcome. This assumption contradicts, however, the basic neoclassical account of market behaviour on two grounds. First, in order for the force leading to equilibrium to be able to operate, we must assume that there is only one market price even at times of disequilibrium, as only in such a case will the interaction between buyers and sellers lead to the disappearance of excess supply and demand. However, this assumption contradicts neoclassical theory itself, according to which the existence of only one market price can be assumed only at the state of equilibrium.[4]

Second, the behavioural assumptions about individual actions at times of disequilibrium contradict the standard behavioural assumptions of neoclassical theory. Again, in order for the force leading to equilibrium to be able to operate, we must assume that whenever we have excess supply some sellers lower their prices while, in case of excess demand, some buyers willingly raise their price offers. Both these actions contradict, however, the second of the listed assumptions of perfect competition, according to which no individual buyers or sellers can affect market prices through their actions. Therefore, Kirzner (1974, pp. 4–5) concludes that while the concept of perfect competition implies a strong tendency toward equilibrium, this tendency is ultimately incompatible with the very assumptions of perfect competition. This was also the essence of Hayek's (1946a, p. 94) conclusion, when he stressed that 'competition is by its nature a dynamic process whose essential characteristics are assumed away by the assumptions underlying static analysis'.

However, in order to fully understand the neo-Austrian position on the question of 'dynamics', the orthodox neoclassical account of the concept of equilibrium must be examined further. Assuming perfect competition, neoclassical theory shows that any exogenous disturbance of the initial equilibrium position will automatically lead to the establishment of a new equilibrium. The automatic nature of this adjustment has two important implications. The first is that the time needed for the transition from the initial to the final equilibrium position can be assumed to be so short that it becomes theoretically irrelevant. Second, the fact that individuals act as passive price-takers means that they do not change their plans during this short period of transition. In its turn, this implies that the characteristics of the new equilibrium position are already inherent in the individuals' plans and are, thus, predetermined.

For neo-Austrians, by contrast, it is pre-eminently during the period of adjustment that competition is most apparent. As Hayek (1946a, p. 103) pointed out, it is competition that determines the path toward the new equilibrium point. Therefore, it is only through understanding of the exact way in which competition operates that we will be in a position to understand the nature of this path and, consequently, the nature of the final equilibrium position. Thus, for Hayek (1968), this final position is not predetermined, but is actually discovered through the process of competition itself.

The individual as creative actor

The principle of methodological individualism requires that the explanation of market phenomena be grounded on assumptions about individual behaviour. The rejection of the automatic nature of market phenomena must be based, therefore, on the rejection of the passive price-taking assumption regarding the behaviour of individuals – the rejection, in other words, of the behaviourist outlook of neoclassical theory. For neo-Austrians, the moving force of market phenomena is not the response of the individual to external stimuli but action aiming at the attainment of ends. The individual of neo-Austrian theory is, above all, a creative actor, who does not simply react to price signals according to a preconceived plan but, instead, makes plans and is free to revise them.

The rejection of passive price-taking behaviour undermines the whole neoclassical edifice of perfect competition and lies at the basis of the alternative view of market activity proposed by neo-Austrians – the view of this activity as a process. The second of the assumptions of perfect competition mentioned above – the existence of a large number of buyers and sellers – now becomes obsolete. In the neo-Austrian account, competition, understood as the never ceasing creative activity of individuals, remains strong regardless of the number of transactors. At the same time, the rejection of the automatic nature of market adjustments reintroduces time as an important variable of theoretical analysis. Thus, if the notion of the market process of neo-Austrian theory is understood as a sequence of constantly changing decisions and actions of individuals, then every step of this sequence of events must be understood as the cause of the one succeeding it. Therefore, as O'Driscoll and Rizzo (1985, p. 3) point out, time cannot be conceived as a dimension of reality that runs parallel to it but, rather, as a factor that causally determines the unfolding of reality.

The major target of the neo-Austrian critique of perfect competition is, however, the last of the assumptions listed above, that of 'perfect knowledge'. The fact that in the neo-Austrian account of the market process every individual is constantly revising his/her plan, means that no individual can treat the actions of his/her competitors as known before they actually appear. Thus, if the neo-Austrian concept of the market participant as a creative actor is accepted, it must also be accepted that he/she functions in conditions of uncertainty. In this framework, however, the question of how the individual discovers the information which he/she needs for the assessment and the revision of his/her plan becomes one of the most crucial problems of economic theory.

Knowledge and market behaviour

For neoclassical theory, the perfect knowledge assumption and the concept of equilibrium constitute the two sides of a theoretical tautology. If the market system is in a state of equilibrium, then all transactors have perfect knowledge of market conditions since equilibrium prices embody all information necessary for the fulfilment of their plans. On the other hand, if the system is momentarily in a state of disequilibrium, the perfect knowledge assumption ensures that all individuals will automatically readjust their behaviour so as to make it compatible with the readjusted behaviour of all other market participants, thus leading to the establishment of a new equilibrium position. Therefore, the rejection of price-taking behaviour also leads to the rejection of this tautology.

From the neo-Austrian point of view, the first criticism against this tautology came from Hayek (1937), who claimed that the simplest concept of equilibrium is the one established in the context of an individual's plan. According to Hayek, a person's actions must, a priori, be supposed to be compatible with each other – or to be in equilibrium – because of the simple fact that they are parts of the same plan. Consequently, they will remain in equilibrium for as long as the specific plan remains unaltered. However, the rejection of the price-taking assumption means that all transactors do not simply react to market signals on the basis of preconceived plans, but are also in a position to alter their behaviour. The equilibrium of a single individual's plan is, therefore, in a process of constant flux.

The question now raised is what aspect of the market process is capable of explaining this constant plan revision. Hayek's (1937, pp. 36–7) answer was that this aspect is none other than the new information which the transactor obtains through his/her participation in market exchange. It is precisely this new knowledge that enables him/her to assess the effectiveness of his/her plan and thus to decide whether to continue to try to fulfill it or to revise it. Even in the context of individual activity, therefore, the new knowledge generated by the market process constantly disrupts the equilibrium of an individual's plan.

Hayek went on to analyse the role of knowledge in the context of the market as a whole. The main difference from the equilibrium of a single individual's plan is that now a large number of persons contrive and revise plans, both simultaneously, as well as independently of each other. Once again, Hayek began his analysis by defining the state of equilibrium as the situation where the plans of all individuals are compatible with each other.

However, the meaning of compatibility is now different from that which can be thought to hold a priori with respect to the different aspects of a single individual's plan. In order for the actions of all market participants to mesh, one must assume that they are all based on the same expectations of external data. However, the meaning of the term 'external data' is now different. In the context of a single individual's plan, external data could be considered as all aspects of reality which lie beyond the individual's control. By contrast, for a society based on exchange, the notion of external data now includes, for every individual, the plans of all other market participants. According to Hayek (1937, p. 38), therefore, the fulfilment of a person's plan depends on his/her ability to foresee the actions of all others. For equilibrium to prevail, the expectations of all market participants concerning their competitors' actions, must always prove correct. For Hayek, however, this assumption did not only seem unrealistic, but would also contradict the view of individual behaviour as creative, and thus unpredictable, activity. Hayek's rejection of the tautological nature of the notions of perfect knowledge and equilibrium is, therefore, complete.

The subjectivity of knowledge

Hayek's criticism of Robbins's famous definition of the 'economic problem' of society can now be understood. Robbins (1962) sees the economic problem that society faces as the need to ensure the optimum allocation of scarce means for the attainment of competing and mutually exclusive ends. Hayek regards as problematic the fact that this definition transcends the level of the individual actor – in which it only implies that actors behave rationally – and concerns the level of the economic system as a whole. In such a way, the term 'economic problem' is objectified and we are, thus, led to the illusion that society can rationally solve the problem by acting as a collective decision-maker.

Hayek's argument began with the question of what the problem we are trying to solve is, when we try to construct a rational economic order. His answer was that if we have knowledge of all relevant information and all available means, and if we can start from a given set of preferences, the problem is one of simple logic. In reality, the solution does not have to be discovered, since it is already inherent in the data and can be expressed mathematically as the equality of the marginal rates of substitution amongst all goods and for all potential uses. However, Hayek (1945, p. 77) emphatically stressed that this is not the economic problem of society, since this data is never concentrated in a single mind. Knowledge of relevant data is fragmented, incomplete and, above all, dispersed among all market participants. The concentration of this data in a single mind is practically impossible. Therefore, the solution of the economic problem of society is not to be sought in the concentration of knowledge but, rather, in the establishment of those conditions which will allow all individuals to make the best possible use of the knowledge they possess.[5] Hayek's logic leads, therefore, to an important reformulation of orthodox neoclassical theory. For the latter, the economic problem of society is how to optimize the use of available resources. For Hayek, by contrast, this problem is how to optimize the use of knowledge.[6]

Up to this point, the term knowledge has been used without having specified its exact nature. In fact, Hayek distinguished between two dimensions of the individual's knowledge. The first is the knowledge of 'time and place', which is the result of the social and market experience the individual has accumulated over his/her social and productive life. The second dimension comprises all information which the individual obtains during the market process itself.

These two dimensions need to be examined in more depth. According to Hayek, the knowledge of time and place can itself be divided into two distinct categories. The first is the category of technical knowledge, which comprises all information that a person has acquired through a teaching process or is in a position to teach to someone else. It is, therefore, an alienable kind of knowledge, in the sense that it can be consciously transferred from one individual to another. The second, and most important, category is that of tacit knowledge. This comprises all rules and social or market practices which a person has learned to obey, although he/she is not consciously aware of them and, thus, cannot articulate them. This knowledge is, therefore, inalienable; the individual cannot intentionally transfer it since it lies beyond his/her consciousness. It is precisely the non-transferability of this category of knowledge which, according to Hayek (1968, p. 182) makes it entirely subjective. Obviously, this is Hayek's notion of supra-conscious knowledge, mentioned in the previous chapter.

The meaning of Hayek's position about the optimization of the use of knowledge can now be understood. Since tacit knowledge is non-transferable, any effort to concentrate it in a single mind is futile. Therefore, the only way that society can ensure that this knowledge is put to the best possible use, is by letting those who possess it use it as they see fit. However, it does not suffice that individuals are allowed freedom to use their knowledge of time and place, as the economic system as a whole must also function in a way that delivers to them all information they need for their activity.

This brings us to Hayek's second dimension of knowledge – all information a person receives through his/her participation in the market process – and to the important question of how this knowledge is dispersed through the market. Hayek's answer was that this information is both dispersed and received through the process of competition. It was on these grounds that he described competition as a discovery procedure (1988, p. 19). Competition is, therefore, the process through which knowledge is both generated as well as discovered.

Systems of knowledge dissemination

There is still the question of how the new information generated by the process of competition is actually dispersed. Of course, the most obvious method is through the price system. In contrast with the orthodox neoclassical view which sees the price system as an allocative mechanism, Hayek stressed its knowledge–disseminating character. As with all social institutions in Hayek's theory, the price system has not been designed by any individual or collective will but is, instead, the product of a long process of natural selection. In Hayek's account (1945, p. 86), there are two fundamental features of the price system that explain its selection as the most effective knowledge-disseminating system. The first is that the information it disperses is freely available to all market participants, and the second that prices convey all information individuals need for their market activity.

Hayek used an example to illustrate the efficiency and the speed with which information is dispersed by the price mechanism. Assume that somewhere in the market a new opportunity for the use of some resource, say tin, is discovered or that some supply source of tin disappears. Whatever the case, the result will be practically the same. The supply will now be diminished and the users of tin must somehow understand that they need to either economize in their use of it or replace it, if possible, with a substitute. This message is conveyed to them by the increase in the price of tin. The increased price will, in turn, induce the users of this material to increase the prices of their products, thus further spreading the information that tin is scarce to the most distant parts of the market system. According to Hayek (1945, pp. 45–6), therefore, the individual market participant does not need to know the reason for the initial drop in the supply in order to plan his/her actions, since prices convey to him/her all the knowledge necessary for this planning.

The price mechanism is not, however, the only knowledge-dispersion system in market society. In Hayek's account, the rules of conduct and the social institutions which have evolved through the centuries of human existence, are not just a historically given framework within which economic activity takes place. They are, instead, part of this activity, as they themselves constitute a knowledge-disseminating system. Through them, the knowledge of the legal, political and moral framework of any social activity is conveyed to all market participants. There is, thus, a major difference between the information-disseminating functions of the price system and those of rules and institutions. The knowledge dispersed by the former is of a dynamic nature, in the sense that it leads individuals to a constant revision of their plans. The knowledge dispersed by the latter is stabilizing, in the sense that it constantly reaffirms the stability of the social framework in which individuals act.

This view of institutions as knowledge-dispersing-systems has important political implications. The fact that institutions are products of a long process of social evolution rather than products of human design, implies to Hayek that their function cannot be analysed rationally. Consequently, the knowledge disseminated by rules and institutions must itself be tacit,[7] in the sense that it is not based on the rational understanding of their role in market society. Any effort to reconstruct institutions is bound, therefore, to distort their function as knowledge-disseminating systems. Since the knowledge they disperse is tacit, the social scientist cannot compare the effectiveness of the reconstructed institutions with that of the old ones. One can only be certain that any such intervention will have a destabilizing effect, as it will tend to destroy patterns of behaviour which were hitherto unquestioned and, thus, the spontaneous ordering forces of modern society.

The notion of error

The radical difference between the neo-Austrian theory of knowledge and the perfect knowledge assumption of the orthodox neoclassical school must be clear by now. There is, however, one strand in the latter, known as the 'economics of information',[8] which must be specifically addressed. In this strand, information is viewed as a commodity, in the context of a general equilibrium system. The equilibrium price in the market for information shows the maximum cost which individuals are willing to incur in order to obtain a certain amount of this good. At first glance, this approach seems to answer the main criticism of neo-Austrians against the perfect knowledge assumption, as it allows transactors to search for information instead of assuming that they know everything in advance.

As Kirzner points out, however, the treatment of information as an economic good poses a fundamental problem. According to neoclassical theory, agents decide to obtain a good because they know the satisfaction it will give them. But how can one know the satisfaction that will be obtained from a piece of information? This knowledge is possible, according to Kirzner (1976a, p. 142), only if the information itself is known in advance. Thus, the real problem in market transactions is not how to obtain information already known to exist – even if one is unaware of its exact content – but how to obtain information, the existence of which one is entirely ignorant.

Moreover, there is an even more important aspect of the economics of information which attracts the critique of neo-Austrians. Since the market for information is supposed to be only one of the markets of a general equilibrium system, the individuals' knowledge-seeking behaviour must always be supposed to be in a state of equilibrium. This means that agents are always assumed to make optimal use of the information they acquire. This account precludes, therefore, any notion of error in their behaviour. For Kirzner, by contrast, error is a fundamental characteristic of the market process, as all information relevant to the fulfilment of the individual's plan may be available to him/her but, at the same time, he/she may be unaware of its existence. What is important for economic activity, therefore, is not the existence but the perception of information by market participants.

Kirzner uses an example to support this claim. Suppose someone walks by a shop selling apples for one dollar a pound. He/she sees the price sign but, either because he/she has not yet decided to buy apples or for any other reason, this price information is not kept in mind. He/she ends up buying apples from another shop for two dollars a pound. In cases like this, Kirzner says, the information that would enable this person to make better use of his/her resources was clearly available but it went unperceived. The concept that neo-Austrians find relevant to this kind of situation is that of error.[9]

Knowledge and the possibility of an objective understanding of economic activity

There are two aspects of the neo-Austrian theory of competition and knowledge which seem to support the claim about its radical nature. First, if we agree with neo-Austrians in viewing the dispersion of knowledge through the market system as the moving force of economic activity, then we also have to agree that the market society is the most equitable system of social organization. This follows from the fact that, contrary to all schools of economic thought, neo-Austrian theory claims that a person's success in market transactions does not depend on factor ownership but on his/her ability to perceive and make use of knowledge which is freely available to all. In addition, we have seen that the knowledge an individual possesses is inalienable from him/her, because it is tacit. This tacitness makes it impossible for the economist to obtain this knowledge and to formulate an understanding of the overall workings of the market system, as he/she perceives the market process as an indeterminate sequence of events. Any objective understanding of economic phenomena is, thus, impossible.

This critique will now focus on these two aspects of neo-Austrian theory. Against the first, we will argue that the primacy neo-Austrians assign to perception over availability of information implies that a person's ability to perceive new information is determined by the knowledge of time and place he/she initially possesses. Thus, the fact that the knowledge disseminated by the price mechanism is freely available does not mean that it is equally perceivable by all market participants. Against the second aspect of neo-Austrian theory, we will argue that the market process itself constantly tends to objectify a part of the knowledge that circulates in the market system, thus transforming it from tacit into conscious.

Knowledge and the justification of market society

This discussion will start with Hayek's two dimensions of individual knowledge – the knowledge of time and place, and the information obtained through current market transactions. For neo-Austrian theory, it is crucial that no systematic relation be assumed to hold between these two dimensions of knowledge; otherwise access to the information distributed by the price mechanism would not be free to all market participants, but would depend on a person's initial knowledge. However, as the important notion is perception of knowledge rather than its availability, the problem arises as to whether perception can indeed be assumed to be independent of an individual's initial knowledge of time and place.

This question can be investigated by examining Hayek's example discussed earlier, that is, the way the price mechanism disseminates information about the availability of tin throughout the market system. The initial rise in the price of tin constitutes a signal which is freely available to all market participants. In Hayek's account, however, the perception of this signal follows a pattern which seems to indicate, contrary to his intent, some link between perception and initial knowledge. The first to obtain this information are the producers who use tin in their manufacturing process; next are those who buy the products of the former; and, even later, those for whom tin represents only a tiny content of a consumer good that has been purchased. It is, therefore, evident that, even in Hayek's account, a person's ability to perceive information is related to his/her initial position in the market system. And, as we have seen, it is a person's initial position that determines his/her knowledge of time and place.

Hayek's view does not, of course, amount to a reaffirmation of the possibility of objective understanding of economic phenomena. The economist is still unable to obtain the individual's tacit knowledge of time and place as well as to predict a person's creative response to price signals. However, our conclusion seems to have important implications for the moral and political justification of the market system espoused by neo-Austrians. If an individual's ability to perceive information is determined by his/her initial knowledge of time and place, then one has to conclude that the circulation of knowledge in the market economy constantly tends to reproduce the initial distribution of knowledge. And since this initial knowledge is determined by a person's position in the market system, this position itself is constantly being reproduced. The justification proposed by neo-Austrians is, therefore, incompatible with the primacy they assign to the perception over the availability of knowledge.

The objectification of knowledge

As our exposition of neo-Austrian theory has made evident, the single most important cleavage between neo-Austrian and neoclassical market theories is the rejection by the former of the passive price-taking behaviour of individual agents. What is important to note is that while individuals are assumed to act creatively on the basis of new information they are, nonetheless, assumed to be entirely unable to consciously control the flow of knowledge in the market system. This is a crucial assumption neo-Austrians need to make, because only if the flow of knowledge is entirely free can it be thought of as being freely accessible to all market participants.

This is indeed a plausible assumption, as long as we agree with neo-Austrians that prices convey all information an individual needs for the assessment and possible revision of his/her plan. This is, of course, true by definition in the state of equilibrium, where prices embody all information relevant to the transactor's decision. The neo-Austrian notion of the market process is, however, based on a disequilibrium conception of market activity, which explains the emphasis placed on perception and creativity as well as the rejection of the price-taking assumption. The question now arises as to whether disequilibrium prices can indeed be assumed to convey all relevant information.

Let us, once again, take up Hayek's example with tin. If price signals are the products of disequilibrium situations, then the rise in the price of tin does not, by itself, convey all information the user of tin needs.[10] For neo-Austrians, error is always an unavoidable characteristic of the market process. The user of tin must, therefore, know whether the price rise reflects an error in the supplier's calculation or a true change in the scarcity of this material. In order to acquire this knowledge, the individual cannot, of course, rely only on the information obtained through the price system but is, instead, obliged to follow certain tactics for its discovery.

What are the nature of these tactics? The individual agent has two aims in mind: he/she must check the validity and the accuracy of the information received through the price system, as well as control the information which he/she feeds into the system through his/her actions. In this second case, what a person aims at is to ensure that the response of other agents to this information will be the one he/she wishes. There is, thus, a dual character in these tactics. On the one hand, the individual is trying to reduce the uncertainty within which he/she operates, while, on the other hand, he/she is trying to distort the information his/her actions generate. All this is actually an effort to manage the flow of knowledge to the agent's advantage.

This is certainly a conclusion well grounded on the principle of methodological individualism, since it has been arrived at through the analysis of the logic of an individual's actions. Moreover, these dual tactics are characteristic of many situations which can be described as games involving many interacting players. According to Hayek (1982, vol. II, p. 71), the market process is, after all, nothing but a game of skill and luck. What neo-Austrians would not accept, however, is the practicability of these dual tactics, as managing the flow of knowledge would be possible only if knowledge could be objectified. For neo-Austrian theory, however, this objectification is impossible. For instance, the knowledge of time and place is taken to be inalienable from its physical bearer, while the information dispersed by the price system is seen as being freely available to all market participants and can, thus, never be appropriated by any single agent.

Contrary to this position, it will be argued that the market process, by itself, constantly tends to objectify a great part of the knowledge which circulates in the economy. The grounds for such a conclusion have been laid in the previous section, where it was argued that the perception of information is determined by the agent's initial knowledge and, thus, his/her initial position in the market system. An agent's initial position is, however, related to the volume of resources that he/she commands, and it is, therefore, reasonable to assume the existence of a positive correlation between the size of an enterprise unit and the volume of knowledge that it perceives and generates. We are not claiming that size insulates the enterprise from the pressures of competition, but only that it gives it an advantage over its competitors. The bigger the size of the enterprise, the greater its access to the relevant information. Therefore, its ability to perceive knowledge, on the one hand, and to control the information it generates through its activities, on the other, becomes greater.

On these grounds, the tendency toward ever larger enterprise size must be seen as a result of the entrepreneurs' effort to control the flow of knowledge, because the greater a person's accumulated resources are, the greater will his/her ability to manage the flow of knowledge be. It is now evident that this tendency is set in motion by the market process itself – by all agents' efforts to compete from a better position. Such a tendency amounts, however, to an indirect objectification of knowledge, as the ability to manage the flow of knowledge is determined by an objective factor: the mass of productive resources which the entrepreneur commands.

Another tendency set in motion by the market process itself arises from the effort of all individual agents to protect the knowledge they possess. The management of the flow of knowledge can be effective only if agents are in a position to hide from the competition part, at least, of the knowledge possessed. The possibility of this hiding amounts, of course to a transformation of this knowledge from tacit into conscious, since one can only hide something of which one is aware. We now have, therefore, a process of direct objectification of knowledge. This is a process, once again, inexorably linked with the size of enterprises, for even if we agree with neo-Austrians that the functioning of large corporations depends on the subjective and supra-conscious knowledge of the individual entrepreneur, we will still have to admit that the running of such a corporation presupposes the transformation of a large part of the entrepreneur's knowledge into explicit operative rules. It is the explicit and conscious character of these rules which makes them suitable to guide the actions of the large group of people that constitute the contemporary corporation.

This objectification of knowledge implies, of course, that some part of the knowledge of time and place is now transferable. As it can now be alienated from its physical bearer, it is transformed into an exchangeable commodity. The moment that knowledge becomes conscious, it is transformed to an object of property, which has exactly the same character as any other economic good. Patents and copyrights are examples of such commodified knowledge. The essence, however, of the category of property is the ability of a good's owner to exclude all other members of society from its use, or to protect this property. Commodified, or objectified knowledge is, therefore, protected knowledge.

It has so far been argued that knowledge can be objectified and that its flow in the market system can be managed, as well as that the effectiveness of this management depends on the volume of resources commanded. It is evident that this conclusion contradicts the neo-Austrian theory of knowledge, as it introduces an element of objectivity in our understanding of the functioning of the market system. The full consequences of this conclusion will, however, become evident in the next chapter, which deals with the neo-Austrian rejection of the concept of market structure.

Notes

1. See Stigler (1957).
2. See McNulty (1967, 1968).
3. This notion is already clear in Cournot (1929, p. 90).
4. This is Jevons's 'law of indifference'.
5. As will be seen in Chapter 11, this was one of Hayek's main arguments against socialist central planning.
6. The emphasis is thus shifted from the scarcity of resources to the scarcity of knowledge. See O'Driscoll and Rizzo (1985, p. 81): 'what the individual has learned ... is the constraint'.
7. Gray (1986, p. 21) claims that on this point Hayek seems to follow Wittgenstein 'in grasping the role of social rules in the transmission of practical knowledge'.
8. See Stigler (1961).
9. See Kirzner (1976b, pp. 129–30) and Loasby (1982, p. 126).
10. It is, of course, true that in his example Hayek implicitly referred to a system in equilibrium, so that the prices are also necessarily equilibrium prices.

4 Competition and market structure

As mentioned in the previous chapter, the concept of perfect competition provides neoclassical theory with not only the foundation for the establishment of the notion of equilibrium, but also a theoretical criterion for the classification of market structures according to the intensity of actual competition. The analysis in this chapter will focus on an extreme form of imperfect market structure, the monopolistic market.

Consider, for a moment, the theoretical and political importance of the problem. If we consider, in the manner of orthodox neoclassicists, the conditions of perfect competition as the ultimate measure of the economy's efficiency, then any deviation from these conditions must be assumed to reduce this efficiency. Thus, for neoclassical theory, perfect competition offers the justification for social interventions in the workings of the market system, aiming at bringing about the conditions of perfect competition.[1] It is precisely these interventionist implications of neoclassical theory which explain the neo-Austrians' reaction against the concept of monopoly.

The neoclassical concept of monopoly

Orthodox neoclassical theory defines a monopolistic market structure as the situation where two of the assumptions of perfect competition have ceased to hold: the existence of a large number of sellers in the market and the perfect mobility of resources across industries.

Let us begin by examining the first of these assumptions. In a perfectly competitive market, the shape of the demand curve faced by each individual seller is horizontal, implying that he/she is a price-taker. By contrast, the shape of the demand curve faced by a monopolist is of negative slope, which means that this seller is now a 'price-setter'. Assuming that all market participants act rationally, the monopolist will set the price at a level maximizing his/her revenue. In contrast with a competitive market, however, this price is entirely independent of the seller's cost. Thus, the monopolist can reap profits which are higher than what he/she would earn in a competitive market. The actual level of monopoly profits depends, of course, on the price elasticity of demand, and the latter is, for this reason, often considered as a measure of monopoly 'power'.

Neo-Austrians agree with the neoclassical account of the characteristics of monopolistic markets, as evidenced from Mises's remark (1949, p. 356) that the shape of the demand curve is the fundamental condition for the existence of monopoly. They also agree with the neoclassical account of the negative distributional consequences of monopoly. By offering his/her product for a price higher than the competitive one, the monopolist offers, at the same time, a lower quantity than he/she would offer under competitive conditions. Therefore, according to Mises (1949, p. 368), the monopolist reaps, in the form of surplus profits, the loss of utility incurred by consumers.

The neo-Austrian rejection of barriers to entry hypotheses

It is the withdrawal of the second of the assumptions of perfect competition mentioned above (the perfect mobility of resources) that brings out the differences between neoclassical and neo-Austrian theories. Neoclassical theory assumes that the mobility of resources is blocked by various barriers to entry in the monopolistic market. According to O'Driscoll (1982, p. 189), this notion of monopoly derives from Ricardo, who viewed monopoly as the consequence of scarcity, while the neo-Austrian notion of monopoly derives from Adam Smith, who considered monopoly as an outcome of privilege granted by government. In this latter view, the only conceivable barriers to entry are not products of the market process but products, on the contrary, of exogenous interventions in its operation. However, in order to sustain this notion of monopoly, neo-Austrians must first show that the market process itself can never create barriers to the free mobility of resources. In this section we will therefore examine the neo-Austrians' rejection of some of the entry barriers most frequently cited by neoclassical theory.

Product differentiation

One such barrier is supposed to spring from the effort of every seller to differentiate his/her product from those offered by the competition,[2] thus segregating the demand for this specific good from the total demand faced by the relative industry. It is precisely in his/her effort to insulate the market for his/her product from markets of substitutes, that the seller is seen as becoming a monopolist.[3] Neo-Austrians base their critique of this view on their notion of competition as a process. Their main argument is that the product differentiation hypothesis seems to be grounded on the view of the monopolistic market which the economist forms only after the differentiation has occurred. However, the tendency toward product differentiation is really a consequence of competition, actually reflecting the effort of every seller to offer a different product from his/her competitors. Therefore, as Kirzner stresses (1973, p. 116), product differentiation must be seen as proof of the presence of competition rather than of its absence.

The natural monopoly hypothesis

According to orthodox neoclassical theory, the category of natural monopoly describes an industry in which the optimum size of the enterprise is so large that no room is left for the operation of more than one firm.[4] The significance of this entry barrier lies in the fact that it seems to be a consequence of the market process itself. By contrast, neo-Austrians claim that the concept of natural monopoly is really arbitrary, because, as Pasour points out (1982, p. 219), it is based on the implicit assumption that there are no close substitutes for the monopolist's products. For neo-Austrian theory, however, the process of competition always ensures that there can be no product without close substitutes.[5]

Advertising as an entry barrier

We can now turn to the situation where the seller has the capacity to spend resources in order to convince consumers that his/her product is both different and better than the ones offered by competitors. Recognizing this situation, Chamberlin (1933/1962) introduced the distinction between production and selling costs. Production costs comprise the total of expenditures required for the production and delivery of a good to consumers. Selling costs, on the other hand, include all expenditures incurred by the seller, which aim at increasing the demand for the specific product. Evidently, a typical example of a selling cost is advertising. However, assuming perfect knowledge, the category of selling cost becomes redundant, since buyers know perfectly well the characteristics of all products, and sellers know perfectly well the consumers' preferences. Therefore, the actual existence of selling costs can only mean that a specific market is not characterized by perfect competition.[6]

Theorists who view advertising as an entry barrier, sometimes also accept its positive side, that of informing consumers about the characteristics of different products.[7] In such accounts, the information conveyed by advertising is supposed to offer a separate product to consumers, which is of a complementary character to the one actually advertised. It is precisely this separation of advertising information from the product itself, which attracts the criticism of neo-Austrians. As Kirzner notes, the important thing for the entrepreneur is not only to inform consumers about the product, but to ensure that they perceive the opportunity offered.[8] In Kirzner's account, therefore, advertising is a part of the product rather than something separate from it. Thus, the distinction between production and selling costs loses any real significance. Instead of a barrier to entry, advertising activity must be viewed as a typical instance of competitive behaviour.

Capital costs and start-up costs

According to the view of capital costs as entry barriers, the cost of raising the necessary capital is supposed to be so high that potential competitors are barred from entering the monopolist's market. High capital costs are, therefore, supposed to discourage potential competition, exactly as advertising by the monopolist prevents competitors from producing a close substitute. According to O'Driscoll and Rizzo (1985, p. 152), however, there can be no absolute definition of the height of the capital cost, as this height is always relative to the profit which is expected upon entering the monopolistic market. The fact that the capital cost is perceived as being high, only implies, therefore, that the expected profit does not, in the potential competitors' view, justify this venture.

The same argument is employed by neo-Austrians against the view of start-up costs as entry barriers.[9] The fact that the monopolist incurred a high cost for the commencement of the enterprise cannot be supposed to prevent potential competitors from entering the market, provided, of course, that they are willing to bear the same initial cost as the monopolist. In this account, a start-up cost is really the cost of waiting until the initial investment starts to pay off. Therefore, the unwillingness of potential competitors to incur such costs only means that they are not in a position to bear the losses which are usually associated with the early period of an enterprise's operation and does not imply the existence of an entry barrier.

Patents and copyrights

The last category of entry barriers to be examined is that of patents and copyrights. It is really the category of trade secrets, which even Adam Smith thought able to lead to a discrepancy between the natural and the market price of commodities. However, whereas Smith assumed that the impact of these secrets can be only temporary, as they will eventually be discovered by all market participants, the modern legal system has granted to patents and copyrights the status of property rights. Therefore, even if they are discovered, their use is forbidden to anyone but their legitimate owner.

Patents and copyrights pose indeed a delicate problem for neo-Austrian theory. On the one hand, they are viewed as having been imposed on the market by the legal system. On the other hand, however, the legal system itself is seen as a spontaneous product of the market order – as are all social institutions. Thus, according to this latter view, the extension of the freedom of property and contract from material to non-material objects must also be considered as a product of the market order. Therefore, the dilemma neo-Austrians are facing is either to pretend that patents and copyrights do not distort the process of competition or to admit that they are entry barriers created by the market process itself.

This dilemma explains why neo-Austrians are not unanimous in their views on this matter. Hayek recognized that the contemporary legal system often creates the conditions for the emergence of monopoly and he urged that the extension of property rights from material to non-material objects should be treated with caution (1947, p. 114). He was also suspicious of the extension of property rights to trade marks, especially where the seller's trade mark tends to be identified with the product (1947, p. 115). By contrast, O'Driscoll and Rizzo (1985, pp. 155–6) express a much less hostile view toward patents and copyrights. They recognize the problem and admit that it needs further theoretical investigation. They hurry to add, however, that they are not ready to argue against the legal granting of patents and copyrights, as they believe that the distinction between those property rights which are essential for the decentralized operation of the market system and those which may lead to the emergence of monopoly is often very fine.

Kirzner's account of monopoly

This discussion of monopoly seems to reveal a paradox. Neo-Austrians agree with neoclassical theory on the characteristics of a monopolistic market – such as the existence of only one seller, the shape of the demand curve and so on. However, their critique of the various barriers to entry hypotheses seems to imply that monopoly can only be a temporary phenomenon which the process of competition constantly tends to dissolve. The paradox, therefore, is that neo-Austrians seem to agree with neoclassical theory about the description of a phenomenon, the actual existence of which they practically deny.

Actually there is one entry barrier which we have not yet considered, and which Kirzner describes as the case of an entrepreneur who exclusively owns an indispensable resource for the production of a specific good. For example, if a manufacturer of orange juice controls the entire supply of oranges, then any potential competitor is barred from entering the market for this beverage. He/she is not, of course, barred from perceiving the entrepreneurial opportunity of entering this market, but the fact that he/she is not in a position to obtain the most essential resource for the production of orange juice means that entry is barred. This is, according to Kirzner (1973, p. 103), the genuine case of monopoly.

Kirzner's monopolist is also a producer. Therefore, it is not the exclusive ownership of oranges that determines his/her monopolistic position, but the fact that this resource is used exclusively by him/herself in the production of orange juice. If the exclusive owner of orange groves sold his/her product to all interested buyers indiscriminately, entry to the market for orange juice would be free for all.[10] We cannot, of course, treat the mere fact of exclusive ownership as an entry barrier, because that would, according to neo-Austrians, lead to the absurd conclusion that monopoly is a result of private property. It is only the element of exclusive use, therefore, that constitutes an entry barrier to the orange juice market.[11]

This notion of monopoly leads Kirzner to an important conclusion. Exclusive ownership of a resource may be viewed as a feature of the initial distribution of resources amongst the members of society. But it may also be viewed as a product of competitive entrepreneurial behaviour, as the individual who first perceived the importance of a resource for the production of a specific good may have bought up its entire supply from its previous owner. This account has important implications for the analysis of monopoly. From a short-term point of view, the behaviour of Kirzner's monopolist-producer can be considered as an entry barrier. From a long-term point of view, however, the monopolist-producer must be perceived as an entrepreneur who has proven more alert than his/her competitors, and thus his/her behaviour must be seen as proof of the operation of competition.

Monopoly as a protected property right

O'Driscoll (1982) considers Kirzner's view of monopoly as only a variation of the orthodox neoclassical position, because it arbitrarily assumes that the exclusive owner of a resource will also take up production of the relative product. However, why would the exclusive owner of orange groves turn to the production of orange juice, when the selling of oranges to juice manufacturers could still earn him/her monopoly profits? Therefore, according to O'Driscoll, the capacity of an exclusive resource owner to make such profits is entirely independent of his/her ability to bar entry into the market for the final product.

On these grounds, O'Driscoll and Rizzo propose an alternative notion of monopoly which does not, in their view, suffer from the arbitrariness of the neoclassical notion. Having rejected the view of monopoly as the consequence of exclusive resource ownership, they claim that the emergence of monopoly is impossible if competition is entirely free. Thus, obstacles to competition may only originate from outside the market process itself. It is on these grounds that they define monopoly as a legally-enforceable property right to a product or a market share,[12] a notion stemming from Adam Smith's conception of monopoly as the outcome of the granting of privileges by political authority.

This view of monopoly reveals some important social consequences of monopolistic markets. We have seen that neo-Austrians agree with neoclassical theory that the major negative aspect of monopolistic structures is that the monopolist offers a smaller quantity of the product than the quantity he/she would offer under competitive conditions. To this quantitative argument, O'Driscoll and Rizzo (1985, p. 147) add a qualitative one: as the monopolist is protected from competition, nothing will induce him/her to offer consumers the product they actually want. Rather, the general tendency would be to offer them the wrong products, which they have no alternative but to accept. On the other hand, while a monopolist can indeed avoid some costs of competition like advertising or frequent technological modernization, O'Driscoll and Rizzo (1985, p. 150) stress that what he/she cannot avoid is the cost of investing in good relations with the political authority, as a way of ensuring the continuation of the monopolistic privilege.[13]

Labour unions as monopolistic structures

Neo-Austrians are unanimous in describing labour unions as monopolistic structures. The monopolistic nature of their functioning is supposed to lie in the fact that they are in a position to restrict the employer's market freedom, as they force him/her to negotiate the purchase of an essential factor of production from a single source. They are seen, therefore, as displaying all the negative aspects of monopoly: being in a position to impose a monopoly price for labour, while, as at the same time, restricting its supply. On these grounds, Mises (1949, pp. 772–3) considered the monopoly power of unions as direct coercion upon the employer.

Contrary to Mises, Hayek (1946a, p. 104; 1988, p. 131) stressed that the main problem with labour unions is not the coercion they exercise upon the employer but upon non-unionized workers. The monopolistic nature of unions allows them to erect entry barriers to all but their members. Moreover, their monopolistic character is not seen by Hayek as a consequence of workers' rights to form associations (a right which he does not question in principle), but rather as a consequence of the coercive powers governments have allowed unions to exercise, especially through exempting them from the ordinary rules of law. As all monopolistic structures, labour unions are, thus, not products of the market process but are, instead, consequences of political interventions in that process.

Competition and market perfection

If one agrees with neo-Austrians that monopolies are by and large consequences of governmental interventions in the market process, then the idea of a government policy aiming at curbing monopoly power appears absurd. Moreover, neo-Austrians find unacceptable the idea that the state could correct market imperfections, not only because it is incompatible with their particular notion of monopoly as the consequence of the granting of privilege, but also because it presupposes the economist's ability to understand and evaluate economic phenomena on an objective basis. On both these grounds, neo-Austrians reject any idea of an anti-monopoly policy.

For neo-Austrians, the advantages of competition for society do not depend on its being perfect. Hayek (1946a, p. 104) admitted that if competition were perfect, the use of society's resources would be optimal. But he hastened to add that even imperfect competition brings about as effective a use of resources as can be brought about. Therefore, what society must aim at is not to create the ideal conditions of perfect competition but, rather, to abolish any barriers to the actual process of competition.

Evidently, the reaction of neo-Austrians against the idea of anti-monopoly policies is not grounded only on their general aversion to the state's involvement in the economy, but also on epistemological principles. This assertion will become apparent if their position is compared with those of other advocates of market freedom. Henry Simons (1948, p. 30), for example (who, together with Frank Knight, is considered to be the founder of the Chicago School of Economics) believed that the only solution to the problem of monopoly is to place under state control any enterprise that comes to acquire a monopolistic control of a specific market. What inspired Simons's position was not his approval of state interventionism but the positivist outlook of neoclassical theory, which lead to the view that the ideal representative of society, the state, must be commissioned to create the conditions of perfect competition.[14]

The neo-Austrians' critique of anti-monopoly policies is grounded on their dynamic notion of competition as a process, in contrast to the static neoclassical concept of perfect competition. According to neo-Austrians, by attempting to create the conditions of perfect competition, the state is actually constructing a static system. Therefore, state interventionism tends to block market dynamics and, even when the state aims at combatting monopoly, it thus ends up erecting entry barriers to the markets it is trying to control. The nationalization of a private monopoly, for example, is bound to create a public corporation which is institutionally protected from competition, in contrast to a private monopoly where freedom of competition may eventually subvert the monopolist's power.[15]

Anti-monopoly policies and the subjectivity of cost

A second type of criticism neo-Austrians raise against anti-monopoly policies springs from their theory of knowledge. The ability of the state to fight monopolies presupposes the ability of the economist-observer to judge whether and in what respects market reality diverges from the ideal conditions of perfect competition. More specifically, he/she must be able to judge whether the price exceeds the marginal cost of the enterprise. However, according to the neo-Austrian theory of knowledge, this ability presupposes the possession of two types of knowledge: the knowledge of time and place possessed by each individual transactor, and the knowledge of market conditions which will actually prevail in the future. Only on this basis can the economist-observer judge whether a monopolistic market structure is a transitory or a permanent phenomenon. But we know, of course, that neo-Austrians see the obtaining of such knowledge as impossible.

What is especially untenable is the assumption that the economist-observer is in a position to know the marginal cost of an enterprise. The neo-Austrian theory of knowledge sees the economist's perception of cost as necessarily different from that of the monopolist, a view grounded on the fundamental subjectivity of the concept of opportunity cost.[16] In order to be able to know the monopolist's opportunity cost, the economist-observer should be in a position to know the monopolist's own evaluation of the revenues foregone for all possible alternative uses of his/her resources. On these grounds, O'Driscoll (1982, pp. 203–4) maintains that the neoclassical theory of monopoly defines costs and revenues not on the basis of an individual transactor's own perception of these categories but according to the perception of an ideal economist-observer who is situated outside the market system. Thus, according to O'Driscoll, what neoclassical theory fails to understand is that the perception of cost varies according to the vantage point from which it is observed.

The institutional argument

Let us return to Kirzner's monopolist-producer who is supposed to have acquired exclusive control over the entire supply of a specific resource. From a long-term point of view, this situation must be seen as a consequence of the superior alertness of this entrepreneur in perceiving a profit opportunity before his/her competitors. Such a monopoly is beneficial to society as a whole, because, according to Kirzner (1973, p. 240), the alertness of this entrepreneur has led to the production of a good which consumers want and which nobody had offered them so far. From a short-term point of view, however, consumers only stand to gain if the monopolist-producer loses exclusive control of the specific resource, in which case there will be a drop in the price of the final good as well as a rise in the quantity produced. From this point of view, an anti-monopoly policy must be seen as beneficial to society.

Kirzner argues, however, against the idea of an anti-monopoly policy even in this latter case. He claims that even though, from a short-term point of view, an anti-monopoly state action seems to benefit consumers, in the long-run it can only harm them, as it will tend to discourage entrepreneurial activity. According to Kirzner (1973, p. 242), entrepreneurship will perish if under the constant threat of state intervention. Evidently, the essence of Kirzner's argument is institutional, in the sense that it demands that short-term considerations should be subordinated to the requirement of ensuring the stable institutional framework which is essential for the flourishing of entrepreneurship.[17]

Enterprise size and the neo-Austrian notion of monopoly

Before proceeding with our critique of the neo-Austrian theory of monopoly, let us sum up its strong points in comparison to the neoclassical view. Neo-Austrians seem to be justified in attacking the static nature of the neoclassical notion of the market structure, as the latter cannot explain how a monopolistic situation is created. In addition, they convincingly reject the only explanation offered by neoclassical theory, the various barriers to entry hypotheses. Finally, they seem right in their criticism of the static nature of anti-monopoly policies and in their conclusion that such policies can only hinder market dynamics.

However, the most problematic element of the neo-Austrian theory of monopoly is that it does not consider enterprise size as affecting the actual process of competition. Neo-Austrians deny any relation between large size and monopoly power, provided, of course, that the enterprise does not own a protected property right to a market share. In the contemporary economy, however, we observe large concentrations of productive resources functioning under a single entrepreneurial control, which, in spite of operating in a competitive environment, are in a position to maintain or even increase their size independently of their shares of the various markets to which they sell their products. Must we, therefore, assume, as neo-Austrians do, that these large concentrations of capital are only transitory phenomena which the process of competition constantly tends to dissolve?

Contrary to the neo-Austrian position, we will try to establish two points. First, we will argue that large size does secure for an enterprise an advantage over its competitors. Secondly, we will argue that this advantage may be shown to be of a monopolistic character. On these grounds, we will conclude that the nature of the concept of the market structure may indeed be static, but the analysis of market dynamics can nonetheless reveal to the economist-observer the structure of the economy as a whole – a structure which the market process itself constantly tends to bring about.

Size as an advantage over the competition

As we have shown, the tendency toward growth of enterprise size – or, more generally, of the volume of resources operating under a single entrepreneurial control – can be assumed even under the neo-Austrian theory of knowledge. In fact, we argued that this tendency is based on the information advantage that large size entails, in the sense that a large enterprise has better access than its competitors to the knowledge which circulates freely in the market system. The conclusion in the previous chapter was that there is a positive correlation between size and access to information. Furthermore, we believe our argument to be of a dynamic nature: large size today cannot necessarily ensure large size tomorrow, but it can certainly enable the enterprise to pursue such a target with better chances of success.[18]

Interestingly enough, Hayek did recognize that the tendency toward larger enterprise size cannot but adversely affect the efficiency of the market system, which is why he argues for some sort of central regulation of enterprise size. The target of his criticism is, in fact, the modern legal system, which grants to the corporation the same transaction rights that it grants to the individual. Hayek did not deny the right of a corporation to own stock of other corporations as an investment. What he insisted upon, however, is that this stock should have no voting rights (1960a, p. 309). Therefore, contrary to most neo-Austrians, Hayek seems to realize that the legal attribution of voting rights to large corporations contradicts the major conclusion of the neo-Austrian theory of knowledge that an efficient competitive order requires every individual to use freely the tacit knowledge that he/she possesses. Evidently, it would be absurd to claim, for instance, that a large corporation owning the majority of the stock of each of ten subsidiaries is also in a position to obtain the tacit knowledge of time and place possessed by each of these ten subsidiaries.

Hayek's dilemma is that while he realizes the above absurdity, he is, at the same time, unwilling to accept that the tendency of enterprise size to grow is a consequence of the market process itself. For if he did so, he would actually be admitting that, in the modern economy, access to knowledge is positively correlated with size and, thus, with factor ownership. To avoid this dilemma, he puts the blame for the growing size of modern corporations on the legal system. Evidently, however, this is a Utopian position, as it contradicts the logic of the institution of private property. His stance against voting rights, for example, actually amounts to a demand that the resource owners (the majority of the shareholders of the holding company) should concede to transfer control of their property to other individuals – the minority of the shareholders of the subsidiaries. Hayek is thus faced with a fundamental contradiction, which characterizes the whole of his philosophy. While he believes that the legal system is a spontaneous outcome of the proliferation of the market culture, he also implies that it tends to produce practices which undermine this culture.

From the structure of the market to the structure of the market system as a whole

We can now take up our second point, that is the monopolistic character of the information advantage of large concentrations of capital. If this advantage is not shown to be of a monopolistic, or protected, character, its existence could be seen as merely temporary. Our argument is once again grounded on our critique of the neo-Austrian theory of knowledge expounded in the previous chapter. We have seen that the market process itself produces forces that lead to the objectification, or commodification, of ever-growing sectors of knowledge. Thus, the ability of market participants to manage the flow of knowledge in the market system is positively correlated with the volume of capital they possess.

The essence of our argument can now become clearer if we use an example. Imagine the economy as a system of simple commodity production in the Marxian sense of the term. In this context, it is reasonable to assume that the knowledge every individual possesses is entirely tacit. A shoemaker, for instance, knows his/her trade, but he/she is not in a position to describe all the details of his/her production process. In the modern economy, where the production of shoes involves complex technical processes and is carried out by relatively large production units, the complex division of labour requires the transformation of the knowledge of production processes into conscious and objective knowledge. If, however, technical knowledge has been objectified to such a degree, then any new technical knowledge (any innovation in the production of shoes) must, from the point of view of the enterprise, now be perceived as an objective factor that can be purchased like any other material resource. In fact, such knowledge *is* a resource and, therefore, the firm's ability to obtain it depends on its economic power.

However, if major sectors of knowledge are transformed into private property, thus ceasing to be freely accessible to all market participants, the efficiency of the system is dramatically reduced. The economic power of large units of capital now allows them to exclude large sections of knowledge from all other market participants and, thus, to protect this knowledge from competitors. What we have here, of course, is the transformation of the information advantage, which was the object of our first point above, into the monopolistic control of a scarce resource.

Although Hayek is the theorist who introduced the notion of tacit knowledge, he seems, at the same time, to recognize that the modern economy constantly tends to transform knowledge from tacit into conscious. He sees such a tendency in the extension of property rights to non-material objects, a view which explains his negative stance toward patents and copyrights. This stance seems to contradict, however, the principle of methodological individualism, according to which all economic phenomena must be studied from the point of view of the individual actor. It is exactly from this point of view that any distinction between ownership of material and non-material objects is meaningless. From the point of view of the acting entrepreneur, whenever a sector of knowledge becomes objectively known, it automatically assumes the same character like any material resource. Therefore, in contrast to what Hayek believes, the extension of property rights to non-material objects is not a distorting effect of the modern legal system but is, instead, a consequence of the market process itself.

However, if the information advantage of large units of capital is, as we have argued, of a monopolistic nature, the insistence of neo-Austrians upon the temporary character of monopolistic situations can no longer be sustained. Nor can the phenomenon of monopoly be viewed exclusively as a product of state interventionism, since it can also be a consequence of the dynamics of competition. We are now led, however, to an even more important conclusion. Although we first agreed with the neo-Austrians' rejection of the static nature of the neoclassical notion of the market structure, we can now substantiate a view of the market system as a structured system. It can, in other words, be shown that market dynamics tends to produce a specific form of the system as a whole. The structure of the market system seems, thus, to take the form of a pyramid. The higher an individual is situated in the pyramid, the greater the amount of productive resources he/she controls and the higher his/her information advantage will be. Conversely, the lower in the pyramid one is situated, the smaller the size of one's property and the lower one's information advantage. Thus, the latter individual will be able to merely respond to the flow of knowledge transmitted from the highest levels.

Such a conclusion constitutes, of course, a first affirmation of the possibility of objective knowledge of economic phenomena. Without having to revert to the perfect knowledge assumption of neoclassical theory, we have shown that the economist-observer is able to perceive the form of the market system which the dynamics of the market process constantly tends to produce and sustain. The neo-Austrian understanding of the market system as the indeterminate outcome of numberless individual actions is, thus, put into question. The dynamics of the market process is, instead, primarily determined by the action of the large concentrations of capital, while the individual who does not own any factors of production is now a genuine price-taker who can never affect prices through his/her actions.

A Marxian view on the problem of size

The neo-Austrian rejection of the orthodox neoclassical notion of the market structure implies that markets are always interconnected, and that competition drives the actions of transactors not only within the context of a single market but in the market system as a whole. How characteristically neo-Austrian is this idea?

We will now present a contemporary Marxist account of the theories of competition and monopoly, expounded by Semmler (1982), which displays extremely interesting similarities with the neo-Austrian critique of orthodox monopoly theory, though it leads to a view of the functioning of the market system which is almost identical with our own conclusion about the structure of the market system as a whole.

Semmler begins with a review of the various Marxist theories of monopoly capitalism, and concludes that they all view monopoly as a consequence of the existence of entry barriers. Thus, they claim that in monopolistic conditions Marx's law of value is invalidated, in the sense that the prices of production are no longer the centres of gravity toward which market prices converge. On these grounds, monopolistic enterprises are assumed to be in a position to systematically extract profit rates which are higher than the economy's average. Thus, instead of a tendency toward the equalization of profit rates, monopolistic conditions create a stable hierarchy of profit rates. Monopolies are supposed to occupy the highest ranks of this hierarchy, as a result of their reaping monopolistic profits, while the lowest ranks are occupied by firms which operate in competitive conditions and earn profits which are lower than the economy's average.

Semmler analyses a number of econometric studies that attempt to prove the existence of a systematic correlation between a hierarchy of profit rates and various barriers to entry in monopolistic markets and shows that none of them manages to prove the existence of such a correlation. Even in cases where a statistically significant correlation seems to appear, Semmler (1982, pp. 97–100) claims that Marx's theory of the equalization process of profit rates could offer a more satisfactory explanation of this phenomenon. According to Marx, the process of competition among capitals produces differential profit rates within each sector as well as an equalization tendency across industries. For Marx, the existence of differential profit rates does not mark the absence of competition but, instead, confirms its presence. Therefore, Semmler concludes that viewing the existence of differential rates as a sign of monopolistic conditions is equivalent to viewing the economy from the static viewpoint of neoclassical theory rather than from the dynamic viewpoint of Marxian theory.

The affinity of Semmler's notion of competition with the process analysis of neo-Austrians is really remarkable.[19] Their final conclusions are, however, very different. Neo-Austrians believe that monopoly can only be a temporary phenomenon. By contrast, Semmler proposes that we should employ the term 'large units of capital' instead of monopoly. The theoretical superiority of Semmler's concept arises from the fact that it can accommodate two phenomena which are characteristic of modern reality. First, these large units of capital are not only formed through the acquisition of a sector's smaller production units by one big corporation, but also through the acquisition by a parent company of firms that operate in sectors other than its own.[20] Second, it is no longer necessary to assume that the behaviour of these large units will conform to the behaviour of monopolies as specified by orthodox neoclassical theory, that they will charge, for example, monopoly prices and earn monopoly profits. On the contrary, says Semmler (1982, p. 111), the main target of these corporations is to secure long-run normal costs, output and prices.

Semmler's account leads, of course, to a very different view of the market system from that of neo-Austrians. The theoretical dissociation of enterprise size from market structure means that competition never ceases to operate, but also never leads the market system in the direction neo-Austrians believe that it does. The market system cannot be seen as a consumers' democracy, as Mises (1927/1985, p. xvi) believed, but as an inherently hierarchical structure. Thus, Semmler's view of the market system is almost identical with the pyramid-like structure which, as we argued, the market process tends to produce.

Semmler concludes that large corporations rely less and less on traditional regulatory institutions, such as monetary and fiscal policy, and thus tend to become increasingly independent from state regulation. More than that, as multi-product and multi-plant corporations, they constantly tend to become independent from the market itself. What is important for the long-run expansion of their capital does not have anything to do with exchange, that is, the market but with developments in the sphere of production. The most important single requirement for the realization of the value of their capital is the constant effort to develop their production processes, so that their cost is constantly suppressed. This is necessarily a competitive effort, and its measure of success depends on the ability of each large corporation to exclude its competitors from new production processes.[21] Therefore, the institutional granting of property rights in the area of patents and copyrights is inexorably linked with the logic of their operation. It is again a conclusion identical with the one we have expressed.

We are now faced with two important consequences regarding the notion of anti-monopoly policy. First, we have shown that the economist-observer possesses a knowledge of an entirely different nature from that of an individual market participant, the knowledge of the dynamics and of the form of the market system as a whole. This is objective knowledge, and such objectivity allows normative analysis. Second, since we have rejected the notion of market structure, an anti-monopoly policy cannot aim to bring actual market conditions closer to neoclassical perfection. As Semmler points out, the aim of such a policy can no longer be the control of market shares but, rather, the control and regulation of the financial resources, the investment and production of large corporations.

Notes

1. It is generally recognized that the theories of monopolistic or imperfect competition which were put forward in the 1930s provided the theoretical and ideological justification for government intervention. See Chamberlin (1933/1962) and Robinson (1933/1979).
2. See Chamberlin (1954, p. 255).
3. In this account, the monopolist's power depends on the value of the cross-elasticity between the demand for his/her products and the demand for the closest substitutes.
4. See Friedman (1973, p. 41).
5. To support this argument, O'Driscoll and Rizzo (1985, p. 154) use the example of railroads. In the 19th century, railroads were considered to be a typical natural monopoly. The development, however, of road transport from the beginning of the 20th century has led to the development of competition in the transport industry and has, thus, subverted the monopoly power of railroads.
6. This view of advertising as a factor of monopolistic control of markets, seems to have been the orthodox view from the 1930s to the 1950s, as evidenced from works such as Pigou (1932, p. 196), Robinson (1933/1979, p. 90), Kaldor (1949–50, p. 118), and Simons (1948, p. 95).
7. See Pigou (1932, p. 196) and Kaldor (1949–50, p. 103).
8. See Kirzner (1973, p. 148). It is clear that the difference between information about and perception of an opportunity stems from the notion of error which we analysed in the previous chapter.
9. For the orthodox view of start-up cost see Bain (1956, p. 55) and Mason (1967, p. 348).
10. For an analytical exposition of this instance, see Kirzner (1963, pp. 226–8).
11. Kirzner's notion of monopoly seems to be rooted in the views of the pioneers of the neo-Austrian school. Mises (1922/1981, p. 349) claimed that a monopolist's position can be secured much more easily if it is grounded on the exclusive control of a natural resource rather than on the control of some intermediate product. Hayek (1960, p. 136), on the other hand, believed that only if a monopolist is the exclusive owner of a scarce resource – as is the case with someone who owns a well in the desert – can he/she exercise coercion upon consumers. Patents and copyrights really belong to this category, as they can be viewed as scarce non-material resources.
12. See O'Driscoll and Rizzo (1985, p. 149). For a similar view of monopoly see Armentano (1978) and Rothbard (1962).
13. Important as the methodological distinction between the Mises–Kirzner and the O'Driscoll and Rizzo notions of monopoly may be, it should not blind us to the fundamental agreement amongst neo-Austrians that the most important cause of monopoly is state interventionism. As Mises (1949, p. 363) emphatically pointed out, monopolies are not consequences of the market process but of the conscious actions of governments. Hayek (1966, p. 176) expressed a similar opinion when he stressed that it is much more important for governments to avoid aiding the emergence of monopolies, than it is to try to fight them.
14. Hayek disapproved of interpretations of Simons's work that viewed it as 'socialist'. At the same time, however, his uneasiness with some aspects of this work – such as Simons's position on monopoly – is quite obvious. See Hayek (1949a, p. 191).
15. Hayek added another doubt on the notion of an anti-monopoly policy. As any act of state interventionism, an anti-monopoly policy is the product of a political decision and is, thus, entirely independent of market signals. However, state interventionism necessarily lacks the flexibility of response to market signals that characterizes the economic behaviour of private transactors. There can be no guarantee, therefore, that an anti-monopoly action will be abandoned as soon as it has achieved its declared objective. As the process of competition will have been suspended, the price system can never reveal when state action will no longer be necessary. Thus, according to Hayek (1966, p. 176), government-supervised monopolies will automatically tend to be transformed to government-protected monopolies.
16. See Kauder (1965, p. 172), concerning the introduction of the concept of opportunity cost by Wieser.

17. The relevance of such an institutional argument is even wider. As shown by Hayek, the market is itself an institution. Viewed as an institution, the market displays the inexorable unity of its two moments: the process of competition and exchange as well as the distributional outcome of that process. Any intervention in the distributional aspects of the market process cannot, therefore, leave the process of competition unaffected but, on the contrary, tends to undermine it. Any anti-monopoly policy can, thus, only lead to the subversion of the spontaneous order of the market. As O'Driscoll and Rizzo (1985, p. 131) put it, we cannot question the distributional outcomes of the market process, without, at the same time, questioning the market process itself.
18. Of course, neo-Austrians can never see the size of enterprise distorting competition – a position derived from their argument against the notion of start-up costs as a barrier to entry. This position does not, however, affect the validity of our argument, since the latter does not rest on the static notion of entry barriers.
19. Semmler (1983, p. 93) explicitly notes the similarities of the concepts of competition in the classical, Marxian and Austrian theories, in contra-distinction to the concept of perfect competition of the neoclassical school.
20. This is the category of multi-product firms.
21. See Semmler (1982, p. 110).

5 The theory of entrepreneurship

Neo-Austrians are very much in need of a theory of entrepreneurship. Their rejection of price-taking behaviour and their conception of the market as a system in constant flux are based on a view of the flow of information as the moving force of economic activity. Therefore, they need a theory describing, on the one hand, the motive that mobilizes creative use of knowledge and, on the other, the exact mode in which this behaviour is expressed in the market process. The theory of entrepreneurship is proposed as the answer to both points. And since creative activity is not, as we have seen, compatible with the concept of perfect competition, entrepreneurial behaviour can only be conceptualized as a phenomenon which springs from the reality of market disequilibrium.[1]

Two aspects of human action

Our reference to entrepreneurial behaviour seems to imply that there are other types of behaviour which do not belong to this category. Indeed, neo-Austrians distinguish between two aspects of human action. The first, which they describe as optimizing, is the notion of human action espoused by orthodox neoclassical theory, according to which, every individual is supposed to maximize the utility he/she can achieve through the use of the means that are available to him/her. Underlying this notion is the assumption that the individual knows perfectly well both the ends he/she is trying to achieve as well as the means that are available – that is, the ends-means framework within which his/her activity will unfold. In such a context, the notion of human action evidently assumes the character of problem-solving behaviour.[2]

However, neo-Austrians consider a second aspect of human action to be more important, namely, all behaviour which does not merely occur within the context of a given ends-means framework, but which also involves the individual's choice of the framework in which he/she will act. From the point of view of the individual actor, the act of choosing the relevant framework is a true act of creation, as this framework did not really exist prior to its having been chosen. According to Kirzner (1973, p. 35), it is actually only this creative aspect of action that deserves to be called entrepreneurial.

The entrepreneurship of Robinson Crusoe

The fact that entrepreneurial behaviour is defined as an aspect of action allows neo-Austrians to claim that it is a category that characterizes the behaviour of even one single individual isolated from society. In order to illustrate this point, Kirzner employs the example of Robinson Crusoe.

Suppose that Crusoe is currently using his bare hands to catch fish. This activity is perceived by him as optimizing, in the sense that he is constantly trying to minimize the time he spends in order to catch the fish he needs. However, one day he decides to devote part of his time in making a boat and a net, as he believes that a new fishing method will allow him to substantially increase his catch. He understands, therefore, that so far his activity was based on an error, even though it was rational within the particular ends-means framework in which he was functioning. As Kirzner (1978, p. 164) notes, Crusoe had not previously perceived that a different ends-means framework would offer him a profit opportunity, and it is precisely the discovery of this error that makes his behaviour entrepreneurial.

Crusoe's entrepreneurial behaviour can be perceived as an effort to overcome the fundamental ignorance within which he, like any individual, has to operate. What Crusoe lacked is not the technical knowledge of how to build a boat and a net but, rather, the knowledge of an alternative ends-means framework that would make his efforts more productive. This framework was always potentially present but Crusoe had not perceived its existence. Its discovery can be seen as a result of his alertness. It is futile to ask whether Crusoe is aware that he possesses alertness or that he is capable of acting entrepreneurially. As Kirzner (1978, p. 169) stresses, the presence of this subjective property can only be perceived at the moment it is actually revealed. Thus, the knowledge involved in entrepreneurial activity is entirely supra-conscious.[3]

Entrepreneurial activity in the market process

As in the case of an isolated individual, neo-Austrians view entrepreneurship as springing from the notions of ignorance and error in the context of the market process as well. Of course, ignorance is really the opposite of the orthodox assumption of perfect knowledge. Therefore, entrepreneurship is incompatible with perfect knowledge, in the presence of which the actor would be under no inducement to search for alternative ends-means frameworks.

The introduction of ignorance has profound implications for the manner in which market activity is understood. The abandonment of the perfect knowledge assumption implies that the market is not in equilibrium and, consequently, that Jevons's law of indifference does not hold. Thus, the same good may be sold at different prices. This is precisely the situation described by Kirzner's example of the two shops selling apples at different prices, discussed in Chapter 3. The knowledge of this market error is freely accessible to all transactors. Therefore, the apple seller – or any other market participant for that matter – who first realizes the existence of this error may act entrepreneurially by offering a price slightly higher than one dollar in order to buy the whole quantity of apples from the first seller, and then proceed to sell it for slightly less than two dollars to all buyers who were previously willing to buy from the second seller. According to Kirzner (1973, p. 16), this is the case of pure entrepreneurship, where an individual takes advantage of a profit opportunity without having to expend any resources. Thus, as in the example of Robinson Crusoe, a profit opportunity is seen as the motive of entrepreneurial activity in the market.[4]

Reekie (1984, p. 45) further analyses entrepreneurship with the aid of an Edgeworth box. The existence of a market error is depicted by the fact that the two transactors do not realize that they can both increase their utility by moving to higher indifference curves. Thus, they remain on intersecting rather than on tangential curves. The distance between the two curves defines the profit opportunity which any pure entrepreneur may perceive and take advantage of. Entrepreneurial activity is thus perceived as an arbitrage function. However, the notion of arbitrage should not be taken to imply that entrepreneurial activity is a phenomenon of the sphere of exchange alone. According to Kirzner (1973, p. 18), entrepreneurial activity is, in the sphere of production as well, motivated by a profit opportunity perceived as the possibility of buying means of production and selling the final product at a revenue higher than total cost.

Entrepreneurship, competition and equilibrium

This leads to two important observations regarding the nature of entrepreneurship. First, that entrepreneurial behaviour is always competitive. As the essence of this behaviour is the discovery of profit opportunities, a successful entrepreneur is one who perceives these opportunities before his/her competitors. Conversely, competitive activity is always entrepreneurial, since the essence of competitive behaviour is the discovery of market errors. Therefore, for neo-Austrians, the notions of entrepreneurship and competition are complementary.

The second observation concerns the role of entrepreneurship in the operation of the market system as a whole. Entrepreneurial activity is a product of market disequilibrium. However, its character is by definition equilibrating, as it constantly tends to eradicate its own cause, for evidently taking advantage of a profit opportunity is equivalent to cancelling it.[5] Therefore, the entrepreneur of neo-Austrian theory is the exact opposite of the Schumpeterian entrepreneur. The latter is an individual who destabilizes the market's equilibrium by introducing revolutionary production and management techniques. Neo-Austrians, by contrast, view entrepreneurial activity as the force that constantly pushes prices toward equilibrium.

Who is the entrepreneur of neo-Austrian theory?

The fact that entrepreneurship is defined as an aspect of human action, implies that its exercise must be considered a general feature of human existence. Thus, as Mises (1949, p. 253) points out, the function of the entrepreneur must not be attributed to any specific individual or social group. It could be argued, however, that an individual's or a group's position in the market system may enhance the cultivation of the properties of alertness and perception, which constitute the essence of entrepreneurial behaviour. Such a view would, of course, tend to link this behaviour to factor ownership. Therefore, the first issue to be investigated is the relation between the entrepreneur and the capitalist.

Kirzner proposes an abstract model for the analysis of this relation. Suppose that market society is composed of two distinct groups. The first includes all those who only act in an optimizing fashion within a given ends-means framework. The second group comprises the entrepreneurs, those who constantly evaluate and choose from such alternative frameworks. The members of this second group are considered to be 'pure' entrepreneurs, as the success of their activity depends on their alertness to profit opportunities and is, thus, entirely independent of factor ownership. As Kirzner (1973, p. 48) stresses, 'a profit opportunity means the discovery of something obtainable for nothing at all'. Therefore, in his account, entrepreneurship does not entail capital ownership.

In the previous section, we briefly touched upon a further sense in which entrepreneurship is independent of factor ownership, the fact that it cannot be considered itself a factor of production. A factor of production is already present prior to its owner's decision to employ it in some particular mode. Entrepreneurial activity, by contrast, does not actually exist before its appearance in practice. Moreover, according to Kirzner (1980, p. 11), an individual can never be conscious of possessing the ability to act entrepreneurially. Therefore, as a typical example of supra-conscious knowledge, entrepreneurship cannot be viewed as a factor of production. Thus, neo-Austrian theory views entrepreneurship as an entirely subjective function.[6]

Kirzner's model of a society made up of an optimizing and an entrepreneurial group is, of course, only a theoretical abstraction. In reality, both of these behaviours occur simultaneously. Moreover, although it is true that the exercise of pure entrepreneurship does not presuppose factor ownership, it is equally true that a capitalist must necessarily be an entrepreneur. Let us analyse Mises's argument in support of this claim. Suppose that an entrepreneur borrows the capital he/she needs. From the legal point of view, this entrepreneur is the owner of this capital but, in essence, he/she remains propertiless since his/her assets equal exactly his/her liabilities. If the profit opportunity is actually realized, the relative profit is reaped by the entrepreneur. If, however, the venture leads to a loss, the burden will fall on the capitalist. Therefore, Mises (1949, p. 254) concludes that a capitalist's function is always entrepreneurial, because the decision to lend capital to a prospective entrepreneur necessarily involves the discovery of a profit opportunity which may or may not be actually realized.

At first glance, Mises's claim that a capitalist is always an entrepreneur seems to contradict Kirzner's view of pure entrepreneurship. However, as Kirzner (1974a, p. 97) himself stresses, the fact that every capitalist always acts entrepreneurially does not mean that every entrepreneur must necessarily be a capitalist. Moreover, he argues that securing the necessary capital for the realization of a profit opportunity constitutes an integral part of entrepreneurial activity.[7]

Profit as an *ex-post* criterion of entrepreneurship

The denial of any link between entrepreneurship and capital ownership leaves unanswered the question of who the entrepreneur is, which formed the title of the previous section. If the exercise of entrepreneurship is independent of any objective feature of an individual's position in the market system, how can the economist distinguish entrepreneurial behaviour from other types of market activity? Kirzner argues that since profit is the motive of entrepreneurial activity, the realization of profits must be treated as an ex-post proof that entrepreneurship has been actually exercised.

Kirzner (1973, pp. 57–62) uses an example in order to show how his criterion might be employed. Suppose that an individual perceives a profit opportunity in the market for meat and decides to rent a gun and hire a hunter. If we assume that this individual initially borrowed the capital required, he/she remains propertiless. The revenue that remains after the repayment of the initial loan is the entrepreneurial profit and, as such, constitutes proof that entrepreneurship actually has been exercised. Of course, this profit opportunity will eventually attract other entrepreneurs into the meat market and, as a consequence, the rent of guns and the wages of hunters will increase until there are no more profits to be made in this business. However, for as long as profits were realized, they must be perceived as a sign of entrepreneurial activity.

We have, so far, implicitly assumed that all guns and all hunters are of exactly the same quality. Let us now assume that one hunter is superior to all others because of his/her ability to find rich hunting grounds. We can distinguish between two possibilities. The first is that this hunter is not consciously aware of his/her exceptional ability. In this case, he/she will secure for the employer a bigger quantity of meat than the competitors' hunters. The enterprise will, therefore, make a profit. Evidently, this profit is a result of entrepreneurial activity, as it springs from the employer's superior alertness, which led to the hiring of the exceptional hunter. The competition among the employers will raise the hunter's wages and profit will eventually disappear. The fact, however, remains that profit, for as long as it was realized, was, again, proof of this employer's entrepreneurship.

The second possibility is that the hunter is fully aware of his/her exceptional ability, in which case two further possibilities arise. The first is that the employer does not realize the superior potential of his/her employee. Thus, the latter may keep the profit to him/herself. The existence of this profit shows, of course, that entrepreneurial activity has been exercised by the hunter. The second possibility is that the employer realizes the hunter's potential. In this case the profit will be the result of the entrepreneurship exercised jointly by both the employer and the hunter, so that both of them must be viewed as constituting the entrepreneur.

The nature of the criterion proposed by Kirzner is now clear. As he points out (1973, p. 51), 'the correct theoretical characterization of a particular receipt depends on the character of the decision responsible for that receipt'. Therefore, in a particular situation, we can always judge who the person, or persons, who acted entrepreneurially is, by observing who actually obtained a venture's profit. In Kirzner's account, entrepreneurship may be exercised by the employer, the employee, or jointly by both.

The entrepreneurial role in the modern corporation

The reality of modern corporations is, of course, much more complex than the possibilities considered by Kirzner. Therefore, a theory attempting to locate the entrepreneurial role in the context of the modern corporation must explain how its owners, the shareholders, exercise their entrepreneurship. Of course, the idea that the owners of capital act entrepreneurially is already accepted by neo-Austrians. However, what is difficult to specify in this context is the role of the pure, or propertiless, entrepreneur.

According to Kirzner (1974a, p. 101), what a propertiless entrepreneur must try to do in order to secure the capital necessary for the realization of the profit opportunity he/she perceives, is to convince a capitalist about his/her personal integrity as well as about the profitability of the project he/she proposes. However, the negotiation between the capitalist and the potential entrepreneur involves a transactions cost. From the latter's point of view, this is the cost he/she must incur in order to convince the capitalist of his/her integrity and entrepreneurial judgement. From the point of view of the capitalist, it is the opportunity cost of choosing the entrepreneur who will secure the highest profit.

Kirzner (1974a, p. 104) believes that the corporate form of business organization is an ingenious device, which enables modern business to avoid this transactions cost. Capital does not have to be lent by the capitalist to the potential entrepreneur, as the latter can hire him/herself out to the capitalist as corporate executive. Thus, the entrepreneurial role is now shared between the owners and the executives of the corporation – a situation that resembles the last case in Kirzner's example (where the entrepreneurship is exercised by both the employer and the employee, jointly).[8]

The fact that entrepreneurship can be shared between the shareholders and the management of the modern corporation, does not mean that neo-Austrians espouse Galbraith's thesis (1967, chapters 5 and 6) on the separation between ownership and control. On the contrary, they stress that the fact that control remains firmly in the hands of the owners is supported by two considerations. First, the shareholders retain the right to sack the management, when the latter's performance is judged unsatisfactory. Second, they can always get rid of their shares by selling them in the stock market.[9]

Entrepreneurship and state interventionism

We have already seen that the exercise of entrepreneurship is independent of factor ownership. However, the logic of neo-Austrian theory leads to a still more important conclusion: the more unequal the distribution of wealth is, the more vigorous entrepreneurial activity will be. Inequality of market outcomes is both the cause and the effect of entrepreneurial activity. Therefore, by discouraging entrepreneurship, any attempt toward a more equitable distribution of wealth necessarily hinders economic development.

For profit opportunities to be perceivable, the market system must function entirely unhindered, as only in this case do price signals transfer correct information about transactors' intentions. This transfer includes information about market errors and inconsistencies, which constitute the profit opportunities the potential entrepreneur is alert to. Any state intervention in the market process tends, therefore, to discourage entrepreneurship, as it hinders the discovery of market errors. Thus, according to Kirzner (1974, p. 92), free entry to all markets constitutes the most fundamental requirement for the exercise of entrepreneurship.

This line of argument leads neo-Austrians to two important conclusions. First, state interventionism distorts market signals by either preventing errors from being perceived or by magnifying them beyond any proportion. These distortions are not confined to the market where the actual intervention takes place, but are multiplied as they are dispersed by the price mechanism through the whole system. Therefore, even if the short-run objectives of the intervention are accomplished, its long-run effect will be the destruction of entrepreneurial possibilities.[10] The second conclusion is that, as it is a function which is independent of capital ownership, entrepreneurship will be present even in a society in which private property has been abolished altogether.

Entrepreneurship and socialism

At first glance, the second conclusion above seems like a paradox, for it raises the question of what would the motive of entrepreneurship be in a society where there was no form of private property. However, neo-Austrians regard profit, in the sense of a personal benefit, as a motive of individual activity which is independent of the institutional framework. Two illustrative cases which seem to justify this view, will now be examined.

The first case is described by the instance in Kirzner's example where the employer is unaware of the hunter's exceptional ability, in which case the hunter is in a position to reap the entrepreneurial profit him/herself. In a socialist system, the state is the only employer and, as there are no markets for capital goods, has no way to judge whether an enterprise is making profits or losses. Moreover, there is no mechanism which evaluates the performance of the management of state corporations. The problem of such a society would be actually twofold. On the one hand, there would be no way of knowing which enterprises are run unprofitably and, as a consequence, social capital would be used inefficiently. On the other hand, there would be no way of knowing which enterprises are making profits, thus allowing the managers of those enterprises to appropriate profits for their personal benefit.[11]

The second case is that of non-pecuniary profits, such as less work pressure or greater appreciation of the manager's performance by the superiors in the hierarchy. For neo-Austrians, this kind of entrepreneurial activity arises because the manager of a socialized enterprise cannot be judged on the basis of any profitability criteria. Thus, some alternative criteria are required. However, as there is no competition amongst producers, consumers' satisfaction does not play any role in evaluating entrepreneurial performance. Therefore, the only reward that the individual manager can strive for has to be sought from his/her hierarchical superiors.[12]

Cultural foundations of entrepreneurship

We have, so far, concentrated on the institutional requirements for the flourishing of entrepreneurial activity. However, the fact that neo-Austrians define entrepreneurship as an aspect of human action implies that there also have to be some subjective requirements. Although entrepreneurship cannot be taught, neo-Austrians argue that it may be promoted or discouraged by a society's culture. The abolition of private property, for instance, does not hinder entrepreneurial activity solely through the institutional barriers it imposes, but also through the proliferation of a culture that destroys the will to act creatively – a culture that tolerates the gradual erosion of liberty.[13]

On these grounds, Kirzner argues against the orthodox theory of economic development. He believes that the latter concentrates on the analysis of the technical requirements of development, like the rise in the productivity of labour, the accumulation of capital, the increase in international trade, and so on. He points out (1969, p. 118) that envisaging these issues as technical problems leads to the conclusion that the best solution must be sought through central state direction. He claims, by contrast, that the most important problem faced by underdeveloped countries is the fact that their cultural traditions do not encourage entrepreneurship. Therefore, instead of the centrally-planned direction of economic activity, the main objective of such societies should be the encouragement of entrepreneurial activity through the creation of a free market environment.

The moral justification of the entrepreneurial function

We may finally turn to the moral justification of entrepreneurship which neo-Austrians propose, and especially their moral justification of profit. In orthodox neoclassical theory, the principle of marginal productivity postulates that, as long as we assume perfect competition, every reward reflects the actual contribution of each factor in production. Neo-Austrians, however, do not view profit as the reward of a factor of production and are thus in need of a different moral justification of profits.

Kirzner claims that the neoclassical theory of profit is grounded in Locke's classical theory of the right to property. According to Locke, the individual has a moral right to own his/her own person and, consequently, his/her labour, as well as the goods that he/she can obtain by combining this labour with freely-available resources. Finally, he/she has a moral right to own all that can be obtained by the expenditure of the property that has been accumulated in that process. Kirzner (1973, pp. 193–4), maintains that factor rewards are, in the context of Locke's theory, viewed as automatic derivatives of property, because they stem from it without its owner having to act in order to acquire them.[14]

As an alternative, Kirzner puts forward a notion of the right to property which attempts to define this right independently of the prior possession of property. As entrepreneurship creates a profit opportunity that did not exist prior to its being perceived, Kirzner (1973a, p. 194) sees the profit earned by entrepreneurial activity as not springing from property but as, instead, created by entrepreneurial action itself. It is this notion of property rights that justifies the entrepreneur's 'ethical deservingness' of the profit he/she created by his/her actions. Kirzner (1978a, p. 212) labels this new moral principle as the principle of the 'finder-creator-keeper'.

An alternative view of entrepreneurship

It should be clear by now why we chose to begin this chapter by stressing that neo-Austrians are in need of a theory of entrepreneurship. In Chapter 3, we saw that they view the circulation of knowledge as the moving force of economic activity. The principle of methodological individualism requires, however, that both the generation and perception of knowledge be linked to a specific individual behaviour. The fact that it is entrepreneurship that is proposed to fill this theoretical need, can be illustrated by a simile: for neo-Austrians, knowledge is the pollen that fertilizes the market system, while the entrepreneur is the bee responsible for the transport of pollen. Without the entrepreneur the market system would collapse, as knowledge would cease to be generated and perceived.

Our analysis of the neo-Austrian theory of entrepreneurship has shown that its truly radical characteristic is its twofold dissociation of entrepreneurial activity from factor ownership. Entrepreneurial activity is neither itself a factor of production nor does it require prior ownership of capital. It is this twofold dissociation of entrepreneurship from capital ownership upon which our critique must focus.

Entrepreneurship and the theory of knowledge

According to the neo-Austrian theory of knowledge, entrepreneurship must be seen as constituting the ultimate type of tacit knowledge. Consider, for instance, its difference from the tacit knowledge of time and place. Although an individual is not in a position to articulate his/her knowledge of time and place, he/she may, at least, be aware of its existence. This is particularly true in cases where this knowledge refers to some process that is being repeated through time. By contrast, the knowledge of the entrepreneur has the character of a discovery. However, the fact that a profit opportunity is discovered today does not mean that another such opportunity will be discovered in the future. Thus, the entrepreneur cannot be aware that he/she possesses some special kind of knowledge. Therefore, neo-Austrians view entrepreneurship as an entirely inalienable kind of knowledge.

However, other aspects of the theory of entrepreneurship seem to contradict this view. We will argue, first, that entrepreneurial knowledge is constantly being objectified in the market process and that it tends to assume the character of a consciously-held technical knowledge, which is perceived as such both by the entrepreneur and other market participants. Second, we will argue that this process transforms entrepreneurship into an alienable and, thus, transferable kind of knowledge. On these grounds, we will reject the strictly subjectivist character of entrepreneurship proposed by neo-Austrians, and we will maintain that the market process itself tends to transform entrepreneurship into a factor of production.

We have already come across an instance involving the transfer of entrepreneurship in Chapter 4. Arguing for the competitive character of advertising, Kirzner claims that what the entrepreneur is trying to achieve through advertising is not to inform the consumers about the positive features of the product but, rather, to make them perceive the opportunity that the consumption of the specific product represents. Kirzner (1973, p. 148) sees the entrepreneur as 'engaged in providing the consumers with the "entrepreneurship" which they ... lack'. It could be argued, though, that the reverse is actually the case. Instead of providing consumers with entrepreneurship, the entrepreneur can be viewed as assuming the entrepreneurship of the consumers by disposing them of the need to search for the product that will offer the highest satisfaction. What is important in either approach, however, is that, implicit in Kirzner's remarks is a view of entrepreneurship as both alienable and transferable.

Let us also recall the model proposed by Kirzner in order to explain the negotiation between the pure entrepreneur and the capitalist. The former must convince the capitalist both about his/her personal integrity as well as about the viability of his/her project. Evidently, the persuasiveness of the potential entrepreneur depends on his/her ability to make the capitalist see the same error that he/she has discovered. This persuasiveness presupposes the ability of the entrepreneur to articulately convey all the details that constitute this profit opportunity. Therefore, the very act of negotiating a project with a capitalist implies that the knowledge of this project has been brought already to the fore of the entrepreneur's consciousness and, consequently, that it can be alienated from him/her and transferred to the capitalist.

Of course, neo-Austrians could still argue that, even though the knowledge of the potential entrepreneur is indeed transferable, the entrepreneurship of the capitalist remains an inalienable and strictly subjective function. Therefore, it is the capitalist's alertness that will, in the final analysis, determine whether the proposed project will be implemented. However, this salvage of the subjectivist character of entrepreneurship raises more questions than it answers, for if the only inalienable type of entrepreneurship is the one exercised by the capitalist, the fundamental conclusion of neo-Austrians that entrepreneurship is independent of capital ownership falls apart.

Entrepreneurship as a factor of production

If the argument that entrepreneurial knowledge is constantly objectified in the course of the market process is valid, then the transaction between the potential entrepreneur and the capitalist can be seen as involving the exchange of an objectively existing commodity. What is actually exchanged is, of course, knowledge. However, the character of this knowledge is now conscious rather than tacit. This can easily be shown if we observe this transaction from the point of view of each of the transacting parties. For the potential entrepreneur, the commodity he/she offers for sale to the highest capitalist-bidder is none other than his/her entrepreneurial discovery. From the point of view of the capitalist, the commodity he/she is trying to buy is an already existing profit opportunity. Therefore, from both points of view, the transaction is perceived as being entirely equivalent to the exchange of an objectively existing factor of production. Consequently, the moment the potential entrepreneur perceives a profit opportunity and tries to sell this knowledge to a capitalist, he/she ceases to act entrepreneurially with reference to the specific opportunity, and is transformed into an owner of a scarce resource.

Of course, Kirzner would disagree with such a conclusion. In his view, when both the capitalist and the potential entrepreneur are fully aware of the latter's ability, the most likely outcome of their negotiation will be a partnership, in which entrepreneurship will be exercised and profits reaped by both. Let us recall that this is exactly the outcome which follows from Kirzner's example with the hunter. This view raises, however, a question regarding the exact meaning of the term entrepreneurial ability. Neo-Austrians view this ability as involving the discovery of market errors. However, entrepreneurial ability cannot guarantee that market errors will always be discovered. Therefore, Kirzner's notion about the sharing of entrepreneurship between the potential entrepreneur and the capitalist faces a paradox. Why would the capitalist enter into a long-term partnership with the potential entrepreneur, if the project the latter proposes is a one-off deal? Evidently, it is much more reasonable to assume that the transaction between the two parties will take the form of a single sale of a factor of production, rather than the form of a long-term partnership, as Kirzner believes.

Neo-Austrians could argue that the notion of entrepreneurial ability implies that the individual who possesses it is able to discover profit opportunities with greater ease than the average market participant, thus assigning to entrepreneurial ability the character of a personal talent.[15] Even so, however, the sharing of entrepreneurship proposed by Kirzner can be disputed. If entrepreneurship has the character of a personal talent, it is difficult to explain why it cannot theoretically be treated as a factor of production. Talent is something that is constantly being revealed and evaluated through the market process. Although it cannot be alienated from its physical bearer, the services of the latter can always be considered an exchangeable commodity. Therefore, the view of entrepreneurship as a personal talent further undermines the neo-Austrian position that entrepreneurship cannot be conceptualized as a scarce resource.

The capitalist as the sole entrepreneur

This line of reasoning leads, of course, to a notion of entrepreneurship which is entirely the converse of the neo-Austrian view. Entrepreneurship cannot be conceptualized as one of the two aspects of human action, but can instead be conceptualized as a type of behaviour that stems from property ownership. Therefore, what mobilizes entrepreneurial activity is not market disequilibrium but property itself. However, if entrepreneurship is linked to resource ownership, why continue to refer to it as if it were a distinct economic function? To put it differently, does factor ownership always entail entrepreneurial activity? Neo-Austrians would give an affirmative answer: in his/her effort to secure the highest return on his/her property, a resource owner always functions entrepreneurially. Thus, an individual who is searching for a banking institution that offers the highest interest rate for his/her savings, is behaving just as entrepreneurially as the owner of a manufacturing plant who is considering which factor mix and which product mix will secure the highest return on his/her capital. Evidently, such an approach trivializes entrepreneurial activity by reducing it to the axiom that every individual is always seeking the best way to achieve his/her ends. Thus, the important issue is whether, theoretically, the entrepreneurial function can be distinguished from the function of an owner of property in general.

To address this issue, let us begin by retaining the notion of profit as the motive of entrepreneurship. Evidently, the identification of entrepreneurship with resource ownership implies a fundamental transformation of the notion of profit, as it is now impossible to distinguish between the reward reaped by entrepreneurial activity and the reward reaped as a return on property. Therefore, profit can continue to be viewed as a sign of the exercise of entrepreneurship, only if its actual magnitude is perceived as a measure of the owner's success in increasing the value of his/her property. This success will necessarily have to be of a comparative nature: the higher an enterprise's profit is compared to the average rate of profit in the economy, the greater the owner's success.

We can now attempt to answer the question raised above, on whether factor ownership always entails entrepreneurship. Since we have retained the notion of profit as the motive of entrepreneurship, the only possible distinction between entrepreneurial behaviour and the behaviour of someone who owns property, is to identify the former with only that part of property that aims at the acquisition of profit – that part which aims at its own expansion. The question now is on what methodological grounds can this distinction be drawn. Evidently, the principle of methodological individualism does not provide these grounds, as it is impossible to identify the part of private property that is profit-seeking on the grounds of the individual's own idea about his/her activity. Thus, in the neo-Austrian analytical framework, the distinction between the function of the entrepreneur and the function of the owner of property is untenable.

However, this distinction is equally untenable for neoclassical theory, which, assuming perfect competition, views all property as bearing the average rate of interest. Therefore, this distinction requires the transcendence of both the neo-Austrian and the neoclassical analytical frameworks, and can only be sustained in the context of Marx's notion of capital as self-expanding value.[16] Thus, entrepreneurship can only be viewed as a function of the individual whose property functions as capital. The salvage, therefore, of some notion of entrepreneurship requires the category of capital.

We will end this chapter with two points that follow from the above conclusion. First, if profit is the motive of a capitalist's entrepreneurship, then its comparability with the profits of other capitals is of the utmost importance. Therefore, the concept of the rate of profit remains central for economic theory.[17] The second point is of a political nature. One of the most influential political slogans of the New Right in the 1980s has been that of 'popular capitalism'. The neo-Austrian theory of entrepreneurship has provided the crucial theoretical foundation of this ideology, as it claims to have shown the possibility of a 'capitalism without capital' through its notion of the pure entrepreneur. The conclusion that entrepreneurship can only be linked with that part of private property that functions as capital undermines, therefore, the persuasiveness of the ideology of popular capitalism.

Notes

1. Mises (1949, p. 253) writes, 'In the imaginary construction of the evenly rotating economy there is no room left for entrepreneurial activity'. The concept of the evenly rotating economy will be referred to in Chapter 6, when Mises's views on the notion of equilibrium are examined.
2. Kirzner (1980, p. 6) notes that 'correct decision-making in this non-entrepreneurial sense, means correct calculation; faulty decision-making is equivalent to mistakes in arithmetic'.
3. On the basis of Crusoe's example, Kirzner (1982a, p. 144) concludes that it is impossible to judge the rationality of entrepreneurial activity. The fact that the alternative ends-means frameworks from which the actor can choose are not known prior to his/her choice, means that they cannot be ranked according to any rational criterion. Thus, entrepreneurship constitutes an activity which transcends the possibility of rational evaluation. This does not mean that it is an irrational activity but, rather, that it is impossible to evaluate it on the basis of a pre-existing frame of reference.
4. As a subjective motive, the notion of profit opportunity is of an entirely ex-ante character. This means that its nature as a motive is independent of whether the opportunity will be actually realized by the actor – in which case he/she will realize a profit – or whether it will not prove fruitful – in which case he/she will incur a loss.
5. See Mises (1949, p. 326).
6. In this context, however, the main motive of this function, which is profit, also takes up an entirely subjective character. Thus, any view of profit as a percentage of an objectively defined magnitude must also be erroneous. As Mises (1949, pp. 294–5) puts it, since profit is independent of the capital employed by an entrepreneur, any reference to the rate of profit, or normal profit, or the average rate of profit is absurd.
7. Kirzner (1980, p. 30) writes: 'The existence of an opportunity implies access to capital, i.e., the discovery of an opportunity includes the discovery of how to raise the necessary capital. ...The brilliance of an idea must include the brilliant discovery of how to raise the capital.'
8. The fact that entrepreneurship is shared, means that the profits are also shared between

the two groups. Of course, the economist cannot actually observe this sharing, since what he/she can register is only corporate profits distributed to shareholders as dividends. The share of the profits reaped by management is distributed by the internal market of the corporation, in the form of special incentives which aim at encouraging the management's entrepreneurship.

9. According to Reekie (1984, pp. 142–3), it is in this sense that the demand for a company's stock, as reflected in its quoted price, can be treated as an index of the performance of its management group.
10. In this context, Kirzner (1980, p. 23) argues that even institutional arrangements, such as child labour laws or imposed health warnings, may be viewed as barriers to entrepreneurial discovery.
11. This was an important argument in Hayek's position during the 'socialist calculation' debate, as will be seen in Chapter 11.
12. For the same argument see Niskanen (1968) and Wegehenkel (1984, p. 228).
13. Writing 12 years after the first edition of *The Road to Serfdom*, Hayek (1956, p. 224) used this argument to counter the critics of his book who claimed that the experience of the first Labour government in post-war Britain did not confirm Hayek's position that state intervention would inevitably lead to a totalitarian regime.
14. According to Kirzner, this view on the moral justification of profit permeates the whole of economic theory, from classical political economy to modern neoclassical theory. He traces the notion of entrepreneurship to classical political economy and Menger's theory, respectively, and claims that some central aspects of this notion can be traced in Menger's thought (see 1975a; 1977).
15. This is a view explicitly expressed in Mises (1949, p. 256).
16. See Marx (1974, vol. I, p. 152).
17. See note 6 above.

6 Equilibrium, dynamics and economic objectivity

The concept of equilibrium is central to orthodox neoclassical theory, as it provides both the methodological foundation for the study of the allocative function of the market system and the basis for the normative evaluation of market exchange. Evidently, the rejection of this concept by neo-Austrians constitutes a major cleavage with orthodox theory. This chapter will begin by examining the foundations of this rejection and will then proceed to analyse its relevance for the issues of objectivity and dynamics, which constitute the central points of this critique.

The orthodox concept of equilibrium

Orthodox theory ascribes four characteristics to the concept of equilibrium.

1. The equilibrium price vector is assumed to constitute the centre of gravity toward which all prices converge under perfect competition.
2. It is assumed that the time needed for the movement toward the new equilibrium vector, following an exogenous disturbance of the original equilibrium position, is negligible.
3. Equilibrium is viewed as defining the representative moment of the market's operation and consequently, the study of this operation and of the possible interventions that might improve it, must begin with the study of the state of equilibrium.
4. Equilibrium is assumed to determine the optimum outcome of market exchange.

The first two characteristics can be considered as describing the technical nature of the market's operation, while the latter two lie at the core of the normative outlook of orthodox theory.

The revolt against the concept of equilibrium is not confined to economists espousing the neo-Austrian paradigm. Joan Robinson (1978) has claimed that the equilibrium concept is not in a position to encapsulate the historicity of the economy's movement through time, while Kaldor (1972) has claimed that its static nature makes it irrelevant to economic theory. The impotence of orthodox theory to explain the manner through which the system approaches the state of equilibrium has even been pointed out by no less a prominent neoclassicist than Kenneth Arrow (1959, p. 41).

However, neo-Austrian economists do not merely point out the shortcomings of the concept of equilibrium, but they also propose its replacement by the alternative concept of the 'market process'. Our analysis of the neo-Austrian critique of general equilibrium theory will begin by examining the positions of various representatives of the school toward the four characteristics of equilibrium, outlined above. We will begin with their positions toward the technical characteristics, showing their relevance to the neo-Austrian notion of dynamics. We will then proceed with their positions on the normative characteristics, and will try to show that they form the foundation of their rejection of economic objectivity.

Hayek: equilibrium as an empirical fact

As was seen in Chapter 3, Hayek draws the distinction between the equilibrium of the individual and that of the market. The former implies that all aspects of an individual's plan are compatible with each other and it is assumed to hold a priori. Market equilibrium, on the other hand, is the outcome of the interaction of many minds functioning independently of each other. Therefore, in the latter case, equilibrium is no more than an eventuality and is thus characterized by a degree of indeterminateness. This indeterminateness can only be diminished if it is assumed that the market process distributes knowledge to all transactors in such a manner that their plans tend to become compatible over time. In Hayek's view, however, this convergence of expectations is not an a priori but only an empirical fact. As he points out (1937, p. 44), it is only because of the observation of this convergence in the real world that 'economics ceases to be an exercise in pure logic and becomes an empirical science'. This idea springs from Hayek's view of competition as a learning process: through his/her participation in the market process, the individual accumulates the knowledge which enables him/her to correctly anticipate market events.

In Hayek's account, the individual's action is determined by the volume of information that he/she possesses at any one moment. This knowledge is, of course, never perfect, which implies that if transactors had different information at their disposal, their plans might be different and perhaps incompatible with each other. Therefore, the state of equilibrium and the tendency toward it are related only to the existing distribution of knowledge at any one time and are, according to Hayek (1937, p. 53), independent of any idea of perfectly distributed knowledge. As will be seen later, this is a crucial point for Hayek's view on the normative aspect of equilibrium.

Mises: equilibrium as an a priori principle

Mises agrees with Hayek that the market system constantly tends toward a state of rest. Instead of treating this tendency as an empirical fact, however, he considers it to be an a priori principle stemming from the theory of praxeology. He sees man acting in order to avert uneasiness and, thus, human action as aiming at the attainment of a state in which there will be no need for further action. Mises (1949, p. 245) described that state by the notion of the 'evenly rotating economy'. This is a model of an economy, all elements of which are being exactly reproduced through time.[1] It is precisely the certainty of this reproduction that renders any change in the actors' behaviour pointless. Mises recognizes, of course, that this notion does not pertain to the actual economy. Thus, in the real world, the existence of uncertainty and change through time make necessary the study of the process toward equilibrium, rather than the equilibrium state itself.[2]

The rejection of the notion of the state of equilibrium bears some important political implications. Mises (1949, p. 698) argues that exclusive focus on the equilibrium state creates the illusion that the economy constitutes an objective system which the economist-observer can either improve or which he/she can imitate by establishing a regime of central planning. In other words, the exclusive study of the state of equilibrium creates the illusion of the viability of socialism. By contrast, the concentration on the concept of the market process as the central notion for the understanding of market exchange leads, according to Mises, to the conviction that the operation of the market system without the institution of private property is unthinkable.

Kirzner: the stabilizing role of entrepreneurship

According to Kirzner (1975, p. 17), the analysis of economic processes 'must establish the determinateness of the course of market events, quite apart from the issue of whether this course of events does or does not tend toward an equilibrium state'. The real question, therefore, is whether the market process is characterized by such a determinateness. Kirzner's answer is that the feature of the market process that establishes this determinateness is none other than entrepreneurial activity. We have seen that what motivates this activity is the perception of profit opportunities in the form of market errors. We have also seen, however, that the discovery of these errors is equivalent to their cancellation. Therefore, entrepreneurial activity is by definition a stabilizing feature of the market process, as it constantly tends to dissolve market disequilibrium.

In Kirzner's account, the determinateness of the market process is based on an a priori principle. However, this principle is different from the general category of human action attested in Mises as it stems, instead, from the idea that in a disequilibrium situation forces will always emerge which will lead to the discovery of profit opportunities. Entrepreneurial activity is thus recognized as the fundamental source of the endogenous movement of the market system. In other words, it is entrepreneurial behaviour which induces individuals to alter their plans, by constantly rearranging the ends-means framework within which they function.

Lachmann: absolute indeterminateness

Contrary to the above positions, Ludwig Lachmann finds the assertion that the market process is characterized by any determinateness, methodologically unsound. In his view, the observed time-path of market events is merely the net result of the interaction between stabilizing and destabilizing forces. Thus, the realization of whether an event tends to stabilize or destabilize the system cannot be grounded on any a priori reasoning but only on the study of the relative strength of the conflicting forces as they appear in every concrete situation.[3]

For Lachmann, therefore, the market process is characterized by a fundamental indeterminateness. At the core of this notion lies his view on the issue of expectations. Lachmann is in accord with Hayek's account of the market as a system generating and distributing knowledge. He points out, however, that nothing can guarantee that the response of all market participants to market signals will be such that their actions will tend to become mutually compatible. The reason is that this information goes through the mental filter of each and every transactor.[4] Even if we assume, therefore, that the information received by all tends to get more and more convergent, there is no guarantee that it will lead market participants to formulate mutually compatible expectations about future events.

O'Driscoll and Rizzo: the idea of pattern coordination

According to O'Driscoll and Rizzo, the orthodox concept of equilibrium describes a situation where any uncertainty about the future has been assumed away. Thus, general equilibrium is an entirely static concept describing a situation characterized by perfect knowledge, in which market participants are under no inducement to act. O'Driscoll and Rizzo admit that it is difficult to imagine an economic theory without some notion of equilibrium. They stress (1985, p. 85), however, that what is needed is a concept of equilibrium that is in a position to incorporate the dynamic character of the notion of the market process. As such, they propose the concept of 'pattern coordination'.

O'Driscoll and Rizzo claim that any economic process is characterized by two types of events: the typical and the unique. Typical are those events which an observer perceives as being repeated regularly for as long as the process itself is being repeated. Unique events are, by contrast, the ones that occur only once and are thus 'time-dependent'. O'Driscoll and Rizzo accept Hayek's account of competition as a discovery procedure, but they point out that what a specific transactor can discover is only the typical events which characterize the actions of the other market participants (1985, p. 107). The unique events can never be discovered, as their emergence always constitutes a surprise.

The concept of pattern coordination is based on the above distinction between typical and unique events. As far as the typical characteristics of human action are concerned, the market process must be seen as promoting their coordination and, thus, as stabilizing the economy. As far as the unique characteristics are concerned, however, the market process is entirely indeterminate. According to O'Driscoll and Rizzo (1985, p. 85), it is precisely these unpredictable characteristics of human action that explain why the market process never reaches a state of rest. Pattern coordination is thus a dynamic concept.

Market dynamics and the concept of order

Having examined the neo-Austrians' critiques of the orthodox concept of equilibrium, we can see that the general consensus on the need to replace it with that of the market process coexists with important differences on whether the market process itself can be seen as a stabilizing or destabilizing phenomenon. In this section, we will try to show that the divergence of opinions on this issue reveals the difficulty of constructing a theory which attempts to describe the operation of market dynamics while, at the same time, explaining the overall cohesion of the market system.

Let us begin by reviewing the neo-Austrians' positions on the technical characteristics of the orthodox notion of equilibrium. As was seen in previous chapters, the rejection of the second characteristic, which is the automatic nature of the adjustment to the state of equilibrium, is unanimous. The unanimity disappears, however, when we consider the various positions on the first of the characteristics of the orthodox notion of equilibrium – the convergence of all prices to the equilibrium price vector. We now find a range of positions that span from Lachmann's view of the fundamental indeterminateness of the market process to Mises's a priori nature of the tendency toward equilibrium. The question is thus raised whether all these views can still be considered as belonging to the same theoretical school.

This question will be considered by first examining Hayek's views. In his account, the state of equilibrium is at any one moment determined by the distribution of knowledge in the economy. If one considers this distribution as given, then equilibrium must be viewed as the centre of gravity toward which market activity converges if the plans of all transactors prove to be compatible.[5] However, the fact that the market process constantly generates and redistributes knowledge, means that these plans cannot remain unaltered and that the point of equilibrium cannot thus be conceived as a static state but as a point constantly moving through time.[6] Therefore, the notion of an equilibrium point has only a momentary significance.

It is important to note, that Hayek's notion of a moving, or intertemporal, equilibrium is not sufficient for a truly dynamic theoretical outlook. After all, an orthodox economist would agree that the point of equilibrium is, in real life, constantly changing, as a result of changes in the external data. The truly dynamic element of neo-Austrian theory stems, instead, from its view of the market process as an endogenous phenomenon. According to neo-Austrians, market participants do not only react to changes in the external data but act creatively, thus constantly changing through their actions the environment within which they operate. Even if we assume, therefore, that the external data remain unaltered, the economy must be conceived as a system in ceaseless motion. This, however, raises a new question: If both stabilizing and destabilizing forces are endogenous, which factor is, in the final analysis, responsible for retaining the cohesion of the market system?

The most convincing answer to this question is the one provided by O'Driscoll and Rizzo through their distinction between the typical and the unique events of human activity. The existence of typical events allows the market process to operate as a discovery procedure and to achieve what they describe as pattern coordination. Although this coordination is never complete, because of the constant emergence of unique events, it is, nonetheless, adequate to sustain the cohesion of the market system, by creating what Hayek has termed the market order. It is precisely this cohesion that allows the use of the term order. For neo-Austrian theory, the market is a system in constant flux but, at the same time, a system constituting an order, in the sense that its cohesion is constantly reproduced.

Therefore, the differing positions amongst neo-Austrian economists on the stabilizing or destabilizing tendencies set in motion by the market process can be explained as springing from the effort to construct a theory which is, at the same time, a theory of endogenous dynamics as well as a theory of overall cohesion. The shortcomings of this approach will be addressed at the end of this chapter.

The optimizing essence of the market process

We can now proceed to analyse the neo-Austrian critique of the normative implications of the orthodox notion of equilibrium, which is the view of the state of equilibrium as the representative moment of the functioning of the system and also as ensuring the optimum allocation of society's resources. Our analysis of the neo-Austrians' arguments against the orthodox notion of equilibrium has already provided some initial clues about their more specific critique of its normative aspects. First, we have seen that the market process is viewed as a dynamic phenomenon. Therefore, even if we accept Hayek's notion of a moving equilibrium point, the mere fact that the coordinates of this point are constantly changing implies that it cannot be viewed as an objectively existing fact – as the moment that encompasses the essence of the functioning of the system. Second, as the coordinates of the moving equilibrium point are constantly being determined by the existing distribution of knowledge, any change in this distribution is bound to affect them. For neo-Austrians, therefore, the claim that equilibrium ensures the optimum allocation of resources is totally unsustained.[7]

The perfect knowledge assumption of orthodox neoclassical theory implies that both individual transactors as well as the economist-observer know fully well all market data. In this context, the normative evaluation of the market process can be based on the comparison of actual market outcomes with the ideal characteristics of the state of equilibrium. Evidently, the rejection of the perfect knowledge assumption also amounts to a rejection of this normative approach. In order to mentally construct the state of equilibrium, the economist-observer would first have to obtain the knowledge possessed by every individual market participant. As we have seen, however, this concentration of knowledge is impossible according to neo-Austrians.

This has profound implications for the orthodox notion of social utility. Since the knowledge that exists in the framework of the market system cannot be concentrated in a single mind, the very notion of an objectively knowable social outcome of the market process is absurd, as it would require the addition of all individual outcomes by an omniscient central authority. Therefore, according to neo-Austrians, a central authority can never optimize the outcomes of the market process in the same manner that the individual market participant optimizes his/her utility.[8]

This line of reasoning raises the question of whether neo-Austrians believe that there is, in the sphere of the economy, any kind of objective knowledge at all which the economist-observer is in a position to obtain. They believe that in the social sciences we are never in a position to predict specific events, but can only establish techniques that allow the prediction of the orders or the patterns of phenomena. Therefore, the economist-observer is only in a position to evaluate alternative orders or patterns which emerge as consequences of alternative institutional frameworks, rather than concrete outcomes themselves.[9]

We have now reached the core of the neo-Austrians' normative outlook. The object of normative judgement cannot be the allocation of resources which the market process brings about – the outcomes, that is, of that process – but only the market process itself. The criterion proposed for this judgement is the speed with which the market system ensures the response of transactors to disequilibrium situations. O'Driscoll and Rizzo (1985, p. 90) further refine this criterion, stating that a system's responsiveness to disequilibrium is related to its effectiveness in generating and discovering knowledge. Thus, the efficiency of the market order depends on the degree of encouragement provided to individuals possessing knowledge to make free and creative use of it – to undertake, in other words, entrepreneurial activity. It is, therefore, evident that the profit motive is now awarded a normative content, as it is viewed as the motive which mobilizes entrepreneurship, that function which ensures the most effective flow of knowledge in the market system. As Kirzner (1973, p. 223) points out, the encouragement of profit is thus the only policy that can lead to optimum results.

The moral justification of the market order

The view of the market as optimizing individual outcomes is not merely a technical corollary to the neoclassical concept of equilibrium. In the course of the development of economic thought, this view has also been employed[10] as an argument for the moral justification of market society. The argument is that the moral superiority of the market system lies in its supposed ability to ensure that the reward reaped by each factor of production is the maximum attainable. Obviously, any rejection of this view creates the need for an alternative justificatory principle.

Neo-Austrians are not, however, unanimous on such an alternative, but actually show two conflicting philosophical strands in their thought. According to the first of these strands – most typically represented by Mises and Kirzner – the fact that the economist-observer is not in a position to judge market outcomes does not preclude the ability of every transactor to evaluate the outcomes of his/her specific contribution to the market process. In fact, Mises believes that what justifies the free market is, in the final analysis, the understanding by all that this freedom ensures the success of each person's actions.[11]

It is evident that the optimization principle remains, in Mises's thought, the major justificatory principle of market society, as the acceptance of this type of society by its members depends on the degree to which they feel that it ensures the maximization of their utilities. Economic theory can supposedly assist this acceptance, by showing that the freedom of the market process tends to optimize individual outcomes. In this context, liberalism is viewed as a system of social organization grounded on human rationality – on the ability, that is, of each member of society to understand the utility the system guarantees for him/her. The philosophical basis of this approach is, of course, utilitarianism.[12]

The second philosophical strand, attested essentially in Hayek, radically dissociates the normative evaluation of the market system from the evaluation of its specific outcomes. According to Hayek, the normatively positive characteristic of the market process is that it tends to achieve the best possible coordination of individual actions – provided, of course, that it operates entirely unhindered. From the point of view of the specific participant, the market process is not thus justified on the grounds that it tends to produce optimum individual outcomes but, instead, on the grounds that it tends to 'produce conditions under which the chances for any individual taken at random to achieve his ends ... will be very high'. (Hayek, 1968, p. 184).

Hayek's approach leads to two important normative implications. The first is that every market participant must accept that the outcomes of the market process that flow from his/her specific activity are entirely independent of any subjective evaluation of his/her merits and needs. Moreover, they are entirely independent of his/her actual contribution to productive activity. Therefore, every individual must accept that market participation is a game of skill and luck and that, as in every such game, the player can never be certain that the results he/she will attain will be optimum. Hayek (1966, p. 172) thus believes that individual participation can only be based on the acceptance of the rules of the game.

The second implication is that the major normatively positive characteristic of the market process is, in contrast to the normative approach that springs from the optimization principle, the fact that some of its outcomes are not satisfactory and thus induce some transactors to alter their behaviour. In such a context, the failure of individual plans evidently acquires a positive character for society, as it provides what Hayek (1982, vol. II, p. 124) describes as 'negative feedback'.

Hayek demands, therefore, that each member of society accept the social utility of the market order, quite independently of the specific utility that this order tends to produce for him/her as an individual. As Belsey (1986, pp. 182–3) points out, Hayek demands that every member of society accepts the discipline of the market. If there is thus a utilitarian element in Hayek's thought, it is very different from that found in Mises,[13] as Hayek sees the utility achieved by the free operation of the market system in the very perpetuation of the market order itself.

Is neo-Austrian theory truly dynamic?

The neo-Austrians' critique of equilibrium combines, as stated at the beginning of this chapter, their claim about the dynamic nature of their theory with their rejection of any notion of economic objectivity. Our critique of their position on the concept of equilibrium must, therefore, address both of these issues and will in fact try to establish three points:

1. that the neo-Austrian view of the economy as a system in constant and endogenous motion is not sufficient for the establishment of a truly dynamic theory;
2. that a dynamic theory can only be based on an objective view of the forces that set the economy in motion;

3. that the affirmation of any objective view of market dynamics necessarily undermines the normative position of neo-Austrian theory.

Our analysis has shown that the dynamic element in neo-Austrian theory stems from the idea of the market as a system in ceaseless and, especially, endogenous motion. The question to be addressed now is whether endogeneity is a sufficient basis for the establishment of a dynamic theory. Let us begin by expounding our own understanding of such a theory. A theory of economic dynamics must be in a position to single out both the forces that systematically set the economy in motion as well as the direction of the latter.[14] In what follows, we will argue that the principle of endogeneity cannot adequately determine either of the two.

Our argument will begin by hypothesizing a model of an economy with no production sector. Every day, a super-human authority sees to it that every individual is provided with consumption goods of unchanging quantity and quality. Thus, the aggregate quantity and composition of these goods will also remain unchanged from day to day. Evidently, this is an entirely static system, as both its quantitative and its qualitative aspects do not change through time. The static nature of the system does not, however, preclude the ceaseless motion of its constitutive elements. The fact that every participant receives an unchanging quantity and composition of goods does not ensure that these goods meet his/her precise requirements and, even if they did, a person's preferences may always change. The need for exchange thus arises and, with it, entrepreneurial activity in discovering market errors. We can now conclude that the ceaseless motion of the system's internal elements does not necessarily provide that motion with a specific direction. Therefore, endogeneity is compatible with the overall static nature of our model, in the sense that it has no systematic effect on the overall characteristics of this economy. Evidently, such a conclusion undermines the neo-Austrians' claim about the dynamic nature of their theory.

Let us now continue by lifting our assumption about the non-existence of production. Sooner or later, some of the entrepreneurial forces which were originally active in the sphere of exchange, will now turn to production. Thus, both the quantities and the composition of the goods available to this economy will begin to change. However, it is important to note that this shift of entrepreneurship toward production is only an eventuality. Just as in the sphere of exchange, entrepreneurial activity in production is mobilized by the discovery of errors. And since the emergence of market errors cannot be viewed as a systematic outcome of a specific process, the activity that it sets in motion cannot be viewed as having any systematic effect on the overall characteristics of our model. The incorporation of production in our model does not, therefore, invalidate our original conclusion that the idea of ceaseless motion is compatible with a static model of the economy. This line of argument shows that, for neo-Austrian theory, any change in the overall characteristics of the market system has the character of an entirely accidental event.[15]

Finally, we can assess the supposedly dynamic character of neo-Austrian theory. Although neo-Austrians single out entrepreneurship as the activity which sets the economy in motion, they are not in a position to establish how it systematically effects the overall characteristics of the economy. Moreover, they are not in a position to establish the direction toward which it will drive the economy. The notion of accident implies, therefore, that both the forces that set the economy in motion and the direction of change are, in principle, indeterminate. All this leads to an important point. Neo-Austrian theory views a phenomenon as dynamic if the direction of its development is indeterminate – a quite different conception of a dynamic theory from our own. What is really important here is that the insistence of neo-Austrians on the dynamic nature of their theory and the rejection of any objectivity of economic phenomena actually form the two sides of the same coin.

Economic objectivity as a requirement of economic dynamics

Our analysis of the neo-Austrians' critique of equilibrium theory reveals the true aim of their rejection of economic objectivity. On the basis of this rejection, they can claim that any exogenous intervention in the market process is not only incapable of effecting the intended objective but is also likely to lead to outcomes which contradict the intended aims. As the economist-observer does not face a static system or a system that can be concisely described by a representative moment of its operation, he/she is not in a position to predict the results of his/her intervention. Thus, the only thing that the economist-observer may be sure of, is that any intervention will tend to destroy the essence of the economy's operation as a spontaneous order.

This observation sheds new light on the normative position of neo-Austrians. We have seen that they consider the normative judgement of the market process as not based on the evaluation of the individual outcomes produced but, rather, on the assertion that the unhampered market tends to ensure the compatibility of individual actions. As this compatibility can only be ensured if the circulation of knowledge in the market system is entirely free, any intervention tends to destroy the efficiency of the system by distorting the circulation of knowledge. The neo-Austrians' normative position is, therefore, essentially of a negative character, as the normatively positive element of the market system lies in the negative outcomes of any exogenous intervention in its operation.

It is now evident that a critique of the notion of a spontaneous order must begin with the reaffirmation of some notion of economic objectivity. The question raised is whether such a reaffirmation can avoid reverting to the perfect knowledge assumption and the static framework of neoclassical theory. In what follows, we will argue that this is indeed possible, within an analytical framework which transcends both neoclassical and neo-Austrian theories. More specifically, we need an analytical framework that reaffirms economic objectivity while, at the same time, reaffirming economic dynamics. We believe that we have already begun to construct this framework in the previous chapters.

Let us begin by considering what such a line of enquiry entails. In order to avoid reverting to the perfect knowledge assumption of orthodox theory, it is necessary to establish a theoretical point of view, which will recognize the ability of the economist-observer to perceive the trends that the market process itself sets in motion, while, at the same time, denying the ability of the individual transactor to obtain full knowledge of market data. Such a point of view is, of course, incompatible with the neo-Austrian outlook. As we have seen with the distinction drawn by O'Driscoll and Rizzo between typical and unique events, it is the latter which constitute the cause of the ceaseless motion of the market process. The very definition of unique events precludes the ability of individual transactors as well as of the economist-observer to know them. For neo-Austrians, there are thus no systematic trends of the market system which the economist-observer can objectively perceive.

Contrary to this position, in previous chapters we have begun to argue that the economist-observer is indeed in a position to perceive the trends which the market process itself sets in motion. If we reflect upon the method we used to establish our conclusions, we will realize that the essence of our position was the ability of the economist-observer to obtain objective knowledge of economic phenomena and, also, the idea that economic objectivity and economic dynamics are interlinked. Chapter 4 showed that the observer is in a position to perceive the structure of the economy which the unhampered operation of the market tends to generate. Our conclusion regarding the pyramid-like structure of the market system was based on the argument that the market process itself produces the objectification of knowledge, which, in its turn, produces the tendency toward ever larger units of capital. Evidently, our conclusions reaffirm both the ability of the economist-observer to obtain objective knowledge as well as the idea that this knowledge is not of static states but only of dynamic processes.

Chapter 5 showed that the major generator of unique events in the context of neo-Austrian theory – entrepreneurial activity – can be salvaged only if linked to the operation of the objective category of capital. Therefore, if we accept the neo-Austrians' position that entrepreneurial activity is the major source of economic dynamics, the study of the motion of capital must be the focal point of any truly dynamic theory. The shift of the analysis from the subjectivist and indeterminate notion of entrepreneurial activity to the study of the objective category of capital reaffirms, once again, the ability of the economist-observer to obtain knowledge of economic phenomena. As will be seen in the following chapter, the fact that the phenomena that the observer perceives are essentially dynamic (the idea of the reproduction of capital), proves that what he/she can actually perceive is dynamic processes rather than static states. Therefore, our critique has so far established the fact that a theory of economic dynamics presupposes the observer's ability to obtain objective knowledge of economic processes.

The problem of social justice

The final issue we have to address concerns the neo-Austrians' position on the normative judgement of the market process. The concept of equilibrium has two important implications for the normative position of orthodox neo-classical theory. The first, which we have already mentioned, is that at the state of equilibrium the remuneration earned by every factor of production is supposed to be at its optimum level. The second implication is that neoclassical theory recognizes that this remuneration is determined by the distribution of initial endowments. Thus, a policy aiming at income redistribution may lead to a more equitable distribution of resources and may, consequently, increase social utility.

Evidently, neo-Austrians could never agree with such a view. The rejection of any notion of economic objectivity is, of course, incompatible with the concept of social utility and, at the same time, denies the effectiveness of any redistributive intervention in the market process. However, the most important implication of the neo-Austrians' position is that it leads to the rejection of any notion of social justice.

According to Hayek (1982, vol. II, p. 33), a social state may be proclaimed as just or unjust only if its emergence can be attributed to a specific human will. The fact, therefore, that the market system has the character of a spontaneous order and, as such, is not the intended outcome of an individual or collective will, implies that its characteristics cannot be judged either as just or unjust. However, whereas the outcomes of the market order cannot be evaluated ethically, the actions that consciously intervene in the market process must be seen as unjust, since they constitute purposeful behaviour and are, as such, consequences of an individual or collective will. Thus, according to Hayek (1982, vol. II, p. 129), any act of intervention constitutes a coercive activity, as it tends to force market participants to act differently from the way they would act if this intervention had not occurred.

How does this approach counter the assertion of orthodox theory that the larger a person's initial endowments are, the greater the share of the social product he/she is likely to appropriate? Hayek simply denies the validity of this conclusion. He claims that the income an individual earns from his/her participation in the market process is solely determined by his/her skill and luck. The size of an individual's endowments is merely an outcome of his/her luck in the past and, consequently, nothing can ensure that this luck will also continue in the future (1982, vol. II, p. 71). Therefore, it is invalid to argue that the unequal distribution of resources is a self-reproducing characteristic of the market system. According to Hayek, the constant reproduction of unequal distribution must not be treated as a scientific observation but, rather, as a sequence of random and causally unrelated states. Of course, the conclusion in Chapter 4 about the self-reproducing character of the market system as a pyramid-like structure undermines Hayek's normative thesis.

Our references to luck and random states in the context of Hayek's theory stem from his account of social evolution as a sequence of accidents – already discussed in Chapter 2. This is actually a verification of our argument that in neo-Austrian theory, and particularly in Hayek, economic dynamics is only a corollary of the more general view that there are no systematic forces at work in the economy, and there is thus no economic change which can be scientifically knowable. However, we have here a contradiction at the core of Hayek's methodology. If we agree with him that the dynamics of the market system is really a series of causally unrelated accidents – and thus a phenomenon not analysable by economic theory itself – we are actually reverting to a historicist methodology. It is really remarkable that a vehement critic of historicism, like Hayek,[16] comes to argue that economic theory can only analyse the emergence of the market order, while it has nothing to say about the dynamics of its evolution. The introduction of the idea of accident seems to reveal a methodological approach which treats the dynamics of the economy as determined at every moment by the specific conjuncture of operating historical facts – an approach that reflects the essence of the historicist method.

Notes

1. According to High (1986, p. 112), the only difference between the notion of the evenly rotating economy and the orthodox concept of general equilibrium lies in the intertemporal nature of the former, as this notion describes a state which is precisely reproduced through time.
2. See Mises (1949, p. 354): 'The sole task of economics is analysis of the actions of men, is the analysis of process'. Mises considers this to be the essential difference between his position and that of neoclassical economists – the mathematical economists as he described them.
3. See Lachmann's position as described by O'Driscoll (1978, p. 129).
4. See Lachmann (1966, p. 113).
5. See Hayek (1941, p. 23): 'the statement of the conditions under which individual plans will be compatible is ... implicitly a statement of what will happen if they are not compatible'.

6. See Littlechild (1982, p. 95).
7. Thus, the neo-Austrian notion of equilibrium is entirely divorced from the idea of Pareto optimum. For an identical conclusion see Boehm (1986, p. 25). One need also remember that, in Hayek's view, the existence of a momentary equilibrium is determined by the existing, and not an ideal optimum, distribution of knowledge.
8. See Mises (1922/1981, p. 466). As will be seen in Chapter 11, this was the essence of the neo-Austrians' position during the socialist calculation debate.
9. One evaluative criterion could be the maximization of the aggregate product of an economy. The economist-observer can never measure the actual size of the aggregate product, but can theoretically establish the kind of order which is most likely to achieve this result. In Hayek's opinion, this is, of course, none other than the market order (1964, p. 36).
10. In the course of the development of economic thought, the optimization principle has been employed both technically [this is the essence of 'Euler's theorem', see Schumpeter (1954, p. 1033)], and in its ideological and political implications [see Clarke (1982, p. 157)], as an argument for the moral justifications of market society.
11. See Mises (1949, p. 147). Kirzner (1963, p. 299) makes the same point even more forcefully by stating that 'participants would hardly be concerned with the efficiency of a market process unless they also knew that the final state of equilibrium the process tended toward was also at least reasonably efficient'.
12. On this basis, however, the views of Mises and Kirzner are reduced to a politically conservative version of orthodox neoclassical theory. Notwithstanding the importance of some technical differences from orthodox neoclassicism, this approach re-establishes the faith that the freedom of the market process generates optimum individual outcomes.
13. See the explicit recognition of this difference by Hayek in his Foreword to Mises's *Socialism* (1922/1981, pp. xxiii–xxiv).
14. A similar view is implicit in Schumpeter (1954, p. 964).
15. Chapter 2 analysed the fundamental importance of the concept of accident for Hayek's theory of social evolution.
16. See Hayek's critique of historicism (1952/1979, chapter 7).

7 The praxeological theory of capital

The different aspects of the notion of the market process have been discussed. The analysis will now turn to the neo-Austrian theory of capital which, together with the theory of money which will be analysed in the next chapter, can be considered as laying the foundations for the study of the motion of the market system as a whole. It is for this reason that neo-Austrians consider their theory of capital as the foundation of their dynamic conception of economic phenomena.

As with all economic categories, neo-Austrians base their analysis of capital on the principle of methodological individualism. Thus, contrary to the orthodox view which treats capital as an objective entity that is independent of the will of individuals, neo-Austrians conceive of capital as a phenomenon which can only be explained through the analysis of human action.

The principle of time-preference

We have seen that, according to Mises (1949, p. 45), human action entails choice, in the sense that, prior to acting, the individual must choose the means through which he/she will act. In addition, Mises (1949, p. 93) maintains that, in its turn, choice entails scarcity, since choice would be pointless if means were abundant. The concepts of choice and scarcity are, of course, of fundamental importance for orthodox neoclassical theory as well. For neo-Austrians, however, their unique character lies in the fact that they are conceived as having a time-dimension.

Let us reflect for a moment on the difference between the neo-Austrian and the orthodox notions of time. The latter assumes that the individual's plan encompasses not only his/her immediate actions but also future actions. Thus, in effect, time is shrunk to the moment the individual is expressing his/her choice. For neo-Austrians, by contrast, the individual is constantly revising his/her plan, as he/she is operating in conditions of uncertainty. Consequently, choices made today affect the data upon which any future plan revision will have to be based. For neo-Austrians, therefore, the individual's actions shape his/her future. In this context, however, time is objectified, as it is itself transformed to an object of choice.

This line of reasoning raises the question of the grounds upon which the individual chooses time. The fact that time is now viewed as a scarce means, leads neo-Austrians to the assertion that the choice of time can be analysed on the basis of the same a priori principles that underlie the category of human action. The most general such principle is that the individual always chooses the minimum possible combination of means for the attainment of the desired end. Therefore, the same principle must also be applicable to the choice of time. In this case, however, what the individual is trying to achieve is not the minimum value of means but the fulfilment of his/her desires sooner rather than later. On these grounds, neo-Austrians claim that the choice of time is based on the praxeological principle of time-preference.[1]

However, if individuals always prefer to satisfy their desires sooner rather than later,[2] how can we account for phenomena like the act of saving? Neo-Austrians point out that the qualitative difference between the sooner and the later may be balanced by the quantitative difference between the means available today and those that individuals expect to obtain in the future. In this way, the a priori character of the principle of time-preference is sustained. It is precisely this quantitative increase which constitutes, according to Mises, the category of 'originary interest'.[3] Interest is, therefore, itself a praxeological category, as it is derived from the principle of time-preference.

The subjectivist character of the distinction between capital goods and consumer goods

The fact that a person chooses not to satisfy some needs at the present moment, implies that the means necessary for the satisfaction of these needs are not consumed. Neo-Austrians believe that it is exactly this choice that changes the economic significance of these means, by transforming them from consumer goods to capital goods. The distinction, therefore, between these two categories does not have any objective character, since it is entirely determined by the individual's time-preference.

This view of the individual's actions as allocating economic goods over time, derives from Menger (1981, chapter 1), who thought that the time-dimension of each good is determined by the time that separates it from the moment of consumption. Goods that are immediately available for consumption are described as goods of first order, while capital goods are thought of as belonging to higher orders. The distance of each order from the moment of consumption is determined by the time periods of production required to transform these capital goods into consumer goods. In Menger's spirit, Mises (1949, pp. 491–2) asserts that what determines a capital good is not its physical features but, rather, the actors' choices – their time-preference.

It is on these grounds that neo-Austrians, and especially Mises, reject the theory of the productivity of capital, which was espoused by neoclassical orthodoxy in the 1930s.[4] The latter viewed capital as a fund or an entity entirely independent of the concrete capital goods that the individual possesses – an entity which has the capacity to reproduce itself and, at the same time, to produce an income for its owner. Mises finds that this neoclassical view treats capital as a tree that bears fruit even if its owner leaves it uncultivated. He believes instead (1949, p. 494), that the advantage which the possession of capital provides does not have the character of an income but, rather, the character of a time-advantage, as the possessor of capital can satisfy his/her needs sooner than a person who does not possess capital.

The theoretical derivation of the category of capital goods from the individual's time-preference implies that the capital goods which exist today are the outcome of the individual's past decisions. Neo-Austrians do not, however, take this to mean that capital goods have an objective character. The means that are available to a person today are, of course, historically given, but it is thought that it is only his/her decision at the present moment that will determine what part of these means will be consumed and what part will function as capital goods in the future. Therefore, the means that exist today constitute the data upon which the individual will base his/her decision, but they cannot be seen as determining this decision. As explicitly claimed by Mises (1949, p. 512), a person's *will* is the sole determinant of the category of capital.

The structure and function of capital goods

So far, the terms capital and capital goods have been used alternately, as if they were practically equivalent. However, the essence of the principle of time-preference is that the individual may choose to satisfy a specific need in the future, because he/she believes that the quantity of goods he/she expects to obtain will be larger than the quantity immediately available. Therefore, the means that are treated today by the individual as capital goods, must have such physical properties as to ensure that the goods which will emerge at some future moment will be capable of satisfying his/her specific need. Thus, from the praxeological point of view, a theory of capital must be founded on the concept of capital goods rather than that of capital.

The methodological primacy assigned by neo-Austrians to the category of capital goods implies that the starting point of any analysis must not be the 'alikeness' between such goods but, rather, their 'differences'.[5] In fact, the existence of such differences is viewed as a sine qua non for the very existence of capital goods. As human needs are themselves heterogeneous, the physical properties of capital goods must also be heterogeneous. Moreover, this heterogeneity does not concern differences among the physical properties of capital goods but, rather, differences in their capacity to satisfy human needs.[6]

The fact that the use of capital goods aims to achieve an outcome in the future, makes necessary a definite preconceived plan on the actor's part. The realization of this outcome depends on the actor's ability to predict all actions that are necessary to ensure the final success. Two problems are then raised. The first is whether the physical properties of the productive means which are initially available are appropriate for the intended outcome. The second is whether the individual's expectations of future events will prove correct, as his/her plan must necessarily take the form of a sequence of actions in time.

Let us begin with the first of these problems. Our reference to the appropriateness of the physical properties of capital goods should not be taken to imply the existence of a one-to-one relationship between specific capital goods and desired ends. On the contrary, according to Lachmann (1956/1978, pp. 2–3), what characterizes capital goods is multiple specificity or the possibility to achieve the same result with various combinations of capital goods. Thus, the physical properties of productive means do not automatically determine a specific kind of production process nor a specific kind of product.[7]

The notion of combination allows neo-Austrians to introduce some further concepts. In the framework of his/her plan, the individual can be viewed as choosing a specific combination of capital goods. However, the very notion of combination, together with the heterogeneity assumption, imply that capital goods must be characterized by 'complementarity'. Through his/her plan, the individual aims at transforming the quantities of heterogeneous means at his/her disposal to complementary means of production which may operate jointly in the context of a specific productive process. Therefore, complementarity requires, according to Lachmann (1947, p. 200), the existence of a specific plan, assigning a function to every specific capital good.

As Lachmann further points out, the individual's plan may be simultaneously characterized by 'functional heterogeneity' and 'physical homogeneity'. In fact, he provides an illustration of this possibility (1956/1978, p. 53): a building made of stones which are completely alike. The fact that these stones are completely alike does not mean that they serve the same function in the preservation of the stability of the building: the ones supporting the walls have a different function from those which form the roof. A process of production can, in this manner, be conceived as constituting a structure of capital goods, where the position of each capital good in the structure is determined by the function assigned to it by the individual's plan.

Let us now address the second of the problems raised above, that which concerned the individual's expectations. A process of production implies, by definition, that the individual is trying to achieve an end at some future moment. It is, therefore, a process unfolding in time, with the consequence that the individual's plan must also be seen as extending in time. But the world of neo-Austrian theory is a world of uncertainty: the more distant each stage is from the emergence of the final product, the more uncertain will its realization according to the original plan be. The plan will thus necessarily be in a process of continuous revision, depending on whether the individual's initial expectations are confirmed or disappointed.

A disappointment of expectations renders necessary the revision of the individual's plan. Evidently, this revision must take the form of a new structure of capital goods. However, we have seen that the same product can be obtained through various combinations of means of production. Therefore, even if we assume that the disappointment of his/her expectations does not lead the individual to alter his/her original goal, it will, nevertheless, make necessary the replacement of some capital goods by others. This leads Lachmann (1947, p. 200) to establish the concept of the 'substitutability' of capital goods, as a major condition for the adjustment of a person's plan to changing circumstances.

Let us end this section by stressing, once more, the entirely subjective character of the concepts of complementarity and substitutability. The former refers to the function which the individual's plan must assign to each capital good, so that a capital structure may emerge. The latter refers to the adjustments of the original structure made necessary by the disappointment of expectations. For neo-Austrians, both concepts are fundamental for economic dynamics, as they relate subjective decisions to real outcomes. This line of reasoning leads, however, to an even more important conclusion. Since both the decision on the structure of the means of production as well as on the final product are entirely subjective, the notion of a process of production itself must be entirely subjective.[8] Thus, both the combination of the available means as well as the choice of the end-product must be seen as outcomes of an individual's will.

The structure of social capital

The analysis has, so far, focused on the category of capital in the context of the economic behaviour of a specific individual. This approach was necessary in order to bring out the praxeological – or subjectivist – treatment of capital by neo-Austrians. We must now proceed to the analysis of capital in the context of the market system as a whole. However, this analysis must, from the outset, confront two questions. The first is whether the notion of the structure of 'social capital' can be used in the same sense that the individual's structure of capital goods was referred to. If the answer to the first question is affirmative, the second question is whether this leads to assigning an objective character to the concept of social capital, contrary to the strictly subjectivist approach of neo-Austrians.

Let us address the first of the above questions. As already defined, the individual's capital structure is determined by his/her plan. The problem with the extension of this notion to the economy as a whole is that the structure of society's capital goods cannot be viewed as the outcome of an individual will but, instead, as the outcome of the interaction amongst countless independently-conceived plans. Thus, any reference to the structure of social capital seems to require the transcendence of the praxeological outlook of neo-Austrian theory. In order to retain this outlook, neo-Austrians are obliged to show that it is possible to relate the structure of a society's capital goods to the decisions of individuals.

Let us return to the issue of expectations. The disappointment of expectations leads the individual to adjust the structure of his/her capital goods to the new data. Given the substitutability assumption, this adjustment must take the form of the replacement of some of the original means of production by others. In our analysis so far, we have implicitly assumed that the disposal of the unwanted means and the procurement of the necessary ones would pose no problems. In the context of the market system as a whole, however, the possibility of this substitution depends on whether the individual will manage to exchange the unwanted means for the ones required by his/her revised plan. Thus, it is precisely the mediation of the market that requires the revision of the original notion of capital structure, so that it is no longer defined as the outcome of an individual will but as the outcome of the market process.

From the individual to the social notion of capital structure

Lachmann (1956/1978, pp. 45–6) describes the adjustment of the individual's capital structure to new data as a 'regrouping process'. The disappointment of his/her expectations leads the entrepreneur to alter the group of his/her capital goods – the complementarity conditions of his/her capital structure. Evidently, any such adjustment alters the data upon which all other market participants base their plans. In order, therefore to be able to refer to the capital structure of the system as a whole, we must be in a position to show that these adjustments will tend to become mutually compatible. Only in this case can we view the capital structure of the whole economy as consisting of a group of complementary capital goods. Of course, this notion of complementarity is different from the one examined earlier, as it is not ensured by the mere fact that the function of each capital good has been determined by an individual's plan but is rather indirectly achieved through the market.

We can now understand the meaning neo-Austrians assign to the notion of the structure of social capital. Lachmann (1956/1978, p. 57) notes that in the social sciences we can consider as a structure a complex of interdependencies which retains its internal coherence and continues to behave as a unique entity, regardless of any exogenous disturbances. We can, therefore, refer to the structure of social capital only if we assume that the revisions of individual plans do not affect the 'structural complementarity' of the capital goods which are available to society as a whole. Thus, the stability of the structure of social capital requires the absence of any regrouping of society's means of production.

This position is, of course, problematic for neo-Austrian theory, as it seems to imply an entirely static view of economic activity. In reality, however, it is possible that the absence of regrouping may run parallel to both a qualitative as well as a quantitative change in the data of the economy. The only condition for this phenomenon is that expectations are not disappointed. In such a case, changes in the structure of society's capital goods can be considered to be consistent.[9] To the extent, therefore, that expectations converge, society's capital goods will tend to assume the form of a capital structure. The issue of the convergence of expectations has already been examined in the previous chapter, with reference to the neo-Austrian critique of the equilibrium concept. It was seen that neo-Austrians believe that it is entrepreneurial activity that leads the economy toward equilibrium. As Lachmann (1956/1978, p. 9) points out, it is once more entrepreneurial activity that brings about the stability of society's capital structure,[10] by bringing about the convergence of expectations.

The notion of value-calculation

Capital has so far been considered as a bundle of physically specific capital goods. However, the fact that the analysis has now shifted from the level of the individual to that of the system as a whole, makes it possible to introduce a notion of capital that allows us to consider an individual's, or society's, means of production as constituting a homogeneous category. This methodological possibility stems from the fact that the category of capital in the context of the market process has been considered and has been, thus, implied that capital goods are exchangeable.

We have seen that, through the use of means of production, the individual aims to obtain an outcome which, by definition, offers higher satisfaction than that provided by the original means he/she possessed. However, the fact, that this individual operates in a social framework now makes it necessary that his/her satisfaction is not only of a qualitative but also of a quantitative character, as both the means of production as well as the final product must be exchangeable in the market and thus possess market value. Therefore, the individual must know not only the qualitative difference between the original means and the final product but also the quantitative difference in their values.[11]

The need to consider the quantitative aspects of action, now leads to the introduction of a new concept, that of calculation.[12] Acting in the framework of the market, the individual must be in a position to calculate both the values of his/her capital goods and the goods which he/she produces. This has two important implications. The first is that it now becomes methodological legitimate to refer to 'capital' as the collective value of the individual's capital goods. Let us stress, however, that the reference to capital as a collective entity does not undermine its praxeological basis, since we have, for the moment, only referred to the calculating behaviour of a single individual. The second implication is that values must be expressible in a common standard: money. Thus, the prices on which the individual can base his/her calculations in real life have to be absolute rather than relative.

Therefore, it is methodologically permissible to refer to a collective category of capital only on two conditions. First, there must be a market economy with free exchange of capital goods. Second, a commonly-accepted medium of exchange must have already emerged. On these grounds, Mises (1949, p. 262) notes that it is a mistake to view capital as a category referring to human production in general. In his view, the collective category of capital acquires meaning only in the context of a monetary market economy.

The neo-Austrian rejection of the measurability of capital

The above line of reasoning seems to introduce an aggregate notion of capital. For if the individual's capital goods can be given a collective meaning through the act of calculation, is there anything to stop us from considering social capital as a collective entity in value terms and, thus, as a 'measurable' and objectively determined category?

To understand why neo-Austrians dismiss this possibility, we must begin with the meaning they assign to the notion of calculation. The fact that the individual is in a position to calculate the value of the original bundle of his/her capital goods does not mean that this value must automatically be seen as expressing his/her capital. According to Mises (1949, p. 477), the value of this bundle has only a historical character, while capital is a category which will emerge only at the moment that the individual decides what part of the original bundle to employ as capital goods in a productive process. Therefore, capital is by its nature a category aiming at the future. Its value does not depend on any historically-given values but, rather, on the value of the final product it will produce. Calculation is, thus, an important requirement for the individual's rational behaviour but it is not sufficient to transform capital into a category independent of the actor's will.

It is precisely because calculation is seen as an entirely individualistic phenomenon that explains why neo-Austrians consider measuring social capital to be impossible.[13] At best, such a measurement would merely express the value of the historically-given means of production. However, it is impermissible to consider the existing bundle of society's capital goods as capital, since only individuals' decisions can determine what means will actually function as capital goods. Therefore, neo-Austrians reject any notion of the measurability of social capital, on the grounds that it would imply the dissociation of the category of capital from the actions of individuals.[14]

Capital and private property

It should now be evident that the theory of capital forms an important link between the neo-Austrians' arguments on the impossibility of objective knowledge of economic phenomena as well as on the dynamic nature of their theory. In what follows, our critique will concentrate upon two points. First, it will be argued that the utterly subjectivist character of the neo-Austrian notion of capital renders untenable any theoretical distinction between capital and private property in general. Second, it will be argued that this untenability leads to an entirely static – or one-dimensional as we will describe it – view of capital, thus undermining the neo-Austrians' claim about the dynamic nature of their theory.

We have seen that the subjectivist character of the neo-Austrians' notion of capital stems from the subjectivist nature of concepts such as capital good, process of production, final product, and so on. From the point of view of the economist-observer, there are thus no objective criteria on the basis of which a productive process can be viewed as involving the use of capital or not. For example, the utterly subjectivist nature of a process of production applies just as well in the case of an entrepreneur managing a large manufacturing plant as in the case of an individual cooking his/her meal.

Mises would, of course, disagree with such a conclusion. In his account, the category of capital acquires meaning only in the context of a monetary market economy, as only in that context does the notion of value-calculation become relevant. Taking the simple example above, it is only in the case of the entrepreneur that the use of capital can be considered to be involved, and this for two reasons. First, it is only the entrepreneur's process of production that aims at market exchange. Second, it is only this process that can be viewed as extending in time and, thus, as being determined by the individual's time-preference. However, any theory attempting to assign to time the role of a criterion of the capitalistic nature of a process of production, must be in a position to define the notion of a cyclically repeated process of production.

Why are we led to such an assertion? The subjectivist notion of a productive process and of the distinction between capital goods and consumer goods implies that a process of production must be conceived as extending in time up to the moment that the final product emerges. From the point of view of the economist-observer, what will follow is entirely indeterminate. The individual may decide to consume the final product or, alternatively, to exchange it for capital goods and start the productive process all over again. The fact that the decision is, in either case, entirely subjective, means that it is unknowable for the economist-observer, who is not in a position to assess whether the individual's productive process will necessarily resume its course. It is precisely because of this indeterminateness that we find neo-Austrian theory unable to sustain the notion of a cyclically repeated process of production.

Mises's argument that the category of capital is only relevant in the context of a monetary market economy, thus loses much of its substance. The subjectivist conception of capital implies that it is impossible to judge in advance whether the outcome of a productive process will be exchanged in the market or not. Coming back to the simple example we have used, there are no methodological grounds upon which to claim that the industrialist's process of production is capitalistic, whereas the process of cooking a meal is a process of consumption. After all, in the subjectivist framework of neo-Austrian theory, there is always the possibility that the industrialist may decide to consume him/herself the entire product of his/her enterprise.

Neo-Austrians would, of course, deny this eventuality, on the grounds that it would constitute an irrational behaviour on the part of the industrialist. In this account, the latter will not consume his/her capital, choosing rationally, instead, to consume the bigger quantity of consumption goods which his/her capital will turn out in the future. However, this seems a problematic assertion as it implies that the ultimate criterion of whether a process of production has ceased or is cyclically repeated is consumption. For this criterion to operate, therefore, capital goods must have ceased functioning as such, having left the sphere of circulation – the market – and entered the area of consumption. On these grounds, Mises's claim about the nature of capital is, of course, undermined, as it now seems that the ultimate criterion of the existence of capital is precisely the opposite of what he claims: not the market process but the cessation of that process.

We have seen that the decision concerning what part of an individual's property will function as capital and what will not, is entirely subjective. We have also seen that neo-Austrians cannot sustain the notion of a cyclically repeated process of production, since there are no methodological grounds upon which to distinguish those capital goods which will continue to function as such from those which will be consumed. We are thus led to the conclusion that there can be no sound methodological grounds upon which neo-Austrian theory can base a distinction between capital and private property in general, as a person's capital cannot be theoretically distinguished from the total volume of his/her assets.

The static nature of the neo-Austrian notion of capital

It is precisely the untenability of this distinction that undermines the dynamic content of the neo-Austrian theory of capital. The fact that the notion of a cyclically repeated process of production is unsustainable, implies that capital cannot be perceived as a category in constant motion but, rather, as an entity that emerges only instantaneously, at the moment an individual decides on the allocation of his/her means between present and future consumption.

Neo-Austrians maintain that the major advantage of their theory of capital is that it is first and foremost a theory of capital goods. In this context, they can claim that subjective decisions on the structure of a person's capital goods have real effects on the structure of social capital, by constantly regrouping the available means of production. Thus, individual decisions can indeed be seen as setting in motion the dynamics of the market system. Our objection against this argument is that the subjective character of this constant regrouping renders any change in the complementarity conditions of social capital entirely arbitrary. This does not only mean that these changes are indeterminate from the point of view of the economist-observer but also that there can be no methodological principle linking the initial structure of capital, which existed before the process of regrouping, with the final structure.

It is precisely because the neo-Austrian notion of capital cannot link the present with the future, that we believe it to be a static notion. The priority neo-Austrians grant to the category of capital goods – or their emphasis on the qualitative aspect of capital – implies that capital has an entirely one-dimensional existence. It exists only for as long as the specific process of production goes on. The moment it ceases, capital goods have themselves ceased to exist. There is no basis upon which to consider the consumer goods which the process of production has turned out as capital, because they will function as such only if their owner decides to exchange them for capital goods so as to begin the process of production all over again. The fact, however, that this is only an eventuality which will be determined by the person's subjective decision, means that we are not allowed to view them as capital.

Our assertion about the arbitrariness of the neo-Austrian notion of capital should now be clear. It is an arbitrariness that springs from the one-dimensional character of capital, or the fact that capital cannot be methodologically seen as linking the present with the future. A process of production certainly extends in time having a beginning and an end, but nothing makes it necessary that it will repeat itself. It seems to us that this argument reinforces the conclusion we reached in the previous chapter concerning the accidental character of the evolution of the market economy within the neo-Austrian approach.

Neo-Austrian theory thus seems permeated by a paradox. On the one hand, its supporters claim that it is a dynamic theory, as it relates the dynamics of the market system to the constant reshuffling of the economy's capital structure. On the other hand, it is not in a position to determine whether a process of production will repeat itself in the future or not. One could argue, of course, that this latter claim only holds at the level of a specific individual, while, at the level of society as a whole, the repetition of productive processes is essential for the sustenance of social existence. This is a valid argument but it seems to reinforce the paradox we described, as it transcends the outlook of methodological individualism and leads to a holistic point of view.

The idea of reproduction as the fundamental concept for economic dynamics

A further problem in the reasoning of neo-Austrians regarding the interaction between the qualitative and the quantitative aspects of capital is now revealed. On the one hand, the entirely subjectivist conception of capital cannot accommodate the idea of a cyclically repeated process of production. On the other hand, however, the notion of calculation implies that the individual is constantly trying to expand that part of his/her property that functions as capital. Therefore, the notion of capital that assigns priority to its physical form cannot really be dynamic. By contrast, the notion that assigns priority to its quantitative aspect poses the need for the constant increase in its value.

This is an insoluble problem both for neo-Austrians as well as for neoclassicists, as neither school is in a position to integrate the qualitative with the quantitative aspect of capital. Neo-Austrians assign priority to the qualitative aspect, while the value aspect of capital is assumed to adjust to qualitative changes. Neoclassical theory, on the other hand, assigns priority to the value aspect of capital, assuming the qualitative data to adjust automatically to value changes. Neo-Austrian theory is in a position to realistically describe changes in the physical characteristics of the economy, while neoclassical theory can attain mathematical rigour through the introduction of the equilibrium concept. What they both cannot do, however, is explain economic dynamics.

A truly dynamic theory must, therefore, be in a position to overcome the problem described, by establishing a link between the qualitative and the quantitative aspect of capital. According to Grossman (1977; 1977a), it is precisely the ability of Marxian theory to establish the relationship between these two aspects that enables it to analyse the dynamics of the market system. Grossman claims that Marx managed to embody in his analysis the element of time. Thus, the 'period of reproduction' – the time needed for the replacement of the original capital – becomes a fundamental concept for the understanding of the process of capital. The period of reproduction is not determined by the value but, rather, by the physical aspect of capital. The fact, however, that the different physical elements that constitute an individual capital employed in a specific process of production do not need the same period of time to reproduce, implies that there is a constant interaction between the physical and the value aspects of capital. According to Grossman (1977a, p. 81), it is this interaction that sets the dynamics of the market system in motion.

Grossman's stress on the importance of the element of time as well as on the importance of the physical aspect of capital, seems to be remarkably close to the approach of neo-Austrians. There is, however, one crucial difference between the two positions: the idea of the reproduction of capital is entirely incompatible with neo-Austrian theory. It is, of course, the same point we have made when we referred to the impossibility of sustaining the notion of a cyclically repeated process of production within the neo-Austrian analytical framework. The idea of reproduction is based on a view of capital as an entity in a continuous cyclical motion, in which the physical and the value aspects represent two moments of the cyclical process.[15] It should be evident, therefore, that the notion of capital as a cyclical motion is entirely incompatible with the static neo-Austrian category of capital.

Let us summarize our argument. A theory of economic dynamics must necessarily be based on a notion of capital as a process in constant motion. Although the subjectivist conception of capital can describe the motion of capital goods as a consequence of individual decisions – something that orthodox neoclassical theory cannot do due to its non-material notion of capital – it cannot explain the necessity of a ceaseless motion of capital. It cannot, in other words, sustain the idea of reproduction. Therefore, in contrast to the claims of its supporters, neo-Austrian theory is not in a position to truly analyse economic dynamics. This does not mean that it is static in the same sense that neoclassical theory is. Its individualist basis, in contrast to the general equilibrium outlook of neoclassical theory, indeed makes possible a view of the market economy as a system in constant motion, but this motion is seen as unpredictable and indeterminate.

In contrast to neo-Austrian theory, we have argued that a theory of economic dynamics must be in a position to analyse the motion of the economy on the basis of the interaction between the physical and the value aspects of capital. This is, however, untenable both to neo-Austrians who emphasize the qualitative aspect of capital, as well as to neoclassical theory which emphasizes the value aspect. It is, however, a condition satisfied in the framework of Marxian theory, where the motion of the qualitative aspect is captured by the 'technical composition of capital', and that of the value aspect by the 'value composition'. The linkage of these two categories in the concept of the 'organic composition of capital' constitutes, therefore, the most decisive step toward understanding economic dynamics.

Notes

1. It is in this sense that Mises (1949, p. 491) considers time as a praxeological concept.
2. See Hayek (1931/1935, p. 38): 'we may increase the output of consumers' goods from a given quantity of original means of production indefinitely provided we are willing to wait long enough for the product'.
3. See Mises (1949, p. 521). Mises uses the adjective 'originary' to denote the fact that interest is derived from the logical analysis of the a priori category of human action. Thus, although the phenomenon of interest actually appears in the monetary sphere, its origin must be located in the real sphere of the economy. On the other hand, although the owner of capital may perceive interest as an income arising from the productivity of his/her assets, Mises claims that interest is not produced by capital but is an outcome of the individual's time-preference.
4. See Knight (1941) for a reference to the productivity theory of capital. See Hayek (1945a; 1941, p. 93) for his views on the supremacy of the principle of time-preference over the productivity theory. Finally, for a detailed reference to Mises's critique of the productivity theory see Kirzner (1974b).
5. Garrison (1985, p. 162) writes: 'But the exchanging of capital goods and the restructuring of production processes cannot be explained in terms of the alikeness of all capital. A satisfactory explanation must be in terms of the differences among capital goods'.
6. See Lachmann (1956/1978, p. 2).
7. If they did, any reference to the individual's choice would be pointless, as his/her actions would be entirely predetermined by the qualities of the capital goods at his/her initial disposal.
8. See Garrison (1985, p. 167).
9. As Hayek (1941, p. 26) points out: 'coincident expectations ... will in effect co-ordinate all these different plans into one single plan, although this "plan" will not exist in any one mind'.
10. It is important to note, however, that the reference to entrepreneurial activity as affecting the stability of the structure of social capital makes now possible a concrete description of the converse situation, that of structural maladjustment in Lachmann's (1956/1978, p. 60) terminology. Therefore, the absence of complementarity amongst the capital goods and the productive processes that constitute the complex of social capital is now transformed into a new concept, which, as will be seen in Chapter 9, lies at the core of the neo-Austrian theory of the trade cycle.
11. If the actor ignored this aspect of his/her activity, he/she would cease to act rationally, as he/she would not really be concerned about whether his/her actions helped to augment the original capital or led to its consumption instead.
12. For the meaning of the concept of calculation, see Mises (1922/1981, part II).
13. As will be seen in Chapter 11, the belief that 'social calculation' is impossible formed the core of Mises's argument during the socialist calculation debate.
14. As Kirzner (1976c, p. 141) points out: 'To view the aggregate capital stock as a fund requires us in the end to give up our concern with individual plans'.
15. See Marx (1974, vol. II, p. 108): 'Capital as self expanding value ... is a movement, a circuit-describing process going through various stages, which itself comprises three different forms of the circuit-describing process. Therefore it can be understood only as motion, not as a thing at rest.' The three forms mentioned by Marx are: the value (money) form, the form of means of production and labour power, and the form of the final product.

8 A theory of commodity-money

In the previous chapter it was mentioned that the theories of money and capital form the groundwork for the neo-Austrian understanding of the motion of the market system as a whole. Our analysis will reveal a significant methodological affinity between the two theories, as neo-Austrians regard both the category of money and that of capital as having a fundamentally subjective as well as physical character. It is precisely the physical character of money that explains the title of this chapter as, for neo-Austrians, money never ceases to be a material commodity.

Money is a social institution, a category whose inner logic requires that it be unconditionally accepted by all members of the community. A subjectivist theory of money must, therefore, be in a position, on the one hand, to attribute the historical appearance of money to the activity of individuals and, on the other hand, to account for the fact that the unconditional acceptance of money by all transactors does not thereby cancel the subjective determination of its function in the market system. This chapter will begin by examining the neo-Austrian position on these two points.

The historical appearance of money

The neo-Austrian theory of money has its roots in the work of Menger, who believed that social institutions are products of a long process of evolution rather than of a directing intelligence. Menger thought that a theoretical understanding of social evolution can only be based on the principle of methodological individualism. Social institutions, including money, of course, are thus seen as stemming from individual actions which, although originating in entirely individual motivations, lead to results which are unrelated to the wishes of the original actors.

Menger began his analysis with the first historical form of exchange, the barter system. When a primitive community first came in contact with another such community, the idea arose that each of them could obtain certain goods not in its possession – or possessed in limited quantities only – by exchanging them for other goods possessed in abundance. As these exchanges, and especially those between individuals, became more and more extensive with time, impediments to the further development of barter trade arose. The difficulty of finding another transactor seeking to carry on the exact type of exchange an individual wished, led the latter to barter the goods at his/her disposal for other goods not immediately desired, which, however, would be easier to barter at some future transaction. Thus, as time went on, a whole range of goods began to be sought not as consumer products per se, but as media of exchange.

Obviously, one cannot predetermine which goods will acquire the role of media of exchange in a given society. This is because the primary characteristic which Menger believed a commodity must possess in order to acquire this role is 'marketability' – the easiness with which it can be exchanged for other goods. Of course, this quality cannot be determined a priori, because a commodity becomes an acceptable medium of exchange only as a result of the activities and customs of a particular community. It is, in fact, the community's general acceptance which gains for this commodity the status of money. Consequently, according to Menger (1985, p. 155), the origin of money is not to be sought in some commonly-agreed contract or in a particular legislative act, but in the unintended outcomes of individual actions.

Subjectivism and the quantitative aspect of money

Neo-Austrians believe that the subjective character of money is not only apparent in the historical process that led to its original appearance, but also in its very function in the modern economy. Therefore, a theoretical analysis of the contemporary role of money must begin with a consideration of the actions of individuals. However, the subjectivism inherent in Menger's conception of the historical appearance of money seems to contradict the view of its contemporary role as that of a generally accepted and thus objective medium of exchange. This contradiction is implied by White (1986, p. 303), when he states that the nature of money is simultaneously subjective and intersubjective.

In reality, however, this contradiction is only superficial, and this becomes readily apparent when we differentiate between the qualitative and the quantitative aspects of money. Menger's theory essentially refers to the qualitative aspect, because it explains how the historical development of the barter system eventually led to the general acceptance of a range of commodities as media of exchange. The qualitative dimension of money is also employed by Rothbard (1978) in order to support his contentions regarding the subjective nature of the money supply. He claims that the individual perceives as a medium of exchange everything which is liquid enough to allow its immediate exchange. Therefore, it is this subjective conception of the nature of money that determines what money is.

However, the qualitative aspect of money cannot explain the amount of money a specific individual wishes to hold. Therefore, it is upon the quantitative aspect that the subjective character of money should be pre-eminently founded, since what is affected by the actions of individuals in modern society is undoubtedly the quantity of money rather than its quality. Neo-

Austrians thus seek to explain how individuals determine the amount of money they wish to hold.

From our analysis of the ideas of Menger, we have seen that money first made its historical appearance when it achieved the status of the most marketable commodity. To the extent, therefore, that money retains the character of a concrete commodity, the individual's desire for its acquisition should be analysed on the basis of the theory of marginal utility.[1] Of course, money is different from other commodities, in that it possesses a two-fold utility. First, it can satisfy certain human needs as a result of its physical characteristics. In addition, it can fulfill an individual's need to have a certain amount of purchasing power readily available. As Moss notes (1976, p. 18), it is precisely this second aspect of the money-commodity upon which neo-Austrian monetary theory is based.

However, in order to establish the validity of this approach, one has to confront two basic questions. First, whether the axiom that marginal utility is a diminishing function of the quantity of a commodity which an individual possesses, remains in force when considered in the context of the marginal utility of the monetary commodity. If it does, then we must also accept a priori that each unit of money that the individual obtains provides him/her with less satisfaction than the one that preceded it – a view which seems to be, at least at first glance, quite paradoxical.

Mises (1949, p. 401) offers a solution by pointing out that one should not confuse the desire to obtain wealth, which is indeed insatiable, with the possession of wealth in the form of money. According to Mises, the amount of money which an individual wishes to hold is not related to his/her wealth but, rather, to the volume of transactions which he/she wishes to complete in the future. Therefore, if at any given moment the individual should come into possession of a larger amount of money than anticipated, he/she will proceed to spend a portion on consumer or capital goods, retaining as cash balances only what he/she expects to need for future transactions.

The second question concerns the very notion of the utility of money. According to neoclassical theory, a commodity's utility depends on its physical characteristics as well as the preferences of consumers. However, the usefulness of money cannot depend on either of these two factors, since the desire to hold cash cannot be viewed as primarily stemming from the ability of the money-commodity to satisfy any human needs.[2] Neo-Austrians admit that it is indeed impossible to directly define the utility of money and propose an indirect definition: they assume that the marginal utility of an amount of money is equal to the marginal utility of those goods which can be obtained in exchange for it. However, a new difficulty now arises. The quantity of goods an individual can obtain in exchange for his/her money is directly related to the latter's purchasing power. We must, therefore, conclude that the marginal utility of money is a function of its purchasing power.

The regression theorem

We are now involved, it would appear, in a vicious circle. The amount of money an individual is prepared to hold is directly dependent upon the utility of that money. This utility depends, however, upon the purchasing power of money. Thus, we are led to the conclusion that the individual can only perceive the utility of his/her money holdings the moment he/she exchanges them for goods. The only way in which we can extricate ourselves from this vicious circle is by presuming that the individual is able to calculate the purchasing power of his/her cash holdings without being obliged to expend it first. The solution to this difficulty is provided by Mises's 'regression theorem'.

Mises admits that the purchasing power of money depends on the prices of goods. Prices are, however, determined through exchange, so that the individual may not know them prior to expending his/her cash holdings. He/she knows, nonetheless, the prices that prevailed on the day before and, as a consequence of this knowledge, he/she is able to calculate the purchasing power of money on the basis of yesterday's prices. The problem with such reasoning is that it seems to conflict with the supposedly subjective nature of human action. The individual's calculation is apparently now based upon an objective factor: the prices which were established yesterday and which constitute an objective knowledge for all market participants.

However, if one calculates the purchasing power of money on the basis of yesterday's prices, and if yesterday's calculation was based on the prices in effect the day before and so on, one should theoretically arrive, through a process of regression, at a particular day in the past which Mises calls the 'last day of barter'. This hypothetical day is the last day on which the utility of the commodity, which was subsequently to assume the character of money, was determined by its physical characteristics and the preferences of consumers like the utility of any other good.[3] Therefore, the calculation of the purchasing power of money is nothing more than a single link in a whole chain of calculations whose starting point is an entirely subjective evaluation.

Transactions and precautionary demand for money

The subjective character of the individual's decision on the quantity of cash balances he/she wishes to hold has been analysed above. In order to proceed to the investigation of the role of money in the economy as a whole, it is now necessary to introduce the concept of the economy's demand for money. This analysis will become clearer if the neo-Austrian notion of this demand is compared with that proposed by Keynesian macroeconomic theory. For the latter, we can theoretically distinguish three reasons why individuals wish to hold money:

1. for future transactions;
2. as a precaution against unforeseen circumstances;
3. for speculative purposes.

The neo-Austrians' consent to the first component of the Keynesian notion of the demand for money is immediately recognized in the Mengerian conception of the historical appearance of a commonly-accepted medium of exchange. According to Menger, people hold money in order to be able to exchange it in the future for consumer or capital goods. Thus, future transactions constitute the major motive of the demand for money.

The second component of the Keynesian notion is known as precautionary demand. Obviously, no provision for the future would be necessary if the future were already known. Therefore, in regard to this component of the demand for money, the agreement of neo-Austrian theory with that of orthodox macroeconomics seems quite natural. If one were to assume the existence of a state of perfect knowledge, then the maintenance of cash reserves would be superfluous. In fact, in a world where there was absolute certainty about the future there would not be any need for the existence of a medium of exchange at all; the institutionalization of a generally-accepted accounting measure of values would suffice. This is precisely the conception of money upon which the general equilibrium theory is based, in which money is relegated to the role of the numeraire. Thus, as Mises (1949, p. 414) points out, the actual role of money is incompatible with the notion of general equilibrium.

The speculative component of the demand for money

It is the third component of the Keynesian notion of the demand for money, the speculative motive, which reveals a significant divergence between neo-Austrian and Keynesian theories. This motive stems from the function of money as a store of value and implies that, apart from exchange purposes, money can also be used speculatively. Keynes defined speculation (1936/1973, p. 158) as the activity which aims at forecasting short-term changes in the psychology of the market. Therefore, the possessor of money is in a position to realize profits not by buying and selling commodities but through purchases and sales of securities. The motive of speculation thus induces individuals to hoard money, thereby removing it from the sphere of the circulation of commodities and allowing it to remain idle for as long as they do not perceive speculative opportunities.

It is precisely this distinction between circulating and idle money that lies at the core of a first point of disagreement between neo-Austrian theory and Keynesian macroeconomics. As Mises notes (1949, p. 399), any attempt to distinguish between circulating and idle money is futile. Money is always held for the realization of future transactions. It is, therefore, immaterial what sort of transactions – speculative or not – the individual wishes to carry out. Thus, cash balances do not constitute withdrawals from circulation, simply because money does not circulate but is, rather, constantly held for the purpose of participating in exchange at some future moment. On this basis, neo-Austrians do not view the speculative motive as being incompatible with their notion of the demand for money. After all, they conceive entrepreneurial activity fundamentally as an effort to buy cheap in order to sell dear. In that context, the precautionary and the speculative motive of money holding are indeed indistinguishable, as they both constitute different aspects of human action under conditions of uncertainty. Basing his view on precisely this alleged equivalence between the two motives, Streissler (1973, p. 167) maintains that Menger had already produced, far earlier than Keynes, a comprehensive theory of the role of speculation in the economy.

This leads to the second main point of disagreement. The logical consequence of the neo-Austrians' refusal to acknowledge that there is anything peculiarly distinctive about the speculative component of the demand for money, is that they end up viewing the demand for money as being independent of the rate of interest.[4] As seen in the previous chapter, this explains why they consider interest as a real, rather than a monetary phenomenon.

To sum up, both neo-Austrians as well as Keynesians base their understanding of why money is held on the motivations of individuals, and both agree that the economy's demand for money is nothing but the sum of individual demands. At this point, however, the agreement ends. According to Keynesian macroeconomics, the demand for money is subjectively based, but it is simultaneously objective in the sense that it is directly linked to the rate of interest. For neo-Austrians, by contrast, both the supply as well as the demand for money are subjectively determined. Consequently, as Mises (1949, p. 418) points out, it is the autonomous activity of individuals which brings about the convergence of the supply and demand for money, just like for any other commodity.

The critique of the quantity theory of money

If the money market functions like any other market, an analysis of its interaction with the markets for other commodities ought to proceed on the basis of the interplay among markets in general. Thus, any change in the supply and demand for money leads to changes in the markets for all other goods and, conversely, all changes in the supply and demand for other commodities lead to alterations in the money market. Therefore, according to neo-Austrians, money is not a neutral factor in the economy but, rather, a factor which causes real adjustments in economic variables.

It is precisely the rejection of the neutrality of money by neo-Austrians, that forms the basis of their critique of the quantity theory of money. In its simplest form, the quantity theory can be presented – as it is by Moss (1976, p. 31) in his interpretation of Wicksell's version of this theory – as a 'proportionality theorem'. The notion of proportionality implies that a change in the quantity of money brings about a proportional change in the money-prices of commodities – the price-level – while their relative prices remain unaffected. The logic behind such an approach is simple: relative prices are determined by the individuals' evaluation of the utility of specific commodities. However, money per se does not enter into these evaluations. Thus, the equality between the ratios of relative prices and those of money prices can only be ensured if it is assumed that a doubling, for example, of the quantity of money would double money prices while leaving relative prices unchanged.

If, however, money is seen as a real commodity, as it is seen by neo-Austrians, then the individuals' evaluation of its utility will interact with their evaluation of the utilities of all other goods. Consequently, an increase in the money supply will have precisely the same effect as an increase in the supply of any other commodity. Thus, it is just as absurd to maintain that doubling the supply of money will result in the doubling of the money prices of all goods, as it would be to assume that a change in the supply of any given commodity will change proportionally its relative prices in relation to all other goods.[5]

Money as a real element in the economy

The rejection of the proportionality theorem means that changes in the quantity of money are bound to have real effects in economic activity, rather than merely bringing about changes in the price level. An increase in the supply of money[6] will result in certain individuals finding themselves with higher cash balances than they desire. Thus, they will now be in a position to spend greater amounts of money for the purchase of goods than they had anticipated. Increased demand from this group of individuals will create an upward pressure on the prices of the goods they decide to purchase. As a consequence, those who produce these commodities will find that their own liquid assets have increased, which will in turn result in increased demand on their part, and so on, as various groups of individuals are affected by this process.[7]

There is, however, something of significance in the above process. Those who are the first to come into possession of this new money are able to purchase the goods they desire at the prices which prevailed prior to the increase in the supply of money. By contrast, those who were the last to obtain the new money are at a comparative disadvantage, since they are purchasing goods whose prices have already risen even before they themselves obtain any additional cash reserves. Thus, changes in the money supply inevitably lead to a redistribution of wealth.

This raises the question of whether governments could effectively intervene in the economy in order to bring about such a redistribution. Neo-Austrians consider this a disastrous policy. Assuming that the new money is injected into the economy through an increase in the lowest wages, the initial result would perforce be an increase in the demand for consumer products. Of course, eventually there will be an increase in demand for capital goods as well. Until this occurs, however, the profits – and with them employment and investment – of enterprises in the capital goods sector will fall. Thus, according to neo-Austrians, a government policy aiming at redistribution can never lead to a permanent increase of aggregate demand, as Keynes maintained.

The logical conclusion of the neo-Austrians' rejection of the quantity theory of money is the denial of any economic significance of the notion of the price level. In their view, the price level is nothing more than a statistical index – a basically 'historical' entity. As has been seen, however, neo-Austrians do not view historical entities as objects of human action. Thus, the price level does not in itself constitute an economic variable. Evidently, this view amounts to a dismissal of the methodological validity of all macroeconomic theories which study the interplay of aggregates and averages.[8]

We shall end our analysis of the neo-Austrian theory of money by noting the special significance which the school attaches to safeguarding the purchasing power of money. Since money is a real element of economic activity, any change in its quantity inevitably affects all economic variables. This view has impelled neo-Austrians to formulate proposals for safeguarding the institution of money from political intervention. In the inter-war years, this position led Mises to champion the gold standard, while in the 1970s Hayek proposed the denationalization of money, as will be seen in Chapter 10.

The inevitable dematerialization of money

Mises's dismissal of the idea of monetary circulation has already been noted. Of course, money constantly changes hands as it is exchanged for other goods. However, from the neo-Austrian point of view, the exchange of money is of importance only to the degree to which it is itself viewed as a material commodity like any other. Our critique must, therefore, focus on the commodity character of money as well as on the rejection of the notion of monetary circulation. In what follows, two points will be argued. First, that the neo-Austrians' category of money cannot sustain the idea of a monetary economy, and thus their analysis always reverts to the barter view of neoclassical theory. Second, that a distinction between the two types of economies necessarily requires a view of money as a unique medium of exchange – a view which is incompatible with neo-Austrian theory. On the basis of these points, it will be shown that neo-Austrians cannot convincingly account for the category of credit money – a category which can only be determined in the context of the notion of the reproduction of capital.

The distinction between a monetary and a barter economy

To the extent that money is a commodity like any other, its role in the economy is determined by the interaction of supply and demand. Consequently, an individual's decision to increase his/her cash balances (his/her demand for money) inevitably presupposes a decrease in his/her demand of certain other goods, thus leaving unchanged the overall supply and demand conditions in the economy. Therefore, an increase in the demand for money by a specific individual only affects the mix of the goods he/she possesses, but has no effect on any other aspect of the functioning of the system.

The situation does not differ substantially if we assume that the decision to increase cash holdings is taken simultaneously by the majority of transactors. Provided that the amount of money remains unchanged, there will now be a smaller amount of money available for transactions while, at the same time, the demand for other goods will also be lower. Therefore, economic data will once again not undergo any systematic change. There will indeed be changes both in the relative prices of commodities as well as in the purchasing power of money, but they will not be systematic, in the sense of propelling the economy toward any specific direction.

This line of reasoning is based on the fact that neo-Austrians define money as the most exchangeable commodity. Thus, they consider money, even in its most liquid form, as always retaining the character of a commodity. This approach raises the question of whether the economy they envisage is truly monetary or whether it is in reality only a barter economy. Clearly, what distinguishes these two economic models is the fact that money is, within the former model, assumed to function as the only medium in any process of exchange. In actual fact, however, the economy neo-Austrians describe is a barter economy, in which every commodity is characterized by a different degree of exchangeability.

In the neo-Austrian model, money cannot thus be assumed to be the only medium of exchange, thereby violating the major precondition for the existence of a truly monetary economy. The fact that money is the most exchangeable commodity does not remove the possibility of engaging in transactions through the mediation of goods with lower degrees of exchangeability than the money-commodity. The neo-Austrians' contention that their theory is capable of analysing a monetary economy, as opposed to the neoclassical barter approach, is thus put into question. Neoclassical theory reduces money to the role of a numeraire – an accounting measure of values. The numeraire is itself a commodity, but this does not necessarily mean that it has to be the sole medium of exchange. Thus, the neo-Austrian conception of money is not substantially different from that of neoclassical theory. The fact that exchanges are greatly facilitated by the mediation of a commodity with a high degree of exchangeability does not alter the barter character of transactions.

The uniqueness of money and the notion of monetary circulation

The conclusion that has just been established evidently raises a new problem. It was contended that the commodity-character of money makes an analysis of the monetary economy impossible, thus shifting the neo-Austrian analytical framework back to the neoclassical model of a barter economy. It was also maintained that this weakness of neo-Austrian theory springs from its denial to accept the uniqueness of money – its function as the sole medium of exchange. We now have to confront a twofold question. First, what is the precise meaning of the term uniqueness and, second, why can't neo-Austrians sustain this notion?

The notion of the uniqueness of money does not detract from its commodity-character. A denial of this character would indeed make an explanation of the historical appearance of money impossible, since any such attempt must start from barter exchange. Thus, the uniqueness of the money-commodity must be based on some peculiarity not characterizing other commodities, and this is none other than the exclusion of all other commodities from the role of media of exchange. This is precisely the conclusion which De Brunhoff (1976, pp. 21–3) reaches in her analysis of the Marxian theory of money.

However, if indeed the uniqueness of money is the major precondition for the transcendance of the barter model of neoclassical theory, the question is why neo-Austrians cannot recognize it. After all, the logic of neo-Austrian theory seems to be moving in that direction. Menger's account, for instance, of the historical appearance of money, can be seen as describing a process of gradual exclusion of all other commodities by the money-commodity from the role of the medium of exchange. What is it, therefore, that prevents Menger – and neo-Austrians following him – from completing this process of gradual exclusion?

The simple answer is that an acceptance of the uniqueness of money would be tantamount to the refusal of its subjective character. For as soon as one, and only one, commodity assumes the status of the sole medium of exchange, this medium must perforce be viewed as an objective category which is independent of the decisions of individuals. Money assumes an objective existence, not in the sense that it has a concrete material form, but in the sense of having a concrete function, which no other commodity is able to fulfill.[9]

This objectification of the category of money now means that the notion of its circulation assumes a major significance. For as long as money is viewed as a commodity like any other, Mises is correct in maintaining that money does not circulate, since at any given instance it is in the possession of an individual rather than being in circulation. However, as soon as money ceases to be viewed in this way, the study of its circulation assumes a major importance, as it now determines the manner in which all other commodities circulate.

The theoretical legitimation of the notion of circulation introduces, in its turn, the possibility that this circulation may be abruptly either inflated or deflated. Thus, the ideas of hoarding and dishoarding are now also theoretically legitimized. Evidently, these ideas are incompatible with a theory of commodity-money, since, when seen like any other commodity, what determines the existence of money is its utility rather than its circulation. By contrast, the establishment of the unique character of money implies that a withdrawal of money from circulation cannot be seen as coinciding with a reduction in the demand for goods but, rather, as a phenomenon which makes exchanges more difficult, because part of the economy's sole medium of exchange has temporarily been withdrawn from circulation.

Therefore, an acceptance of the concept of the circulation of money inevitably leads to the conclusion that the hoarding or dishoarding of money directly influence the entire economic activity. The nature of this influence is unquestionably related to the temporal structure of production and, consequently, to the temporal requirements for the reproduction of the various components of social capital. Evidently, nothing can guarantee that the increases or decreases in monetary circulation will necessarily ensure the smooth reproduction of capital. As De Brunhoff shows (1976, p. 42), hoarding can be seen as a destabilizing factor for the smooth circulation of commodities, assuming that this circulation was indeed smooth prior to the phenomenon of hoarding. However, it can also function in a stabilizing fashion, if it occurs in reaction to some pre-existing disequilibrium.

On the notion of credit money

Despite their insistence on the commodity-character of money, neo-Austrians are compelled to accept the concept of credit money. If they did not, they would be forced to maintain that banks ought to extend credit or to issue paper money only up to the amount that matches their real deposits. Such an approach, however, would come into direct conflict with the actual historical development of the banking system and its traditional role in creating credit money. Even so, neo-Austrians cannot but view the phenomenon of credit money with some suspicion.

Mises (1946, p. 218) distinguishes between two types of credit: commodity and circulation credit. The first type refers to the banking system's transfer of savings to entrepreneurs – a transfer of unspent purchasing power from savers to investors. Circulation credit, on the other hand, refers to those credits which are created by the banks, either in the form of paper money or by opening new lending accounts. With this type of credit, the banks do not simply transfer unspent purchasing power from one sector of the economy to another but, instead, create new purchasing power. As will be found out in the following chapter, the increase of circulation credit is, according to neo-Austrians, the main cause of trade cycles. Thus, even though they are compelled to accept, for the reasons mentioned above, that there is a role in the economy – albeit a limited one – for credit money, they maintain, at the same time, that this phenomenon is the main destabilizing factor in the economy.

Let us see how neo-Austrians attempt to resolve this apparent contradiction. The fact that money is viewed as always retaining its commodity-character, implies that banks should be obliged to convert credit money to real money on demand. Given this basic assumption of convertibility, coupled with the further assumption that the banking system operates entirely freely, increases in credit money will be limited by the activities of the credit market itself. On the one hand, competition among banks leads them to increase the amounts of credit money offered. On the other hand, however, the demand for convertibility imposes limits on that activity, in the form of restrictions which the banks impose upon themselves in order to ensure their own solvency. Therefore, as Mises (1928, p. 139) maintains, it is the self-regulating character of the money market which ensures that the issuing of credit money will be kept at a minimum.

Thus, while neo-Austrians see credit as a distorting element in the economy, they hold, at the same time, the optimistic view that the credit market itself can ensure that distortions will be kept at a minimum, assuming convertibility and freedom from governmental interventions. Neo-Austrians can indeed afford to be optimistic as long as they assume that it will be the self-regulating character of this market – like that of any other market – that will restrict any distortions. However, the problem with this approach is that it cannot envisage credit apart from the operation of the credit market. Neo-Austrians, for example, present no explanation for the role of commercial credit, a phenomenon which historically preceded the banking system in its modern form. This phenomenon implies that the demand for the creation of credit money does not stem from some institution outside the market process, but from the requirements of this process itself. Therefore, it is the workings of the market process itself which culminate in what De Brunhoff (1976, p. 81) calls the dematerialization of money – the creation, in other words, of credit money.

Therefore, the concept of credit money is incompatible with the view of money as a commodity. Consequently, it is a phenomenon whose appearance must be explained by seeking a different conception of how the economy functions, the conception we have termed 'cyclical reproduction'. As Grossman (1977a, p. 81) has observed, credit is not an exogenous phenomenon but is, rather, directly linked to the mechanism of the turnover of capital. The consequences of such a conclusion will become apparent in the following chapter, where the neo-Austrian theory of the trade cycle will be examined.

Notes

1. See Mises (1912/1934, p. 119) and Hutchison (1962, p. 332).
2. Of course, since money retains the character of a physical commodity, it will indeed be in a position to satisfy at least some human wants. The point is, however, that individuals do not hold money for this reason alone.
3. See Mises (1912/1934, pp. 97–123).
4. See Moss (1976, p. 23). It is precisely this refusal to attach any significance to speculative activities, which is characteristically expressed by Mises (1949, p. 460), as he includes bonds in the category of 'secondary media of exchange'. On this basis, Hayek (1976a, p. 47) describes money as a continuum of objects of various degrees of liquidity.
5. See Mises (1928, p. 91; 1912/1934, p. 139).
6. It is theoretically immaterial whether it is an increase in metallic money, for example because of higher production of gold mines, or an increase in the printing of paper money by the government. See Mises (1928, p. 95).
7. The process just described also holds true if we assume that the new money is divided up equally at the outset among all members of the community. See Rothbard (1976a, p. 163). In this case, the cash holdings of transactors would increase by the same amount. However, since the estimations of the utility of different goods vary among individuals, the mode of spending of this new money will not be the same for everyone. Thus, even in this hypothetical situation, the inflow of new money leads to changes in the relative prices of all goods in the economy.
8. As Hayek (1931/1935, p. 5) points out, 'from the very nature of economic theory, averages can never form a link in its reasoning'.
9. It is not necessary to assume that money retains a concrete physical form. Thus, its uniqueness is an attribute holding just as well in the case of credit money – as will be seen later – as in the case of metal money.

9 The theory of the trade cycle

We are now in a position to investigate the neo-Austrian ideas regarding the motion of the market system as a whole, as they are put forward in the theory of the trade cycle. The analysis will focus primarily on the most comprehensive exposition of this theory, in Hayek's *Prices and Production.*[1]

Hayek begins his analysis with a model of a monetary economy in full employment equilibrium. The existence of equilibrium implies that the plans of consumers and those of producers are mutually compatible, so that the portion of their income which consumers wish to save is exactly equal to the volume of investment which producers wish to undertake. If Hayek's model described a barter economy, the equality of savings to investment would be self-evident, as it would amount to a mere description of Say's law. In a monetary economy, however, it becomes necessary to assume the existence of some mechanism which equalizes savings and investment in money terms. According to Hayek, this mechanism is the credit market, in which the equality of supply and demand is ensured, as in any other market, as long as the price remains at equilibrium. In the case of the credit market, the price is the rate of interest, and the existence of a state of equilibrium implies that the interest rate itself remains at equilibrium.[2]

The meaning of the structure of production

Hayek views the saving behaviour of consumers as actually determined by their time-preference. Thus, the portion of income which is transferred via the credit market from consumers to producers can be thought of as a signal from the former to the latter, informing them about the time they are prepared to wait for the acquisition of consumer goods. The fact that Hayek's model economy is in a state of equilibrium, implies that the value of the quantity of consumer goods which producers offer for sale is precisely equal to the portion of income actually consumed. Therefore, the capital structure of this economy is such that, at each point in time, the quantity of consumer goods offered is exactly equal to demand for such goods.

Neo-Austrians see a process of production not as an instantaneous activity but as unfolding in time. Thus, for the economy's capital structure to remain stable, the period of time required to transform a given quantity of original means of production into the quantity of consumer goods which are demanded, must also remain constant. If such temporal stability did not exist, the appearance at the desired moment of the exact quantity of products consumers demand would not be guaranteed. For if the time needed for production decreased, at some given moment a bigger quantity of consumer goods would appear on the market, while if production time increased, the opposite would occur. The material conditions of complementarity among the economy's capital goods, together with the temporal dimension of the economy's capital structure, constitute what Hayek (1931/1935, p. 38) calls the economy's 'structure of production'.

The Hayekian triangle

One can conceive of an economy's structure of production as the temporal hierarchy of all productive processes according to the time that separates each of them from the moment of consumption. The further removed a process is from the moment of consumption, the more 'capitalistic' it must be considered to be, in the sense that its product is seen as a higher-order commodity – in Menger's sense of this term. This hierarchy is depicted by Hayek as shown in Figure 9.1, which is usually described as the 'Hayekian triangle'.

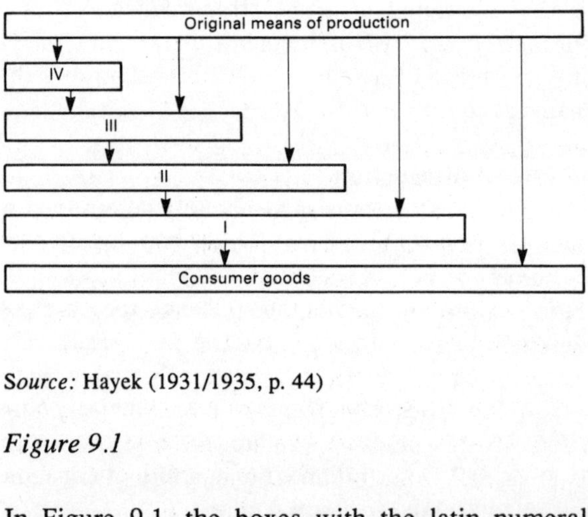

Source: Hayek (1931/1935, p. 44)

Figure 9.1

In Figure 9.1, the boxes with the latin numerals represent processes of production. The closer to the base of the triangle a process is, the shorter the time period that separates it from the moment of consumption. The area of each box represents the product of the specific process, which is itself an input to the next stage. On the other hand, the inputs of each process include the product of the one preceding it as well as a part of the original means of production. The base of the triangle represents the quantity of consumer goods produced by the economy, while its apex can be interpreted in two ways. On the one hand, it represents the sum total of intermediate goods produced by the various stages of production and, on the other, the time required by the capital structure of the specific economy to transform the original means of production into consumer products. Thus, any reference to the stability of the economy's structure of production means that the relationship among the various productive stages remains constant – productive processes are neither added to nor subtracted from the existing structure.

Assuming that the rate of interest remains at equilibrium, the stability of the economy's structure of production will be preserved. Producers will carry out all investment projects which they believe profitable in terms of the specific rate of interest. The fact that the economy is in equilibrium means that the expectations of entrepreneurs are systematically fulfilled and, thus, that they are under no inducement to alter their investment behaviour.

Voluntary savings and the structure of production

We are now in a position to determine what will happen in the event that consumers change their saving habits. Suppose that they now decide to consume a smaller portion of their income, thus increasing their voluntary savings. The increased supply of savings will lead to a fall in the rate of interest. In this event, certain investment projects which were previously disadvantageous will now appear promising. However, these new projects will not be directed toward productive processes which are temporally close to the moment of consumption, as we have assumed that the demand for final products has declined. They will, instead, be directed to stages which are distant from the moment of consumption. Moreover, the fact that the rate of interest has fallen makes it possible that the new investment will be directed to entirely new productive stages, which are even more distant from the moment of consumption than the previously most distant stage.

The drop in demand for consumer goods leads to a drop in the sales of firms which produce these goods, thereby freeing means of production formerly engaged in these processes. Consequently, the prices of these means also decrease. Therefore, not only are producers now in a position to borrow on more favourable terms than before, but they can also purchase the means of production at lower prices. Thus, they can initiate processes of production which are temporally further removed from the moment of consumption. Machlup (1974, p. 21) describes this phenomenon as a 'deepening' of the structure of production. The new situation is depicted by Hayek as shown in Figure 9.2.

The narrower base of the triangle in Figure 9.2, compared to Figure 9.1, represents the fact that the consumer goods the economy is now producing are fewer than before. On the other hand, the greater height of the triangle

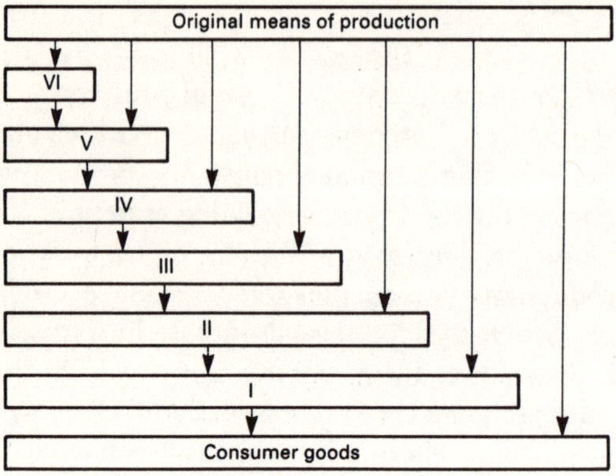

Source: Hayek (1931/1935, p. 52)

Figure 9.2

represents the fact that the structure of production is now deeper, as two new processes have been added – V and VI. Assuming that the new saving habits of consumers remain constant, the new structure of production will also remain stable. Therefore, for as long as the rate of interest remains at its new equilibrium level, forces will not be created which would lead to a transformation in the structure of production.

The above should not lead one to believe that Hayek's model is one of static equilibrium. In reality, what he asserts is that, assuming that the original disturbance of equilibrium is not caused by a dislodging of the rate of interest from its equilibrium level, a tendency toward equilibrium will be a constant feature of the economy.[3] The fundamental characteristic of Hayek's model is now clear. Hayek describes a monetary economy, albeit one in which the role of money is entirely neutral. His notion of neutrality is, however, completely different from that implied by the quantity theory of money. Hayek does not claim that variations in the quantity of money affect merely the price level but, on the contrary as will be seen shortly, that such variations affect the economy through their effect on the relative prices of commodities.[4]

The concept of forced saving

Let us now assume that, while the saving behaviour of consumers remains unchanged, the banking system increases the quantity of money it funnels into the economy. Like an increase in the supply of any commodity, the increase in the money supply will lead to a drop in its price – that is, the rate of interest.

At this point, Hayek introduces the additional assumption that the banking system extends credits only to producers. We are, thus, dealing with an economy where consumer credits do not exist. The drop in the lending rate will encourage investment projects which previously seemed unprofitable. The greater amount of money in the hands of producers will translate into new demand for capital goods, thereby raising their prices. Thus, the processes of production which manufacture capital goods become more profitable, which in turn strengthens the tendency for new investments to be concentrated in stages ever more distant from the moment of consumption. On the other hand, producers have more money at their disposal and can thus offer more for the acquisition of the means of production they require. Therefore, they are also in a position to win over primary means of production from the stages closer to the moment of consumption.

The situation of producers of consumer goods as well as of intermediate products temporally close to consumption is quite the reverse. The demand for their products has not decreased, since, for the time being, neither income nor saving habits have changed. However, their profits are now under severe pressure, since costs are rising under the competition of producers investing in the new more capitalistic processes. They are thus compelled to curb production, as raw materials and labour have grown both more costly as well as scarce.

The end result of this process is a deeper structure of production, as depicted in Figure 9.2. The only difference is that the new structure is not a result of a change in the saving behaviour of consumers but of the increase in the quantity of credit money issued by the banking system. Nevertheless, the fact that the production of consumer goods decreases, means that consumers will not be able to spend the same portion of their income as they did previously for such goods. Thus, the increase of savings – depicted by the shorter base of the triangle – is no longer voluntary but 'forced'.[5]

The expansionary phase of the cycle

The second main difference from the case where the deepening of the structure of production was a result of a change in saving habits, is that the new deeper structure is now unstable, because the plans of producers and consumers are no longer compatible with each other. Of course, producers have reacted to the drop in the rate of interest exactly as they did before, by investing in more capitalistic processes. However, the stimulus to which they are now responding does not stem from the free functioning of the market but from an arbitrary action by the banking system. As O'Driscoll and Shenoy (1976, p. 205) stress, like any intervention in the free operation of the market process, an increase in the money supply disseminates misinformation to producers about the intentions of consumers.

The important thing to note in this case is that the incompatibility between the actions of producers and consumers tends to grow ever more severe. The forced savings of consumers can only be a temporary phenomenon, since, as the costs of means of production increase, so do the incomes of those who own them. Consequently, consumers begin to obtain a share of the money which producers had originally acquired. They are thus in a position to increase their demand for final products, thereby increasing their prices as well as the profits of those who produce them. As a result, the latter can again effectively compete with the investors in the more capitalistic processes for the purchase of primary means of production. Therefore, if we are correct in assuming that investments in more capitalistic processes generally require a considerable amount of time before they begin to yield profits, it is obvious that the cost of such investments will tend to rise over time.

Thus, the deeper structure of production can only be maintained if the banking system continues to increase the supply of credit money, thereby progressively lowering the lending rate, as it is only in this way that producers can overcome the increasing cost of the new investment projects. In other words, the effects of this inflationary process can only be offset by even greater inflation. According to Hayek, this process describes the boom of the cycle and the longer it continues the deeper and more long-lasting will be the phase of the depression which will inevitably follow.

Crisis and depression

There are three reasons why inflation cannot continue indefinitely. The first is that, even if there are no institutional regulations on banks' reserves, each bank has to impose some limit on the amounts of credit money it creates, in order to safeguard its solvency. The second reason has to do with how producers' expectations change in the face of galloping inflation. Even though they may believe that inflation will continue, there will come a point where they will begin to doubt whether a rising inflation can help them beat the rise in the cost of raw materials. Their expectations about the future will, at this point, become more pessimistic and, as a result, their demand for loans will drop. The third reason is that a steady rise in inflation will ultimately lead to the collapse of the currency, thereby rendering money unusable as a medium of exchange and thus transforming the economy into a barter system.

The abrupt cessation of monetary expansion marks the moment of the crisis and the beginning of the phase of the depression. Even if we assume that the amount of money undergoes no absolute decrease but simply ceases to expand, the rate of interest is bound to rise. The reason is that the steady rise in the costs of the means of production will also raise the demand for capital. Thus, investment projects which at the lower lending rate seemed profitable, cannot be continued and will have to be abandoned. As a result, large quantities of capital goods are entirely dissipated or they are, as Haberler notes (1937, p. 52), employed in a manner in which their marginal product does not cover the cost of the investment. Therefore, unemployment will inevitably rise in the more capitalistic process.

However, the drop in economic activity will not solely be confined to those processes of production which are the most distant from the moment of consumption, but will extend to all stages. The unemployment in the most capitalistic stages results in lower incomes and thus lower demand for consumer goods. The producers of these products see both their sales as well as their profits drop. Therefore, the repercussions of the crisis spread throughout the economy. The intensity of the depression will obviously be more severe in the event that the banking system does not merely cease to increase the quantity of credit money but actually lowers it. The occurrence of this phenomenon, which Haberler (1937, p. 58) termed 'secondary deflation', is quite plausible as the banks will try to restore their solvency the moment the signs of the crisis are perceived. Therefore, the depression will continue to spread, with high unemployment and idle manufacturing capacity.

Eventually, of course, this process will be reversed, as the demand for loans will begin to rise. The reason is that at the end of the depression the demand for loans will still be very low – due to the pessimistic expectations of producers – while the solvency of the banks will have been restored. Thus, the interest rate will be at a level lower than equilibrium, thereby making investments attractive once again. However, the new investment will primarily be directed toward processes which are temporally closer to the moment of consumption, since any rise in demand will primarily be for consumer products, and the structure of production will once more tend to assume the characteristics it possessed before the equilibrium was disturbed by the increase in the quantity of money. Thus, the economy will again arrive at the full employment equilibrium and it will remain there for as long as the banking system maintains the stability of the money supply.

The Ricardo effect

In 1939, Hayek slightly altered his argument by introducing the phenomenon which he termed as the 'Ricardo effect'. The main reason for this shift was due to the fact that his theory was, in its original form, based on the assumption that there is an automatic tendency toward full employment, an assumption which had, however, ceased to be regarded as self-evident after the publication of Keynes's *General Theory* (1936). Hayek thus had to show that his conclusions remained valid even when the analysis of the trade cycle began from a state of underemployment.[6]

As observed above, all turning points in the evolution of the trade cycle are, according to Hayek, characterized by an initial increase in demand for consumer goods. For orthodox theory, however, such an increase should inevitably also raise the demand for capital goods. Thus, increased consumption at the end of the boom will lead to increased demand for means of production and capital equipment, thereby tending to preserve the deep structure of production. Conversely, the increase in consumption at the start of economic recovery will once again lead to increased demand for capital goods, thereby tending to accelerate the recovery.[7]

By introducing the Ricardo effect, Hayek tried to show that an increase in consumption will not necessarily raise the demand for capital goods. He based this view on Ricardo's contention that, by reducing profits, wage increases lead capitalists to replace labour with machinery and the reverse when wages fall. Thus, in order to determine whether an increase in consumption will result in greater demand for capital goods, its effects on the profits of the industries producing consumption products must be studied. If the profits of such businesses fall, we ought to expect increased demand on their part for capital goods; if, on the other hand, profits rise, the opposite should result.

We are now in a position to analyse the way in which the Ricardo effect operates at each of the two moments of the cycle in which there is a rise in demand for consumer goods. The first such moment occurs during the final stages of the boom, when new investments in more capitalistic processes have increased incomes and consumption. The wages of those employed in consumer-goods industries are already relatively high when the increase in demand occurs, because competition for labour with the investors in the more capitalistic processes has already raised wages.

However, the increase in demand and the concomitant rise in prices will result in an increase in the rate of profit in the enterprises producing consumer goods. Thus, real wages, as perceived by the entrepreneur in comparison with his/her rate of profit, will begin to drop. As a result, the aim of these businesses is not to mechanize production in order to lower costs but, rather, to achieve a short-term increase in production by hiring more workers, introducing overtime, and so on. Therefore, the increased demand for consumer goods need not necessarily result in increased demand for new capital equipment. Whatever demand for capital equipment does occur, will now primarily be directed toward simple machinery and to a far lesser degree toward complex capital goods which economize labour. Therefore, even if we assume that the interest rate remains at equilibrium, the operation of the Ricardo effect makes the crisis unavoidable, since it renders impossible the continued existence of the deep structure of production.

For Hayek, it was, however, more important to show how the Ricardo effect operates during the final stage of the depression, since only in this way could he rebuff the criticism that his theory is only valid in the event that the economy is in the state of full employment. This stage is characterized by large-scale unemployment and idle production capacity. However, these phenomena are not so acute in the consumer-goods sector, since the demand for such products is less elastic than the demand for capital goods. Consequently, unemployment in this sector is relatively low and, thus, wages remain comparatively high. Nevertheless, the high level of unemployment means that sales and, consequently, profits in this sector will also be low.

In these circumstances, the Ricardo effect induces investment in the consumer-goods sector to be directed toward the acquisition of complex machinery which economize labour. However, this results in a lowering of unemployment in the more capitalistic processes and, consequently, demand for consumer goods begins to rise. It is at this point that the Ricardo effect begins to work in reverse. The unanticipated rise in profits leads producers in the consumer-goods sector to adopt a course opposite to the one which they had originally taken. The demand for complex capital equipment now ceases, while demand for labour and simple machinery intensifies. Thus, in this case the operation of the Ricardo effect seems to delay the process of recovery and the establishment of full employment.

The fundamental importance of the neutrality of money

We have already seen that Hayek considers changes in the money supply as the root cause of the trade cycle. In his view, however, although the cause of cyclical fluctuations originates in the monetary sphere, the cycle itself is a real phenomenon.[8] Such a conception has profound implications for monetary policy. Not only is an increase in the quantity of money incapable of bringing about full employment but it is, in fact, bound to generate a cycle. Therefore, the only policy which can prevent cyclical fluctuations of economic activity is one which ensures the neutrality of money. Moreover, since the notion of neutrality is not based on the manner in which money affects the price level, it can only be ensured if the quantity of money is kept constant.

A Keynesian economist might agree with this view, if the increase in the quantity of money is effected while the economy is already at full employment. He/she would counter, however, that it could indeed accelerate the recovery if it were introduced in the final stages of the depression. Hayek (1939/1975, p. 63) admits that such a policy can lead, in the short term, to full employment. It is his contention, however, that by distorting the price mechanism, its positive effects cannot continue indefinitely but will necessarily lead to further distortions and thus to a renewal of cyclical fluctuations.

Hayek's argument is based on his account of the operation of the Ricardo effect at the final stages of the depression. The introduction of the Ricardo effect endows the phenomenon of the trade cycle with a more endogenous character, because it shows that changes in the structure of production do not only come about as responses to changes in the interest rate but also to changes in profits, wages, and so on. However, this endogeneity actually reinforces Hayek's argument that fluctuations of the quantity of money cannot bring about full employment, in the sense that such exogenous interventions in the functioning of the system cannot but reinforce in any case the disequilibria created by its endogenous motion. Thus, as utilized by Hayek, the Ricardo effect appears to be an entirely anti-Keynesian construct, in the sense that it sheds doubt on the effectiveness of any form of exogenous intervention for the attainment of full employment.

This line of argument raises the question of what Hayek actually proposes as a policy aiming at countering the phenomenon of the trade cycle. Hayek's (1931/1935, p. 99) major contention is that monetary policy should be such as not to allow a cycle to begin, for once the cycle has started there is no policy that can place it under control. Therefore, as Barry (1979, p. 177) has shown, Hayek's proposal amounts to the demand to abolish the very idea of a monetary policy. In essence, what Hayek is proposing is that the only effective policy against the cycle it to 'wait it out' and, according to Machlup (1974, p. 26), it was precisely this attitude which led to the rejection of the neo-Austrian theory of the cycle by the economic orthodoxy of the crisis-ridden 1930s.

The role of the banking system

However, if the manipulation of the quantity of money by the banking system constitutes the main cause of business cycles, the question arises as to why the banks do not learn from experience. Mises believes that this is due to the institution of central banks, which supposedly distorts the operation of the credit market in two ways. First, a central bank is empowered to be the official instrument of state policy in the management of the credit market. However, this results in lessening the responsibility of individual banks, since the avoidance of bankruptcy is now seen to be the responsibility not of each bank but of a centralized policy-making institution.

Secondly, even if the original reason for instituting a central bank was simply to supervise the workings of the credit market, as soon as such an agency is created it immediately becomes a focal point for political controversy concerning the monetary policy it is to pursue. Thus, pressures are created which tend to alter its original role and transform it from a simple control mechanism into a highly-politicized agency. In Mises's view (1928, p. 136) it is the predominance of an 'inflationary ideology' among businessmen, economists and bankers which determines this policy and thus converts the demand for reducing lending rates by increasing the supply of credit money into an indisputable dogma of monetary policy. Therefore, the intervention of central banks in the free workings of the credit market is seen as the major destabilizing factor in the economy.

Hayek does not differ from Mises in his attitude toward what he considers to be the destabilizing role of any governmental intervention in the credit market. Indeed, he notes (1976a, p. 89) that a further reason why such interventions will inevitably deepen economic fluctuations stems from the fact that in a democratic political system, monetary policy is constantly under pressure from various organized groups of sectional interests. However, Hayek (1928/1933, pp. 143-8) is critical of Mises's central thesis that the cycle is initiated exogenously. According to Hayek, even if the banks consciously aimed at maintaining the lending rate at its equilibrium level, this aim would be very difficult to achieve, because the equilibrium rate may change due to changes in the real elements of the economy – for example, a change in the saving habits of consumers as he has shown. Thus, it is impossible for the banks to set their rates at the actual equilibrium level at any one moment, even if they wish to do so. Therefore, in Hayek's view, although the trade cycle is unavoidable, it is government interventions which have, in modern times, consistently made it much worse than it had to be.

Sraffa's critique of Hayek's theory

Among the critiques that Hayek's theory attracted, Sraffa's review of *Prices and Production* in 1932 stands out as the most comprehensive and penetrating. What makes Sraffa's critique especially relevant at this point, is that the core of his argument concerned Hayek's conception of money solely as a medium of exchange – an argument which we have also employed in our critique of the neo-Austrian theory of money.[9]

The role of money as a medium of exchange

Interestingly, neither Hayek himself in his reply (1932a) to Sraffa, nor Lachmann (1986) in his review of the debate 50 years later seem to understand the specific criticism levelled by Sraffa against the view of money exclusively as a medium of exchange. Apparently, this view was so deeply rooted in the minds of both, that they were simply incapable of grasping Sraffa's objection, even though it is a point of central importance and one upon which a whole series of further criticisms was based.

Sraffa begins his review of Hayek's book by declaring his agreement with the concentration of the latter's analysis on the effects of monetary fluctuations on relative prices rather than on the general price level. He immediately notes, however, that a theory which seeks to show how money affects relative prices should begin by placing money on a par with all other commodities. Sraffa (1932, p. 44) then argues that money is, in Hayek's theory, deprived of the most essential characteristic of all commodities: the possession of value. Consequently, Hayek's central thesis that the role of money remains neutral only as long as its quantity remains stable, amounts to a mere tautology, since the neutrality of money is not due to the fact that its quantity remains stable but, rather, to the fact that it has been rendered neutral by the a priori assumptions of Hayek himself.

Of course, it is not entirely accurate that Hayek's theory does not contain any notion of the value of money. We have seen that inflation constantly reduces this value during the boom, thus inducing producers to demand ever larger amounts of credit in order to complete their investments. However, Sraffa's objection is essentially correct because, in Hayek's theory, the notion of the value of money takes on significance only at the actual moment of exchange, while the value of money hoardings is not taken into consideration. From what we have seen in the previous chapter, this view of the role of money is not surprising, since neo-Austrian theory finds the concept of hoarding unacceptable, as it is incompatible with the view of money solely as a medium of exchange.[10]

This view of money also lies at the core of a contradiction in Hayek's theory, which springs from the fact that he assumes, in several instances, that producers and consumers are the same individuals, while, at other times, claims that they are different. Sraffa (1932, p. 45) observes that only in the first case can Hayek's hypothesis that a change in the saving habits of consumers affects the allocation of funds for consumer and capital goods, make any sense. Conversely, only when we assume that they are two distinct groups of individuals does the distinction between consumers' and producers' credits have any validity.

In his rebuttal, Hayek once more seems not to grasp the essence of Sraffa's criticism, for he replies that when a consumer decides to save a portion of his/her income, he/she is simultaneously choosing to lend it to producers. Thus, the consumer is in a position to affect the allocation of expenditure between consumer and capital goods even though he/she is not transformed into an entrepreneur. Therefore, for Hayek, savings are automatically converted into investment.[11] This is a self-evident hypothesis in the context of a barter economy, but it can only be valid in a monetary economy as well if money is assumed to function exclusively as a medium of exchange. Evidently, if Sraffa's view of the contradiction between the roles of producers and consumers in Hayek's system is correct, then Hayek's distinction between those economic developments which are the result of voluntary choices by consumers and those which are forced, is completely undermined. For if entrepreneurs may hoard the amount of savings they obtain in the form of loans, nothing guarantees that they will transform them into investment in more capitalistic processes, as it is assumed by Hayek's theory.

The problem of the dissipation of capital

The second target of Sraffa's criticism is Hayek's conclusion that the deepening of the structure of production, brought about by the increase in the money supply, will tend to be reversed as soon as the process of inflation stops. This reversal is supposed to result in the dissipation of capital which has been invested in the new and more capitalistic productive stages. According to Sraffa, such an outcome is by no means inevitable.

There is here a fundamental point which must be elucidated. At the moment the banks halt the increase in the money supply, some of the new investments in the more capitalistic processes will have already begun to function productively, while others will still be incomplete. Sraffa admits that capital invested in this second category of processes will indeed be entirely destroyed, but he adds that the same phenomenon would arise if the increase in the interest rate had been brought about by a drop in voluntary savings (1932a, p. 249). The major disagreement between Sraffa and Hayek concerns, therefore, the investment projects which are already operational when the rate of inflation falls. The central tenet of Hayek's theory is that capital invested in these projects will also be dissipated, because the rise in the lending rate is bound to lead to a drop in the demand for complex capital equipment – the products of the more capitalistic processes. This was the essence of Hayek's reply (1932a, p. 243) to Sraffa, in which he claimed that what matters for the producer of capital goods is not the preservation of their material form but his/her ability to sell them.

We are thus led to the core of the matter. In Hayek's theory, the deepening of the structure of production will begin to be reversed the moment that the incomes of the owners of means of production begin to rise. However, as Sraffa points out, the deepening of the structure of production implies that the number of productive stages in the economy also rises and with it the number of intermediate products and the number of transactions. Thus, the demand for cash balances must also be higher. As a result, Sraffa maintains that the deeper structure of production will absorb the entire amount of money created by the banking system. Therefore, this new money is destined never to reach the pockets of consumers – the owners of the means of production – since it will be absorbed by the increased demand for liquid assets which results from the larger number of exchanges which now occur because of the deeper structure of production.[12]

Thus, the major disagreement between Hayek and Sraffa is not whether capital can be dissipated, but whether this is the inevitable outcome of the inflationary phase of the cycle, as the former believed. Evidently, Sraffa's argument amounts to a complete rejection of the causal relationship between fluctuations in the quantity of money and the trade cycle, which is implied by Hayek's theory.

Equilibrium and natural rates of interest

The third point of Sraffa's criticism concerns the mechanism by which changes in the money supply affect the structure of production; this mechanism is the divergence of the lending rate from its equilibrium level. Hayek (1931/1935, p. 23) believes that this may only occur in a monetary economy. By contrast, Sraffa argues that such a divergence is equally possible in a non-monetary economy. In that case, the equilibrium rate would have the character of an abstract ratio capable of ensuring the general equilibrium of the system, while the lending rate would have to be expressed in a natural form: as a percentage of the quantity of each commodity which the borrower would be obligated to pay to the lender. In a barter economy, Sraffa observes (1932, p. 49), there exists at all times one, and only one, equilibrium rate. However, there would be as many natural lending rates as goods produced and exchanged, without these rates having to be equal to each other or to the equilibrium rate. Thus, the divergence between the equilibrium and the lending rate is a general characteristic of any economy rather than the result of the arbitrary functioning of the banking system.

Sraffa admits (1932, p. 50) that in the state of general equilibrium all the natural rates will equal the equilibrium rate. The point at issue is whether this equality will persist if the general equilibrium is disturbed. Let us suppose, as Sraffa does, that we observe a shift of demand away from some goods toward others. The immediate result will be a fall in the prices of the former and a rise in the prices of the latter and, as a consequence, the market will expect that production of the former will drop while that of the latter will rise. This also means, of course, that the natural lending rate of the former will drop, while the natural rate of the latter will rise.

The importance of Sraffa's point is now obvious. In Hayek's theory, a rise in voluntary savings is equivalent to a shift of demand away from consumer goods and toward capital goods. Thus, the natural interest rate of capital goods will now be higher than that of consumer products. Therefore, if, as Sraffa maintains, any disturbance of equilibrium will result in the coexistence of a multitude of natural lending rates, how can the banking system ensure the neutrality of money? Hayek's actual prescription that the lending rate be maintained at its equilibrium level, ceases to have any validity, since, as Sraffa notes (1932 p. 51), in such a situation 'there is no such thing as an equilibrium (or unique natural) rate of interest'.[13]

Of course, Hayek's proposal can still be valid if we assume that the money rate of interest is, at any moment, related to all natural lending rates in a manner that counterbalances the differences among them and thus brings about the general equilibrium of the system. According to Sraffa, Wicksell indeed made such a proposal in claiming that the banks should maintain the money lending rate at a level determined by the average of all natural rates weighed in the same way as the index number of prices. However, Sraffa (1932a, p. 251) stresses that this assumption is not permissible to Hayek, as he has 'emphatically repudiated the use of averages'. In this context, Hayek's prescription for economic stability thus breaks down entirely.

The trade cycle and the concept of the reproduction of capital

This chapter will end by noting an apparent paradox in the neo-Austrian theory of the trade cycle. Even though neo-Austrians themselves consider this theory as an indication of the dynamic character of their approach, their fundamental conclusion is that the economy is basically a stable system. Trade cycles are not caused by the market process itself but are, instead, produced by exogenous manipulations of the money supply. On these grounds, we will argue that the difference between neo-Austrian theory and the neoclassical idea of general equilibrium is rather insignificant and that the transcendence of this static outlook requires the introduction of the notion of the cyclical reproduction of capital.

We have already observed that the neo-Austrian theory of capital is essentially a theory determining the physical characteristics of the economy. Conversely, the theory of money should be considered as referring to the value aspect of the economy. Considered in this way, the theory of the trade cycle can be seen as a synthesis of the processes which occur on these two spheres. It is precisely the a priori view that the two spheres constantly interact in a manner that ensures their mutual coordination, that allows neo-Austrians to claim that the market system is inherently stable.

We now have all the elements which describe the paradox mentioned. On the one hand, the insistence of neo-Austrians on the materiality of capital goods and the search for causal relationship between economic variables are, of course, incompatible with the exclusive concern of the neoclassical model with price adjustments and with the simultaneous interdependence of all economic variables. On the other hand, however, neo-Austrians insist on viewing the economy as an inherently stable system, in which any endogenously created destabilizing tendency is quickly reversed. In what follows, we will argue that the failure of neo-Austrians to decidedly sever their links with the general equilibrium model stems from their inability to incorporate into their analytical framework the idea of the cyclical reproduction of capital.

As shown in Chapter 7, the absence of the idea of reproduction implies that neo-Austrians view the category of capital as always retaining its physical character – that of capital goods. In that context, the sole phenomenon relevant for the determination of the value of capital is the process of exchange. This is precisely the conclusion reached previously when we asserted that the concept of the capital structure is pre-eminently static. Without the idea of cyclical reproduction, neo-Austrian theory is evidently unable to differentiate its position from the neoclassical conception of the economy as an aggregate of interdependent markets. By accepting the idea of reproduction, however, the problem of the economy's equilibrium is placed on an entirely different theoretical basis. For equilibrium to exist, what is now required, as Grossman has noted (1977a, p. 82), is that, in each time-period, social capital is exactly reproduced both in its physical and in its value form.

The question which now arises is whether the activities aiming at the reproduction of the value aspect of capital can be a priori thought of as being in coordination with those aiming at the reproduction of capital in its physical form. Only if this is the case can the economic results of these two activities be considered to have a stabilizing effect on the economy as a whole. If one accepts the idea of cyclical reproduction, disturbances of equilibrium can be seen as stemming both from the physical and the value spheres of the economy. This is possible because capital is no longer considered to be an exclusively physical category, but a category undergoing constant mutations from physical to value form and the reverse. Viewed in this way, production is no longer thought of as the automatic consequence of individual decisions on the structure of particular capital goods but, rather, as the economic activity which aims at the unimpeded reproduction both of the physical and the value aspects of capital.

We are now in a position to clearly understand how the sphere of production can generate disequilibrium and, in particular, how such disturbances are directly connected with changes in the value sphere of the economy. As we have seen, neo-Austrians perceive the economy as an aggregate of activities which are all unfolding on the level of exchange. They thus reach the logical conclusion that the market process is constantly disseminating accurate information which will result, if followed, in the overall stability of the system. Given such a theoretical basis, it is logical to suppose, for example, that a producer will react to an expected decline in demand by lowering production.

However, if we base our approach on the concept of cyclical reproduction, such a reaction will no longer seem to be the most rational response by a producer. Rather, such a reaction would mean that the producer should not be expected to make any effort to avoid the devaluation of his/her capital. A more logical response would be for each individual producer to attempt to revolutionize his/her production methods by investing in fixed capital of a new kind, so that he/she can sell at a cheaper rate than the competitors. However, this logical response from the individual producer would act as a destabilizing force on the economy as a whole, as it would lead to instability in the conditions of supply and demand in the markets of commodities. Thus, we are now faced with a disturbance of equilibrium which directly stems from the sphere of production.

As Grossman notes (1977a, p. 86), the marked tendency in the capitalist mode of production toward the constant revolutionizing of production methods is, in turn, responsible for a further tendency toward overproduction of items of fixed capital. Neo-Austrian theory thus shares a common descriptive element with the Marxian theory of crisis. In both, the moment of crisis is characterized by the overproduction of capital goods. We must conclude, however, that neo-Austrians, unlike their Marxist counterparts, do not attribute the appearance of this phenomenon to the unimpeded activity of the market system. Precisely because they do not, they are led to hypothesize that the sources of disturbance are located outside the system, in the arbitrary activities of the banking system. Operating from such a theoretical foundation, however, neo-Austrians can no longer persuade us of the dynamic character of their theory. Consequently, we must conclude that neo-Austrian theory conceives of the economy in the same way as orthodox neoclassical theory does. For both, the economy is a system characterized by inherent stability, and the only systematic disturbances derive from extra-economic sources.

Notes

1. The foundations of the neo-Austrian theory of the trade cycle were laid by Mises (1912/1934). However, in the 1930s, the major exponent of the theory was Hayek (1928/1933; 1931/1935; 1939/1975).
2. Hayek (1931/1935, p. 23) notes that this is Wicksell's 'natural rate', although he prefers the term 'equilibrium rate'.
3. See O'Driscoll (1977, p. 80).
4. In reality, this conclusion is rather oversimplified. Hayek maintains that money is neutral not as long as its total quantity is kept stable but, rather, when this quantity multiplied by the velocity of circulation remains constant. Thus, any fluctuation in this velocity is bound to affect the real elements of the economy. However, it is evident that Hayek does not believe that such fluctuations suffice to explain the phenomenon of the trade cycle, as they cannot be assumed to occur systematically.
5. See Hayek (1932) for a reference to the historical appearance of the concept of forced saving.
6. See Barry (1979, p. 166). As an explanation of Hayek's original position, Lachmann (1940, p. 269; 1976a, p. 60) claims that, in the 1930s, Hayek's work was still under the influence of the general equilibrium model, and further maintains that Hayek's insist-

ence on the full-employment hypothesis was one of the main reasons why the neo-Austrian theory of the trade cycle was rejected by the orthodoxy of the time.

7. This is usually referred to as the accelerator principle.
8. Machlup (1974, p. 23) writes, 'The fundamental thesis of Hayek's theory of the business cycle was that monetary factors cause the cycle but real phenomena constitute it'. Machlup is here paraphrasing a remark made by Hayek himself (1931/1935, p. xiii).
9. See Sraffa (1932, p. 44): 'The money which he [Hayek] contemplates is in effect used purely and simply as a medium of exchange. There are no debts, no money-contracts, no wage-agreements, no sticky prices in his suppositions. Thus he is able to neglect altogether the most obvious effects of a general fall, or rise, of prices.'
10. In fact, there is one instance in *Prices and Production* (1931/1935, pp. 66–8) in which Hayek has to admit the possibility of hoarding. This is the case of integrated firms – the case, in other words, where two consecutive stages of production are merged in the operation of a single enterprise, thereby removing from circulation the amount of money that would be required for the purchase of the product of the higher stage. However, Sraffa (1932, p. 46) claims that this is really a contradiction in Hayek's theory, as 'he is driven to assume that the money saved is hoarded for a time, thus contradicting his postulate that the quantity of money multiplied by its velocity is constant'.
11. See Hayek (1932a, p. 241). In fact, this was the main point of disagreement in the debate between Hayek and Keynes, which began in 1931 with a review by Hayek of Keynes's *A Treatise on Money* (see Hayek (1931; 1932b) and Keynes (1931)). Hayek's basic argument during the debate was that the only possibility that savings and investment may not be equal, is when investment is generated by an arbitrary increase of the quantity of money by the banking system.
12. At this point, Sraffa (1932a, p. 250) becomes sarcastic: 'if Dr. Hayek had taken as much pains in writing his book as his reviewer has taken in reading it he would remember that under his assumptions such cash holdings will absorb not merely certain exceptional amounts, but the whole of the additional money issued during the inflation; that consequently incomes cannot rise at all, and there will be no occasion for any dissipation of capital'.
13. Hayek's reply to this last criticism seems to weaken his own position even further. On the one hand, he admits that, in the circumstances described by Sraffa, there will not be merely one but a vast number of natural rates. He maintains, however, that all these natural rates will, at the same time, be equilibrium rates (1932a, p. 245). This contention of Hayek's is so contradictory that even Lachmann himself (1986, p. 237) does not attempt to defend it, but simply admits that it is a fatal concession on Hayek's part.

10 The depoliticization of the economy

The neo-Austrian theory of the trade cycle views the manipulation of the supply of money by governments as the major cause of trade fluctuations. We must, therefore, turn our attention to the neo-Austrian proposals for depriving the state of any ability to intervene in the economy.

Orthodox theory views the implementation of anticyclical policies as the necessary means in the fight against inflation and unemployment. This view is based on the orthodox Keynesian idea that inflation and unemployment constitute two mutually exclusive phenomena. Evidently, the neo-Austrian theory of the trade cycle leads to a very different notion, as it considers these phenomena causally related. Inflation is an indispensable characteristic of the boom and, since crisis and depression are its unavoidable consequences, unemployment – the major characteristic of the depression – must be considered as the result of the inflationary stage of the cycle.

The priority of combating inflation

This view leads neo-Austrians to articulate a proposal for fighting inflation and unemployment, which is radically different from that of Keynesian economics. What they are aiming at is not the formulation of two sets of policies which can be applied alternatively in order to combat either inflation or unemployment,[1] but the definition of the principles which the state must abide by in order to avoid the start of a cycle. And since the cycle is set in motion by the increase in the quantity of money, the main such principle must be the restriction of the state's ability to manipulate the money supply.

The theoretical and political priority of the struggle against inflation rather than unemployment, explains why the analysis of the negative consequences of the former is really exhaustive in the neo-Austrian literature. Let us briefly present the most important such consequences. As seen in Chapter 8, a first negative effect of inflation is its impact on the distribution of income. Related to this, is the effect of inflation on taxation. As prices and incomes are continuously rising, tax brackets either remain stable or are readjusted periodically. Thus, as Shand (1984, p. 162) notes, the state is able to extract, through inflation, resources from its citizens of greater real value than the nominal value that tax brackets represent.

A further consequence of inflation, as Moss (1976, pp. 29–30) shows, is that it tends to favour the maintenance of monopolistic market structures. In periods of inflation, consumers concede to paying prices constantly higher than those they would be paying in a period of stability – as they are afraid that prices will increase even more in the future – thus allowing monopolies to continue to reap extra profits. On the other hand, consumers will try to compensate for their loss by offering the means of production they possess at higher prices than before.[2] On the one hand, the power of monopolies increases and, on the other, the spiral-like inflationary process is reinforced.

According to Hayek (1950, p. 276), however, the most important consequence of inflation is that it prevents the market process from disseminating correct information. The theory of the trade cycle shows that producers interpret the fall in the rate of interest as a signal that the saving behaviour of consumers has changed, rather than as a sign of inflation. Consequently, the deepening of the structure of production that follows can be considered the correct response to a wrong signal. Moreover, there is a secondary distortion of the knowledge-disseminating function of the market, which derives from the political process. In contemporary democracies, where governments are under constant pressure from their voters, the social groups affected by inflation have the means to achieve the government's intervention in favour of their specific interests. These interventions – incomes policies, price controls and so on – distort the knowledge spread by the price mechanism even further. Thus, state interventionism and inflation are two inter-reinforcing phenomena.

Unemployment as a result of the violation of market freedom

As already mentioned, in comparison to their exhaustive analyses of the negative consequences of inflation, the neo-Austrians' references to the phenomenon of unemployment are rather sparse. These references could be categorized, according to the point of view from which the phenomenon of unemployment is being examined, as the macroeconomic, the political-institutional and the microeconomic approach.

According to the macroeconomic approach,[3] the continuation of inflation can only conceal unemployment, which will inevitably appear with greater intensity when inflation stops or when its rate falls. The distortion of market signals drives workers to enterprises whose viability can be secured only through the continuation of inflation. Thus, as soon as the rate of inflation slows down, the unemployment which was hitherto concealed will openly appear. Consequently, the longer inflation lasts, the greater will be the unemployment which will inevitably follow.[4]

The second approach, which we have termed political-institutional, views unemployment as a product of the monopolistic status of labour unions. As any monopolist, the latter try to maximize total revenue by limiting supply. Labour unions can succeed in obtaining higher wages for their members only by limiting the supply of labour, thus condemning the non-unionized workers to unemployment. Therefore, the abolition of the monopolistic privileges of the labour unions will lead to the increase of employment. Hayek confesses that such a goal seems to be politically unattainable, because even governments that share this point of view are usually eager to avoid labour unrest and, thus, prefer to follow an inflationary policy.[5] On this basis, he concludes that the limitation of the ability of governments to increase the quantity of money at will, does not simply aim at the removal of an impediment to the smooth functioning of the price mechanism but also has a positive political effect (1976a, p. 76). By revealing the unions' responsibility for unemployment, it facilitates the acceptance by public opinion of a policy aiming at restricting their privileges.

The microeconomic approach treats unemployment as a market phenomenon. As any such phenomenon, unemployment is created by the market process, while, at the same time, it is again the market process that constantly tends to efface it.[6] Mises terms this notion of unemployment 'catallactic', precisely because he wants to show that it is a product of catallaxy – or market dynamics.[7] In this context, any intervention in the functioning of the labour market that aims at reducing unemployment tends to distort market signals. More specifically, such interventions delay the adjustment of the expectations of the unemployed regarding the wage rate and, as a consequence, keep them unemployed as they are searching for higher wages longer than they should. On this basis, Mises (1949, p. 770) claims that unemployment benefits not only fail to limit the rate of unemployment but contribute, instead, to its perpetuation.

A dual political irresponsibility

The neo-Austrian view of inflation and unemployment can help us understand why neo-Austrians reject any notion of an anticyclical policy. Since state interventionism is considered to be the major cause of trade cycles, the idea that governments should be entrusted with the responsibility of securing economic stability, brings to mind the story of the naïve shepherd who commissioned the wolf to take care of his herd.[8] Neo-Austrians are, therefore, primarily concerned with establishing the institutional restriction of the state's ability to implement any form of anticyclical policy. Obviously, this is a matter extending beyond economic theory, as it is principally a political issue.

According to neo-Austrians, the notion of an anticyclical policy is grounded on a theoretical fallacy of Keynesianism: the attempt to describe the economy on the basis of the interaction between aggregate variables.[9] According to Keynes, the state cannot diminish unemployment by lowering nominal wages because the labour unions will strongly resist such a measure. In addition, effective demand will decline and unemployment will rise. Therefore, the only way through which the state can create full employment is by lowering real wages – by reducing the value of money through mild inflation. This is, according to Hayek (1958, p. 295), Keynes's proposal.

Hayek believes that such a policy can only be effective for as long as the workers are being 'deceived' by the stability of their money-wages. As soon as they become aware of the reduction of the purchasing power of their earnings, Keynes's logic leads to the necessity of still greater inflation and, consequently, to the further destruction of the stabilizing role of the price mechanism. Hayek maintains (1975, p. 201), however, that the most profoundly negative consequence of Keynesianism is apparent at the level of politics. By justifying the manipulation of the money supply by governments, Keynesian theory has in effect armed politicians with a method of increasing their popularity. The important thing to note, however, is that it is a method that lies beyond the control of the market's spontaneous stabilizing mechanisms.

According to Hayek, the fact that Keynesian policies allowed the economic functions of the state to become independent of market control, has had important implications for the political system that emerged in the West after the Second World War. A consensus was created, according to which the responsibility for economic stability could not be entrusted to the market, but had to be shared between governments and the labour unions. This division of roles is seen by Hayek as having led to a dual irresponsibility. On the one hand, labour unions were expected to negotiate ever higher wages, without regard for the consequences of such a policy on employment. On the other hand, governments strived to achieve full employment by constantly raising the rate of inflation, without regard for the destructive consequences of such a policy on the operation of the price mechanism.[10]

It thus becomes evident that neo-Austrians see the restriction of the role of the state in the economy as requiring reforms on the level of the political system. In what follows, we will concentrate on Hayek's proposals which attempt, on the one hand, to deprive governments of the means of exercising an anticyclical policy and, on the other, to restrict their constitutional powers to intervene in the economy.

The denationalization of money

Hayek's most significant reform aims at the restoration of the stabilizing role of the price mechanism by depriving the state of the monopoly of issuing currency. The denationalization of money is thus Hayek's most daring proposal, aiming at a monetary reform which will subject money to the operation of the market process.[11] In Hayek's account, if the economic role of money were determined by the market process in exactly the same way as any other economic variable, money would obviously lose the character of the means for the implementation of policies, which it has while under the exclusive authority of the state.

According to Hayek's proposal, every private bank would have the right to issue its own currency and, at the same time, every transactor would be able to keep his/her money holdings and carry out his/her transactions in any of those private currencies. The various currencies would be freely exchangeable at exchange rates determined by the interaction of supply and demand and announced daily, in the same way as stock exchange quotations.[12] Hayek maintains that the supply and demand for the various currencies would be determined by the stability of their purchasing power. Therefore, every bank would be trying to keep the purchasing power of its currency stable in relation to a set of goods. Every individual, on the other hand, would be able to choose the currency that is more stable in relation to the set of goods in which he/she is usually dealing. If a bank failed to keep the purchasing power of its currency stable, the demand for it would drop and, consequently, the bank would be forced to support it by immediately restoring its purchasing power.

The issuing of currency by the state is not forbidden in such a system. However, in a regime of competitive currencies, governments would be obliged to safeguard the stability of the purchasing power of their currency just like the private issuing banks would be. Consequently, the denationalization of money would deprive them of the ability to fluctuate the quantity of money at will and would oblige them to compete with the private sector on equal terms. Hayek's proposal would, however, also lead to a further restriction of state authority. The fact that governments would be managing a competitive currency, would subject their activity to the discipline of the market, thus making it impossible for them to sustain budget deficits.[13]

Hayek (1976a, p. 99) concludes that, compared to the reintroduction of the gold standard, a regime of competitive currencies would be a far more radical solution to the problem of state interventionism. He admits that, if currency-issue were to remain under the exclusive authority of the state, the gold standard might indeed restrict the unaccountability of governments in the management of the money supply. However, the effects of denationalization would be much more far-reaching; not only would it make governments more accountable for their actions but it would also render any state intervention absolutely impossible, by depriving governments of their authority on the major tool of any intervention, money.[14]

Money and currency

The main objective of neo-Austrian theory is to abolish the state's ability to implement any form of economic policy. It is, therefore, reasonable to concentrate our critique on the most radical reform put forth by neo-Austrians:

the denationalization of money. Of course, we are not going to dwell upon the technical and institutional requirements for the implementation of Hayek's proposal. An investigation of this aspect of the problem would require a detailed reference to the conditions governing the operation of the international banking system – an issue lying beyond the scope of this book. We will, therefore, assume that Hayek's proposal is indeed realizable.

We will begin the critique by placing the denationalization proposal in the context of the neo-Austrian theory of money. We have seen that Hayek's major aim is to transform money into a variable determined by the market process – an object of consumers' choice. The view of money as an object of choice is, of course, consistent with the neo-Austrian theory of money, which perceives the latter as always retaining its subjectivist and, at the same time, its commodity character. However, the fact that we have presumed that Hayek's proposal is realizable, seems to imply that our argument in Chapter 8 for the unique character of money is now completely undermined, because uniqueness is hardly compatible with the existence of many competitive currencies.

If, however, we delve deeper into this matter, we will discover that this incompatibility is only superficial. Hayek may be proposing the coexistence of many competitive currencies, but he does not deny that their sum total constitutes the generally-accepted category of money. Thus, the character of money as the sole means of exchange – as a good that has already excluded any other good from this role – is reconfirmed. The validity of this argument is attested by the fact that Hayek maintains that the issuing function of a bank differs from the rest of its activities, since the principal criterion for its success is the maintenance of stability. Evidently, in Hayek's idea of the economy, there has to be a commodity the value of which in terms of all others must remain stable. It is precisely, therefore, the demand for stability that unifies the many private currencies into one category, money. The uniqueness of money is thus retained, despite the fact that it may be expressed in many different forms – as many different currencies. The importance of the fact that the denationalization proposal does not invalidate our idea of the uniqueness of money will soon become apparent.

Production and credit money

Hayek sees an issuing bank as performing two parallel functions: issuing currency and transforming its deposits into credits. In the context of the former function, the bank's entrepreneurial activity aims at safeguarding the stability of the currency issued. In the context of the latter, however, it is in the bank's interest to increase the credits offered to its customers independently of its deposits. These two activities are interrelated, as constant credit expansion will lead to the depreciation of the currency in which the credits are issued. Thus, the objectives of the bank's two entrepreneurial activities are contradictory. Hayek believes that it is precisely this contradiction that will force the bank to restrict its credits in order to restore the stability of its currency.

The question now is whether such a prudent policy by each individual bank is sufficient for the stability of the system as a whole. In Chapter 8, we showed that the rejection of the commodity-character of money and of the exclusiveness of its function as a means of exchange, introduces its function as a store of value, and, consequently, the possibility of hoarding. This possibility implies, in its turn, that the flow of money is not necessarily smooth, but that it is liable to fluctuations which are independent and uncontrollable by the banking system. Therefore, the creation of credit money is not necessarily the result of the banking system's speculative behaviour and certainly not the result of the state's inflationary policy. It is the result of the market process itself. Contrary to the view of neo-Austrians, therefore, it cannot be supposed that the creation of credit money is an a priori destabilizing factor.

This argument is reinforced by the conclusion in the previous chapter that the disturbances of economic stability do not necessarily spring from the monetary sphere but may also originate in the sphere of production. In this context, the possibility of hoarding, or of its opposite, is not merely a theoretical probability but a rule for the functioning of the system. The various components of capital are being reproduced at various time-periods. Thus, the cyclical reproduction of the whole of an individual capital requires that its owner has the ability to hoard money so that he/she will be able to continue production until the moment that the whole capital will realize its value. This means that the stages of hoarding and dishoarding will be succeeding one another, in a different frequency for each individual capital. Hence, our conclusion that the phenomenon of credit money is an outcome of the market process itself, constitutes the complete reversal of the causality implied by the neo-Austrian theory of the trade cycle. It is not the creation of credit money that destabilizes the structure of production but, rather, the instability of this structure that requires the creation of credit money.

The consequences of this reasoning for the denationalization proposal should be apparent. Even if it is presumed that a bank's credit and issuing activities tend to keep each other in check, it is not at all necessary that they also stabilize the economy as a whole. On the contrary, such a prudent bank activity might hinder the adaptability of the credit system to the financing needs of the cyclical reproduction of capital.

Production and the money supply

The above conclusion is not sufficient for a refutation of Hayek's proposal. The reason is, as pointed out at the end of Chapter 8, that neo-Austrians, on the one hand, consider the creation of credit money as a destabilizing factor, while, on the other, they recognize it as an unavoidable phenomenon and express the belief that the free operation of the banking system will keep it at a minimum. Contrary to what we have argued, therefore, they could still insist that the interaction between the issuing and the credit activities of each issuing bank will keep the creation of credit money in balance with the requirements of the stability of the market system. Hence, the rejection of the denationalization proposal requires us to show that the balancing of these two activities cannot effectively respond to the credit needs of the reproduction of capital.

Our argument will be based on the notion of the uniqueness of money. A bank's issuing activity is carried out within the framework of supply and demand for the specific currency and aims at keeping its value stable in relation to other private currencies. The credit activity, however, is in fact independent of the currency of the specific bank. What determines this activity is not the demand and supply of the specific currency but the demand and supply of the unique category of money, as we have defined it. The uniqueness of money implies that every bank is offering a means of credit similar to that offered by its competitors. Moreover, the demand for this means is independent of the bank itself as well as from the banking system as a whole, since it is, as we have argued, determined by the fluctuations of productive activity – the demands of the reproduction of capital.

The question now arises as to in what way this situation differs from the case in which currency-issue is a state monopoly. In the latter case, the value of the currency does not concern every individual bank but the central monetary authorities. On the other hand, the credit activity of each bank is subject to the restrictions imposed by the monetary authorities on liquidity and on the aggregate supply of money. The question that should now be answered, is whether free competition among issuing banks can be a satisfactory substitute for the role of the central monetary authorities in coordinating the credit market. Of course, Hayek's answer is positive: competition forces every issuing bank to maintain such a liquidity level so as not to threaten its ability to protect the value of its currency. On the other hand, the aggregate money supply is no more than the sum of the quantities of the various private currencies.[15] Therefore, as every bank is trying to maintain control over the quantity of currency it issues, the aggregate supply of money is also being controlled.

If, however, the banks offer a homogeneous means of credit, as we have argued, then the problem of the coordination of the credit market acquires new dimensions. The fact that there is now not one single currency renders the concept of the aggregate money supply void of any meaning and, therefore, unable to respond to the needs of the reproduction of capital. Competition amongst issuing banks cannot guarantee this responsiveness, because the effects of competition become noticeable through the fluctuations of the exchange rates amongst the various bank currencies. However, if, for example, all banks increase their credits to the same degree, it is possible that the exchange rates amongst the various currencies remain steady. It is, therefore, possible to have an increase of credit money and, at the same time, stability of exchange rates.

The political implications of the denationalization proposal

The denationalization of money, instead of driving the economic system to stability, as neo-Austrians believe, might lead to constant instability and to the danger of total collapse, mainly because of the abolition of any centrally determined aggregate supply of money. However, since we have presumed that the denationalization proposal is technically realizable, the question is how the banking system will attempt to prevent such a possibility.

In the situation described, it will be in every bank's interest to know how far it can extend credits without endangering its liquidity. The only way this can be ensured is through an agreement among issuing banks on commonly acceptable rules governing liquidity and the aggregate supply of money. It is, in fact, the appearance of a credit monopoly, which will be controlling the money market with exactly the same mechanisms and the same efficiency, or inefficiency, as the state monetary authorities. Thus, the final consequence of Hayek's proposal would be that the control of the credit market would be taken away from a public monopoly, only to be handed over to a private one. Therefore, the hope that by denationalizing currency we will be led to an absolutely competitive money market seems Utopian.

There is still one possible argument in favour of the denationalization proposal; a private monopoly is preferable to a public one because it is obliged to function according to market rules, instead of being liable to political pressures. The problem with this type of argument is that it views public and private institutions as strictly separated from each other. In fact, the transfer of the control of the credit market from a public to a private monopoly will simultaneously transfer political pressures from the former to the latter. It will, in effect, transform the private monopoly into a political institution. It is essentially the same argument Bosanquet (1983, pp. 70–1) puts forward: the state is exercising coercion as a representative of private interests. The abolition, however, of the state's ability to act coercively does not limit the ability of private interests themselves to exercise coercion through other, now private, institutions.

Hayek's proposal for constitutional reform

If we agree with neo-Austrians that the role of the state is, by definition, destabilizing, we must also espouse their belief that the most decisive reforms in the direction of limiting the role of the state should be concentrated on the level of the political system. Therefore, such reforms should not merely aim at depriving governments of the tools through which they can intervene in the private sphere, as with the denationalization proposal, but at invalidating the deeper political causes of state interventionism.

Hayek believes that the major cause of state interventionism is the transformation of the democratic principle from a mere procedure for selecting rulers into a principle allowing the absolute rule of the majority over the minority. The reason that governments have almost unlimited power is that their mandate is usually accompanied by a parliamentary majority which allows them to determine the very legal framework within which they are acting. Thus, in contemporary western democracies, the authority of governments has supposedly ceased to be restricted by the law.[16]

More precisely, state interventionism springs, according to Hayek, from the specific development of the political system of western democracies during the past two centuries, which brought about the concentration of executive and legislative power in the authority of the same elected assembly – Parliament.[17] Therefore, a constitutional reform aiming at the restoration of the 'rule of law' should abolish this merging of executive and legislative authorities. Hayek proposes the creation of two separate assemblies. The first, which he calls 'governmental', will be charged with the responsibility to select the government and to daily control its function. The second, the genuinely 'legislative', will be completely independent of government responsibilities and its only duty will be to legislate.

The different character of each of the two assemblies must, of course, be reflected in the manner their members are elected. The election of the governmental assembly will be carried out in the same way as contemporary parliamentary elections: by general poll and party-competition. The legislative body, however, should be elected in a different way, since law-making should reflect the acceptance of general principles and rules, rather than party politics. Therefore, the members of the legislative assembly should not be elected for more than one term of office, so that their legislative work will be unobstructed by any contemplation of re-election and, therefore, from any temptation to give in to pressures by organized groups. On the other hand, every member's term of office should be long enough – Hayek proposes 15 years – so that his/her contribution to the legislative work can be as independent as possible from short-term influences and, therefore, more in accordance with the general moral rules.

Since the duties of a legislator have more to do with his/her judgement than with his/her opinions on specific issues, Hayek proposes a series of other regulations in order to render the election of the members of the legislative assembly as personalized as possible. First, he proposes that the candidates should be at least 45 years of age and that they should be elected by their peers, so that the electors can have as accurate a personal opinion of the candidate as possible. Thus, one-fifteenth of the assembly's members will be annually renewed. Hayek also provides for the strict institutionalization of the procedure followed in preparing every generation for the moment of the election. As soon as individuals finish school, they automatically become members of a club consisting of all their peers and to which they will belong for the rest of their life. Nobody is allowed to switch to an age-group club other than the one to which he/she was initially appointed. In addition, nobody has the right to found such a club, since only one such club is allowed for every generation in every geographical area.[18] The members of each club will discuss public affairs and will get to know each other well, so that the judgement of all future candidates will be fairly assessed.

We can now turn to the responsibilities of the two bodies. The fact that the governmental assembly will be controlling the daily operation of the administration does not mean that it will have no right to make decisions or that it will not have the ability to impose those decisions through its prerogative to exercise coercion. The essential point is that this function will not have a legislative character. Only the legislative assembly will have the right to establish, as Hayek notes, 'universal rules intended to be applied in an unknown number of future instances' (1982, vol. III, p. 109). Consequently, the government's ability to exercise coercion will now be strictly limited, as it will be subject to the rules issued by the legislative assembly.

Let us now cite some examples of the effects Hayek's constitutional reform would have on the economy. The majority of the governmental assembly could decide on the allocation of state expenditure, but it could not rule on matters such as the revenue it will raise from citizens or the personal contribution of each citizen. Those matters would be decided by the legislative assembly, according to the general rules of just conduct. The governmental assembly could also enforce an expenditure policy in order, for instance, to combat unemployment. It could not, however, finance this policy by issuing inflated money, as this would mean that the government is deceiving its citizens by reducing the purchasing power of money – a practice violating moral rules. It is, therefore, obvious that Hayek's proposal is depriving the state of any power to intervene in the economy.

A fundamental contradiction

Evidently, the constitutional reform proposed by Hayek poses great problems to constitutional theory, which, of course, lie beyond the scope of this book. We will, however, focus our attention on a methodological paradox. In Chapter 2, we saw that Hayek considers the uncritical acceptance of the traditions that constitute the culture of market society as a fundamental condition for the preservation of the market order. However, the constitutional reform he is now proposing contradicts his insistence on the uncritical acceptance of tradition, as he seems to be implying that the evolution of social institutions and practices creates mutations which may threaten the viability of market society. For example, he now claims that the evolution of the political system of western democracies has led to the appearance and the constant growth of an institution – the contemporary state – which tends to destroy the spontaneity of the market order. In his account, therefore, the survival of the social organism demands the timely diagnosis and removal of the cancer growths it tends to produce.

Even enthusiastic supporters of Hayek's work recognize that this is a fundamental inconsistency in his thought. Gray (1986, p. 139), for example, believes that Hayek's system ends up facing a 'crisis': a contradiction between its 'rationalist' and its 'sceptical' aspects. By following the rationalist aspect of Hayek's thought, one arrives at Buchanan's public choice approach – the demand for redesigning the political system as an indispensable requirement for the survival of market society. By following, on the other hand, the sceptical element of his thought – his mistrust of the possibility for objective knowledge on the requirements for the preservation of the market order – one will, according to Gray, end up with a theory that may perhaps explain the spontaneous character of the social process, but which cannot be used as a 'guide to action'.

Gray (1986, p. 134) adds, however, that this contradiction is arming Hayek's philosophy with a political advantage. The coexistence of the two elements in his thought seems to allow the coexistence of conservatism with radicalism. On the one hand, Hayek demands the uncritical acceptance of tradition while, on the other, he seems ready to propose radical reforms of those elements of the tradition that may potentially endanger market society. The political impetus of this combination should not be underestimated, as it has proved of fundamental importance for the growth of the New Right movement during the 1980s. This subject will be returned to in Chapter 12. Let us, however, note here that the political aspect of the matter does not cancel the existence of a serious methodological inconsistency in Hayek's thought.

The depoliticization of politics

We are now able to face the essence of Hayek's model constitution. Evidently, his objective is to prevent any conscious effort to redesign society and, hence, any conscious intervention in the social process. In his account, any such effort would be based on the illusion that there exists the possibility of an objective knowledge of social phenomena. As we will argue, however, this position amounts to the absolute elimination of the sphere of politics.[19]

Our argument will be grounded on two considerations. The first concerns the right of citizens to voice an opinion on the quality of contemporary society, in the context of Hayek's model constitution. If we consider that real power to influence social processes rests exclusively with the legislative assembly, it is obvious that every member of society obtains the right to express an opinion on the social system only once in his/her lifetime when, at the age of 45, he/she is called upon to elect some of his/her peers to the legislative assembly. Hence, Hayek's proposal actually forbids political activity, if we interpret this term not merely as the daily control of the administration but, predominantly, as the conflict of ideas about the future of human society. Thus, in the context of Hayek's model constitution, the rejection of economic objectivity is transformed from a scientific theorem into an institutionally imposed feature of the political system.

The second consideration concerns the procedure followed for the election of the members of the legislative assembly. In fact, what Hayek is trying to institutionalize is the individualization of this procedure, by excluding the expression of any collectivity. We have seen that party competition should not, according to Hayek, be influencing the selection of the legislative assembly members, even though it is not at all clear how such a possibility could be totally excluded. What is, of course, apparent, is that the constitutional regulations he is proposing are aiming directly at hindering the expression of any collective position. The regulations concerning the citizens' preparation for the moment of the election, and the insistence on the candidates' judgement as the decisive selection criterion, aim at ensuring that this election procedure will be the outcome of countless individualities. The essence of these problems will be considered in Chapter 12.

This chapter will now conclude by pointing out some of the implications of Hayek's proposal. If we are correct in arguing that his model constitution would inevitably lead to the elimination of the sphere of politics, it is not hard to understand the kind of society Hayek envisages. It is a society where the relations amongst individuals will be exclusively governed by the institution of the market. Nobody will have the right nor the possibility to judge this institution or its effects. Such a judgement would be grounded, as seen in Chapter 2, on the primordial instincts of solidarity and altruism, instincts that should be suppressed by contemporary society. In this context, the family should be the only social organism within which those instincts may be even nowadays allowed. Consequently, Hayek envisages a society consisting of thousands of autonomous family units, whose interrelations will be exclusively limited to exchanges mediated by the market.

Apparently, such a view of human society can make sense only if one accepts Hayek's conception of the market. If we view the market as a game in which every member of society can compete on equal terms on the basis of his/her skill and luck, then its unobstructed operation becomes the most essential factor for safeguarding the cohesion and harmony of human society. If, however, as we have repeatedly argued, the market tends to produce results which are, on the one hand, predictable and, on the other, determined by the individual's command over productive resources, then the neo-Austrian justification of the system is falling apart. In this context, the elimination of the sphere of politics, instead of leading to the emancipation of the individual from state coercion, as Hayek presumes, leads to his/her subjugation to a regime over which he/she is not even allowed to utter an opinion.

Notes

1. This is, according to Hayek (1950, p. 271), the most dangerous legacy of Keynes.
2. For the analysis of this process see Mises (1912/1934, p. 162).
3. The term macroeconomic is employed as a reference to an overall view of the functioning of the system and not as a legitimation of the study of aggregate variables.
4. This view of the relation between inflation and unemployment also lies at the core of the neo-Austrians' argument that their theory can convincingly explain the contemporary phenomenon of stagflation. According to Hayek (1978a, p. 114), the continuation of inflation for a long period creates inflationary expectations. But from the moment the rate of inflation is predictable, the increase of the quantity of money ceases to have any, however short-term, effect on employment. Thus, in their effort to reduce unemployment, governments can only raise the rate of inflation so that it exceeds the rate anticipated by transactors.
5. See Hayek (1958, p. 299). The experience of the 1980s must have made Hayek more optimistic about the ability of New Right governments to restrict the privileges of the labour unions.
6. In this context, Gunning (1985, p. 228) notes that the use of terms such as involuntary unemployment is methodologically unsound. In the same sense that it is meaningless to characterize the absence of exchange as involuntary, it is equally meaningless to characterize as such the absence of an agreement of employment.
7. See Mises (1949, pp. 597–8). Evidently, this is a notion of unemployment which is similar to the orthodox notion of frictional unemployment.
8. As Shand notes (1984, p. 166), the major difference between neo-Austrians and monetarists stems from the formers' mistrust of the ability of governments to stabilize the economy through the manipulation of the money supply.
9. This methodological point lies at the core of the difference between neo-Austrians and monetarists. For the former, the fact that monetarism relies on the study of aggregate variables is, of course, unacceptable. See O'Driscoll and Shenoy (1976, p. 191).
10. Underlying Hayek's view of the impact of Keynesian policies in the post-war era, is the idea that this whole period is characterized by a continuous rise in inflation caused by the increased role of the state in the economy. However, as Tomlinson (1990, pp. 68–80) observes, Hayek avoids to offer convincing proof to support this idea.
11. See Hayek (1976a). Even though the denationalization of money has not been imple-

mented in any country, one should not underestimate its political and ideological thrust. Hayek's argument was apparent, for example, in the polemic of the Thatcher government against the establishment of a European currency and a European central bank. Hayek himself criticizes this prospect in the first page of the 1976 edition of his book.

12. The circulation of these currencies is, of course, not restricted by national borders. Thus, the power of governments to manipulate foreign relations through an exchange rate policy is removed.
13. See Hayek (1976a, p. 89).
14. Hayek (1986) has recently put forward an alternative proposal. Although he continues to support the coexistence of many competing currencies, he admits that governments will never abandon their monopoly of issue. Thus, he proposes that, instead of actually issuing their own currency, banks could rather accept deposits and issue credits on the basis of an artificial 'standard' of money – a weighed average of the prices of a basket of commodities. However, since Hayek's new proposal does not require as significant institutional arrangements as the denationalization proper, what it is unable to explain is why it has not arisen as a spontaneous outcome of the market process.
15. In the second edition of Hayek's book (1978b, p. 102), he poses the question whether the existence of competing currencies makes redundant the role of central banks in regulating the 'elasticity' of circulation. His answer is that, provided that each bank knows that the increased demand for credit will not increase the volume of transactions but only the liquid holdings of its clients, the regulative role of the central bank is redundant. However, from the point of view of each issuing bank, the distinction between these two aspects of the demand for credit is entirely arbitrary. Thus, although Hayek obviously recognizes the problem of the aggregate money supply, the solution he proposes seems to be just wishful thinking.
16. In this context, the term 'law' implies not just any decision of the majority but a universal legal code, which springs from the generally-accepted rules of behaviour and has universal validity.
17. Note that, according to Hayek (1982, vol. III, pp. 105–6), this assessment holds just as well in political systems, such as that of the US, where the distinction between the legislative and the executive branches of government is much more clearly established than in the parliamentary systems of western Europe.
18. Hayek (1982, vol. III, p. 118) explicitly admits that he is inspired by the organizing principles of the Rotary Club.
19. Dahrendorf (1990, p. 32) expresses essentially the same conclusion about Hayek's philosophy, when he argues that by raising all social issues to the level of the constitution, 'a total constitution emerges in which there is nothing left to disagree about, a total society, another totalitarianism'.

11 The socialist calculation debate and the historicity of state interventionism

The famous problem on the possibility of 'socialist calculation', which was the object of the major theoretical debate between neo-Austrians and socialist economists in the 1920s and 1930s, is now examined. In a socialist system, the means of production would belong to the community and, consequently, productive activity would have to be centrally planned. Therefore, the major issue of controversy was whether a centrally-planned socialist economy could guarantee as rational a use of its resources as that achieved by a capitalist society. This chapter will begin with a presentation of the different arguments and will, subsequently, proceed with some critical conclusions regarding the neo-Austrian view of state interventionism.

The introduction of the problem by Mises

Mises was the first to speak of the inefficiency of socialism.[1] This position came as a reaction to the views of socialist economists who maintained that in a socialist society the category of value and thus of money as a measure of values would be redundant.[2] Mises claimed, by contrast, that the process of imputing values to the means of production through the valuation of consumer products is the major prerequisite for the rational functioning of any economic system. Therefore, rational economic activity requires that individuals are in a position to calculate the values of goods and, especially, of the means of production they possess.[3]

Mises stresses that what is required in order for calculation to be possible, is the objectification of subjective valuations, so that the value of each consumer good or means of production reflects the average of the valuations of all members of society. This is realizable only on two conditions. First, all consumption goods and means of production must be exchangeable and, second, the calculation of values must be based on a commonly-accepted measuring unit.

These conditions are, evidently, fulfilled in the capitalist system. The fact that property is private creates the need for exchange and, with it, the need for a commonly-accepted measure of values. In their turn, exchange and money provide the foundations for the emergence of the price mechanism. Price fluctuations reflect changes in subjective valuations and thus provide the signals the producers need in order to adapt production to the preferences of consumers. Hence, the functioning of the price mechanism is the major guarantor of the rational use of resources in a capitalist society.

Can this rationality also be achieved in a socialist system? Mises assumes that exchange of consumers' goods will exist even in such a society, as it would be impossible for the socialist authority to reward every worker with the exact set of goods he/she wishes to consume. In its turn, exchange will make possible the emergence of a kind of money which could technically simplify transactions. However, the role of such a means of exchange will be different from the role of money in a capitalist economy, because its use will be necessarily restricted to the exchange of consumer goods. In a socialist society, the exchange of means of production is impossible, as they exclusively belong to the community. What Mises (1920, p. 104) points out, therefore, is that we cannot have prices without exchange and, in turn, that the calculation of the values of the means of production is impossible without prices. Thus, in a socialist economy the allocation of resources will inevitably be arbitrary, making the wastage of resources not only unavoidable but, rather, the rule. On these grounds, Mises concludes that it is impossible for a socialist economy to function rationally.

One could argue, however, that socialist enterprises would still be able to exchange resources, and that this exchange could lead to the formation of a market and of prices even if the latter were not expressed in money but only in exchange ratios between commodities. Mises (1922/1981, p. 119) vehemently attacks this idea, by pointing out that the market is inexorably linked to the institution of private property. The fact that there can be no competition among enterprises renders the functioning of the price mechanism ineffective and value-calculation unattainable. According to Mises, therefore, even if socialist enterprises may exchange means of production, the fact that these means are not their property renders the emergence of a market impossible.

The mathematical solution

The possibility of exchange between socialist enterprises lies at the core of the solution to the problem of value-calculation, which was proposed by a series of economists during the 1930s.[4] Contrary to Mises's position, they believed that the central planning authority of a socialist economy would be able to set the prices of goods through the solution of a system of simultaneous supply and demand equations. In what follows, the analysis will focus on the first version of the 'mathematical' solution, put forward by Dickinson in 1933.

Dickinson proposes a model of a socialist economy, in which labour and consumption goods are exchangeable in free markets. The means of production, except for labour, are, of course, owned by the community, but enterprises operate independently of each other. The form of the economic system is thus identical to that of the capitalist economy, except for two differences. First, the prices of commodities are not determined on the corresponding markets but are set by the central authority. Second, enterprises are obliged to publish all information relating to their operation. Thus, as Dickinson (1933, p. 239) puts it, they operate within 'glass walls'.

In order to simplify the analysis, Dickinson assumes that consumer goods are not marketed by the enterprises that actually produce them but by 'selling agencies'. He also assumes that retail prices are not, at a first stage, set by the central authority but are freely determined by their supply and demand. When the stock of a commodity held by a selling agency declines, the retail price rises and vice versa. Price fluctuations render the formation of the corresponding demand schedule possible. Evidently, this schedule is known to the central authority, as we have assumed that all terms of an enterprise's operation are transparent.

The orders placed by the selling agencies to the manufacturing enterprises depend, of course, on the wholesale prices. Thus, these orders reveal the corresponding demand schedules, which are again known to the central authority. On the basis of these schedules, manufacturing enterprises place orders for intermediate products, a fact that simultaneously leads to the formation of the corresponding demand schedules, and so on. This procedure obviously ends up in the formation of the demand schedules for the ultimate factors of production.[5]

For the determination of the system's equilibriums the supply schedules for each good are also required. The procedure by which they are formed is identical to that of the formation of the demand schedules, only in a reverse direction, as the quantities of the immediately available ultimate factors of production determine the supply conditions for all goods. The central authority sets the prices of these means at the level that ensures the total absorption of each specific factor. Based on those prices, each manufacturing enterprise will set the wholesale price of its product at the level that equals exactly the cost of production. The consumer prices of the goods produced by the economy will finally be set in this way. Apparently, these will be the equilibrium prices for every specific market as well as for the economy as a whole,[6] as they emerge from the equality of supply and demand in all markets. Once the supply and demand schedules for all goods have been determined, prices no longer have to be formed in free markets. Since all the data are known to the central authority, the latter can set prices through the mathematical solution of a system of simultaneous supply and demand equations.

What remains to be shown is the method by which the central authority can determine the rate of capital accumulation. According to Dickinson

(1933, p. 244), every enterprise can draw its demand-schedule for capital in relation to the rate of interest by ranking the various investment programmes it could alternatively undertake. Adding up the capital demand schedules of all enterprises, the central authority can form the aggregate demand function for capital. The level of accumulation can now be determined in two alternative ways. The central authority can either establish the desired interest rate and thus determine the part of the social product that should be dedicated to the increase of social capital, or it can determine the part of the product that should be saved, thus determining the corresponding interest rate. In both cases, the solution of the accumulation problem ensures equilibrium and thus the possibility of value-calculation.[7]

Central planning and knowledge

Hayek begins his critique of Dickinson's proposal by admitting its logical consistency (1935b, p. 207). He maintains, however, that it is practically unfeasible as a method of directing a socialist economy. Hayek grounds his argument on his theory of knowledge. The substitution of individual economic activity by the central authority is possible only if the latter can utilize in its calculations all the knowledge which individuals possess. Therefore, in order to function at least as efficiently as the capitalist economy, a socialist system should be in a position to utilize a huge volume of knowledge. The greater the volume of the knowledge utilized, the bigger the system of simultaneous equations to be solved and, therefore, the more difficult the solution becomes. Moreover, in a socialist economy, this knowledge cannot be used freely by every individual but must first be transferred to the central authority. However, this transfer is not only technically unfeasible but is also actually impossible, especially with regard to knowledge which is inalienable from its physical bearer because of its tacit character.

Hayek also directs his criticism against less extreme versions of the mathematical solution than that of Dickinson. According to these versions, the central authority would not have to determine every minute detail of economic activity but only some mathematical rules for the running of enterprises. Thus, every enterprise would be operating in a competitive manner, while the authority of the centre would be restricted to the role of auditing. In his criticism, Hayek poses two questions. The first is whether those systems in fact indicate a restriction of the central authority's planning role, while the second asks what is required in order for the central authority to be able to effectively fulfil its new auditing function.

Hayek's answer to the first question is negative. In his account (1935b, p. 232), the planning role of the central authority would not really be diminished in such a system, as it would retain the important function of ensuring the effective use of social resources. The crucial issue is, bringing us to the second of the above questions, the manner through which the central authority can ensure the efficient use of resources. Clearly, since every enterprise is being run as an autonomous unit and in a competitive relation to all others, the role of management assumes particular importance. However, how can the central authority select the appropriate managers and judge the efficiency of their work?

One could propose that the central authority should auction the management of each enterprise and finally assign it to the person promising the greatest returns. However, since this is a system in which private property does not exist, the highest bidder would not be risking anything and, consequently, his/her bid cannot be seriously considered as a selection criterion. Therefore, if the central authority restricts itself to an auditing role, it will not be in a position to appoint the most competent managers and to ensure the effective use of social resources. On the other hand, if it tries to fulfil its role by getting involved in the day-to-day management of each enterprise, then the problems associated with the impossibility of concentrating knowledge re-emerge.

The solution of the Walrasian auctioneer

Lange proposed a model of 'competitive' socialism which he claimed to be free from the practical difficulties of the mathematical solution.[8] In his model, enterprises are allowed to compete with each other on two conditions. First, their main objective is not to maximize profits but to minimize the cost of production and, second, prices are not determined freely by the market but are set by the central authority. Lange's aim is to prove that this kind of price-setting need not be the result of the solution of a system of simultaneous equations, but that it can be effected through a much simpler process – the same process that actually operates in a capitalist system.

Lange (1938, p. 63) begins his analysis by claiming that in Hayek's critique of the mathematical solution there is already an implicit retreat from Mises's original position in the fact that Hayek does not question the logical consistency of this solution but only its practical feasibility. According to Lange, this implies that Hayek actually accepts the 'parametric' function of prices: the idea that prices can effectively direct production even if they do not emerge on free markets but are centrally set.[9] Thus, if it could be proven that parametric prices can be set centrally by a simpler method than the one proposed by the supporters of the mathematical solution, the neo-Austrian argument against central planning would be undermined.

To sustain this conclusion, one should address two questions. The first concerns the rules which must be guiding the running of enterprises, thus inducing them to make the most efficient use of social resources. The second concerns the way in which the central authority can set prices, so as to achieve the optimal use of resources.

Any answer to the first question should take into account that the required rules need to ensure the production of every good at the lowest possible cost and that the total quantity produced precisely equals demand. Lange (1938, p. 75) proposes three general rules. The first is that every enterprise must aim at minimizing average cost, and the second is that every enterprise must extend production up to the level where the marginal cost equals the price. Provided that all markets are perfectly competitive, these two rules replace the incentive of profit maximizing which constitutes the basic moving force of capitalist society. The third rule does not concern individual enterprises but whole industries. Every industry must extend production up to the point where its marginal cost equals the price of its product. This rule determines the production level of each industry and provides the basis for all decision-making concerning the expansion or the contraction of production, new investment and so on. It is a rule that performs, according to Lange (1938, p. 77), the function which is, in a capitalist system, performed by the free entry and exit from every branch.

We now come to the second of our questions. The optimization of the use of social resources is ensured when the economy is in a state of general equilibrium. Thus, the objective of the central authority is to discover the equilibrium price vector. However, instead of trying to determine this vector mathematically, Lange proposes an 'experimental' method. Let us suppose that, at a first stage, the central authority sets the prices of goods entirely at random. This will naturally result in disequilibrium in most markets and, as a consequence, the central authority will have to reset prices, raising them on the markets where excess demand appeared and lowering them on the markets with excess supply. Through such a procedure of consecutive approximations, prices will gradually converge to the equilibrium price vector.[10]

Therefore, Lange assigns to the planners of the socialist economy the role of Walras's auctioneer. The central authority in Lange's model does not have to interfere in the daily activities of enterprises, but only to try and coordinate the actions of buyers and sellers. According to Lange, the observance of his three rules is sufficient to ensure that the response of enterprise managers to the prices set by the planners will lead the system to general equilibrium.

Socialism as a system of general static equilibrium

Hayek (1940, p. 185) responded to Lange's solution by pointing out that it too constitutes a retreat from the original positions of the socialist economists, because Lange's competitive model of socialism is closer to the capitalist system than the older socialist proposals. However, if Lange is correct in believing that his model can limit the role of the central planning authority,

Hayek wonders about the advantages of such a system over the system of the free competitive market itself. Leaving aside questions of social justice, Lange (1938, p. 89) believes that the main advantage of socialism is that the central authority has a much wider knowledge of the functioning of the system and is thus in a position to react to market disequilibria more efficiently than the individual entrepreneur who possesses only partial knowledge. This alleged advantage of socialism constitutes Hayek's focal point of criticism, as he stresses that the method of central price-setting proposed by Lange is primarily static.[11]

According to Hayek, the effectiveness of the price system should not be judged by its ability to approach a static equilibrium, but by the speed with which it reacts to changing circumstances. Consequently, the major criterion for the assessment of Lange's solution is whether the speed of adjustment is greater in a system where the reaction to changes in the data is expressed only after some central authority has perceived disequilibria and has appropriately altered prices, or in a system where the individual entrepreneur can act freely as soon as he/she perceives an opportunity.

This raises the question of the time-period within which prices would be valid – what Hayek terms the 'period of fixation' (1940, p. 191). The very logic of Lange's experimental method demands price-setting at regular intervals and, as a consequence, Hayek concludes that prices would be generally set later than they would under free market conditions (1940, pp. 192–3). Of course, if the central authority reviewed prices on a continuous basis, it would indeed be in a position to replace the entrepreneur's function in the capitalist system. In doing so, however, the planners would have to face all the practical difficulties Hayek was pointing out in his criticism of the mathematical solution: the difficulty of transferring to the central authority the knowledge possessed by individuals. Moreover, such a function would cancel one of the major advantages of the experimental method over the mathematical solution – the non-interference of the central authority in the daily activities of enterprises.

There is a further problem with Lange's model, which springs from the fact that Lange views all markets as being perfectly competitive. Hayek examines an instance in which such an assumption is problematic, that of products 'made to order'. In this case, the central authority can either set prices arbitrarily or study each case separately in order to discover the specific cost. Hayek points out (1940, pp. 188–9) that if it follows the first path, the arbitrary basis of the calculation will invalidate any rationality of this function. If it follows the second, it will apparently fully undertake the entrepreneurial role with all the negative consequences he has already pointed out.

Entrepreneurship under socialism

Hayek is thus led to the conclusion that Lange's experimental method will deprive the managers of socialist enterprises of any possibility to act entrepreneurially. He points out that the application of Lange's three rules for the running of enterprises is unattainable, if the managers are not allowed to set the prices of their products. The cost curves are not given facts, as neoclassical theory supposes, but data emerging through the process of price-competition. On these grounds, Hayek maintains that only if every manager is able to set the prices of his/her products, is the discovery of the lowest cost feasible (1940, p. 196).

Moreover, as the managers are obliged to simply react to prices set by the planners, Hayek wonders how they should act in cases where they believe that a good's current price does not reflect the supply and demand conditions the managers expect to hold in the future. Lange's idea of the parametric role of prices actually demands that the manager continues his/her transactions at the current price, regardless of his/her expectations of future prices. Lange is thus trying to transform every manager into a typical price-taker, in the spirit of the static neoclassical model. According to Hayek, however, this is equivalent to the final abolition of the economic role of the individuals' expectations (1940, p. 197).

This line of argument raises the problem of the relation between the central authority and the managers of the socialist enterprises. Contrary to the mathematical solution, which considers the managers as executives of the central authority, in Lange's model the role of the planners is allegedly restricted to the setting of prices. Hayek points out (1940, p. 201) that if Lange's socialist system is even slightly to approach the efficiency of capitalism, this restriction of the role of the central authority is impossible. If the latter limits itself to price-setting, the economy will not be functioning efficiently, since Hayek has proven that Lange's three rules cannot guarantee production at the lowest cost. The effective functioning of the system demands entrepreneurship and, as the managers of the enterprises are not allowed to apply it, it must necessarily be applied by the central authority. In that case, however, the main advantage of Lange's solution – the decentralized and antibureaucratic character of central planning – is undermined.

Hayek ended his critique of the model of competitive socialism with a political argument (1940, p. 206). Planning on an extensive scale requires a much wider consensus on social priorities than is realistically possible and, thus, any achieved consensus can only be the result of force and propaganda. Therefore, central planning inevitably ends up in totalitarianism – the imposition of the values of the planners on the individual not only in the sphere of the economy but also in every aspect of his/her private life. Thus in Hayek's account, the prevention of the absolute direction of the economy by the central authority is not only significant for economic efficiency, but is also critical for the maintenance of personal and political freedoms.

The orthodox assessment of the debate: a neo-Austrian defeat

Lange's proposal and Hayek's response marked the conclusion of the socialist calculation debate.[12] The orthodox view at the time was that neo-Austrians had been decisively defeated.[13] We will attempt to offer two explanations for this verdict. The first stems from the dominance of philosophical positivism in the orthodox paradigm. Let us recall the major theoretical developments of the 1930s: welfare economics, the theory of imperfect competition and, of course, Keynesianism. What characterizes all these theories is a conception of the economy as an objective system, the operation of which can only be improved through exogenous interventions. Thus, for the majority of economists at the time, Hayek's distinction between the appropriateness of the general equilibrium model as a description of the logical cohesion of the economic system and its appropriateness as a tool for the actual administration of economic activity must have been rather unintelligible.

A second explanation of the orthodox verdict stems from the very political and social situation in the West during the 1930s and 1940s. The depression, the war and the effort of reconstruction after 1945 naturally encouraged views that were aiming at the rapid improvement of the situation through planning, as opposed to views laying their hopes on the freedom of the market.

What makes the socialist calculation debate especially relevant today is that the political climate now favours the neo-Austrian views. One reason for this resurgence is, of course, the collapse of the central planning systems of eastern Europe, a development which undoubtedly seems to justify the neo-Austrian argument that the imposition of a regime of central planning inevitably leads to economic decay and political authoritarianism.[14] Another reason is the failure of the orthodox version of Keynesianism to ensure economic stability. Contemporary supporters of market freedom consider the mixed economy as only an incomplete version of a socialist system, and thus see the failure of Keynesian policies as an instance of the state's inability to manage the economy. The view of state interventionism implied in this approach will be the object of our critique.

The end of history?

The neo-Austrian insistence on the impossibility of consciously and rationally redesigning human society on the basis of some socialist blueprint raises the question whether we should also perceive market society as the final stage of social evolution. This discussion will subsequently focus on three elements of the neo-Austrian arguments on the impossibility of socialist calculation that remain relevant in any discussion on the historical evolution of the market economy.

First, the fact that neo-Austrians perceive the market order as the outcome of a process of natural selection, implies that they deny the existence of historically-specific forces that systematically and predictably tend to alter this form of social organization.

A second element emerges as a consequence of the first. Neo-Austrians perceive the market economy as an entirely self-regulating system. On these grounds they see any intervention in its free functioning as distorting its operation and leading to further interventions. A mixed system is thus bound to be unstable and can only evolve into a system of comprehensive central planning.[15] Note that Hayek's major objective in *The Road to Serfdom*, his most widely read book, is to prove that state interventionism, even in an economy in which private property has not been entirely abolished, will eventually lead to the establishment of a regime of central planning. Evidently, the major target of this position is not the socialists but Keynes.

The third element is, in its turn, a consequence of the second. The fact that any intervention constitutes a step toward a complete central planning of the economy, implies that it also embodies a threat to personal liberty. Thus, liberty is not only threatened in a system of comprehensive central planning but also in a mixed economy.

The historicity of the market order

The discussion will begin by pointing out that the arguments of both parties in the debate seem to share one common characteristic: they both perceive their respective ideal societies as static and ahistorical models. Socialist economists try to construct models of socialism, but they do not specify through what processes and forces a capitalist society will come to be transformed into a socialist one. Neo-Austrians, on the other hand, consider their notion of a spontaneous order as a model of society which does not set into motion any kind of forces that may tend to alter its essential character.

Delving deeper into this assertion, we start with the arguments of the socialists. Their conception of socialism is grounded on the conviction that the Walrasian system of simultaneous equations can describe equally well the functioning of an economy based on private property as well as an economy where the means of production belong to the community. Hence, they consider the economy as a sum of objective processes leading to the optimal point of general equilibrium, independently of whether the type of social organization is capitalist or socialist. The abolition of private property in the socialist system is considered a fact stemming from the sphere of politics and lying as such outside the analytical framework of economic theory. As a consequence of this approach, they are not in a position to show that socialism is the outcome of systematic and historically specific forces operating in the context of market society. It is for these reasons that this theoretical creed has been aptly described as 'neoclassical socialism'.[16]

The same criticism can, however, be directed against the neo-Austrians. Hayek's critique of the neoclassical socialists offers an alternative model; to the model of general static equilibrium he juxtaposes that of the spontaneous order. We see, therefore, that while neoclassical socialists consider the process of the transformation of social relations as already accomplished without explaining the way it has been achieved, Hayek denies that such a process can even begin. As the former believe that this process springs from the sphere of politics, Hayek holds that it is political interventions that lead to increasingly greater state interventions in the economy. However, both sides fail to surpass their static point of view and are thus unable to study the dynamics of the market order.

The static character of neoclassical theory is, of course, well-grounded on the concept of general static equilibrium. Neo-Austrian theory is, however, equally static as we have argued in our critique of the neo-Austrian rejection of equilibrium. We have seen that even though neo-Austrians themselves claim that they are proposing a dynamic theory, the only thing they can explain is the ceaseless motion within the system while the general characteristics of the market order are considered to be unaffected by this motion and unalterable through time. By conceiving of human society as the outcome of a process of natural selection, they come to the conclusion that social mutations have the character of accidents which are independent of the operation of specific historically-given forces.

More specifically, neo-Austrians deny the existence of any dynamic interaction between the market and the modern state. They are thus obliged to presume that state interventionism is not a requirement of the market process itself, but that it springs instead from the sphere of politics. If interventionism were seen as a requirement of the market process, their main conclusion that state interventions destroy the efficiency of the spontaneous order would be invalidated. But on these grounds, the neo-Austrians' notion of market society lacks any historicity, in the sense that it is neither the product of historically specific systematic forces nor does it create forces which may eventually alter its essential character. The analysis will now focus upon the creation of forces which tend to link the modern state to the requirements of the market process.

State interventionism and the process of reproduction

We will now try to sustain two points: state interventionism constitutes a need of the market process itself and this very necessity creates, in turn, the demand that the state's role in the economy be socially controlled. If valid, the first point clearly undermines the fundamental neo-Austrian proposition that the efficiency of the economy is guaranteed only by the absolute absence of state interventions. The second point directly questions Hayek's view that state interventionism necessarily limits personal and political freedoms.

The investigation of the interaction between the market and the modern state requires a view of the latter which does not restrict itself solely to the political dimension of the state but perceives it instead as an institution actively involved in the market system. It is obvious that this involvement can be analysed neither on the basis of the neoclassical view which considers the issue of the state as lying outside the scope of economic theory, nor on the basis of neo-Austrian theory which a priori denies the necessity of any such involvement.

We believe that the interaction between the market and the state can, instead, be studied on the basis of the concept of the reproduction of capital, which we have repeatedly defended in this book. The idea of reproduction raises the question of whether the dynamics of the capitalist economy necessarily reproduce the compatibility of the economy's elements. For the reproduction of capital to proceed smoothly, we would have to assume that the compatibility of the value and the qualitative aspects of every individual capital, and of social capital as a whole, is constantly and automatically reproduced. Of course, we have already argued against this idea.

In fact, the view of the modern economy as lacking any automatic mechanisms which ensure the compatibility of the value sphere with the real sphere, is shared by a wide spectrum of economic theories critical of neoclassical orthodoxy, such as the various theories of underconsumption, the Marxian theory of the tendency of the rate of profit to fall, the Keynesian theory of effective demand, as well as theories of economic historians like Karl Polanyi.[17] The common element in all these approaches is that the stability of the economy – especially in the contemporary capitalist system which is characterized by the domination of large units of capital – cannot be ensured by the market process itself but requires, instead, the intervention of a supra-economic force, which in contemporary society can only be the state. It is precisely the fact that the modern state fulfills this role, that transforms it into a supra-economic institution which is simultaneously an economic subject – a participant of the market process.

However, our insistence on the priority of the idea of reproduction implies that the functions of the state are not confined to attaining the compatibility of the economy's elements – the general equilibrium of the system – but must be seen as part of the process of accumulation itself. On these grounds, the state must be seen as playing an essential role in creating the conditions which ensure the continuation of capital accumulation.[18] Therefore, the functions of the state cannot possibly be limited to the creation of a stable institutional framework. Since the forces obstructing the even development of the reproduction of capital are being created at the market level, the functions of the state that are aiming at the reversal of those forces cannot but be expressed at the same level. Therefore, the creation of the conditions that ensure the continuance of the accumulation of capital must be seen as involving both economic as well as supra-economic – that is, institutional – moments. It is precisely this dual character of the state's role in the economy which is, of course, completely missed by neo-Austrians, who perceive the state primarily as a political institution.

However, participation in the market process is inconceivable if the participant is not an owner of resources. Therefore, state interventionism and state ownership are bound to be complementary concepts. We have consciously chosen such a general term, as it would be useless to determine a priori which of society's resources should be owned or managed by the state. The needs of the reproduction of capital are bound to constantly change and, consequently, are bound to affect the form of state interventions. Therefore, state interventionism is a historically-specific concept, as its character is bound to change as a result of the changing needs of the process of the accumulation of capital.

This line of argument leads to some important implications concerning the privatization trend of the 1980s. Contrary to what the supporters of neoliberalism believe, this trend does not necessarily signal the limiting of the state's role[19] in the economy. A serious investigation of the phenomenon should examine whether the contraction of the state's role in some sectors coexists with its expansion in other sectors – a possibility very much implied by the huge public sector deficits – as well as with the possible transfer of interventionist functions from the national to the supranational level.

The problem of the social control of state interventionism

We can now turn our attention to the question of the social control of state interventionism. If the state's involvement in the economy is indeed such as to be in a position to act coercively, as Hayek believes, the only way that this coercion can be restricted is through supra-economic methods. Evidently, the market process itself cannot restrict this coercion, since the latter stems from the supra-economic character of the state rather than from its character as a subject of the market process.

If we understand the term coercion as meaning that individuals are hindered from achieving their aims in the market system, then the state's involvement in the economy must itself be perceived as coercive in the sense that it inevitably brings about different outcomes from those which the unhindered market would create. Of course, if the outcomes of the market process were indeed unpredictable, as neo-Austrians believe, then the freedom of the market process should be seen as the sole guarantor of liberty. If, however, market outcomes are to a large extent predictable, as we have repeatedly argued, and if the state's involvement in the economy is a requirement of the market process itself, then the only way that the coercive potential of the state can effectively be restricted is through social control of this involvement. It is therefore the mode of state interventionism, as it is expressed in different historical periods, that is being constantly evaluated by the community through the political process.

The question that now emerges concerns the procedure through which society can evaluate and select among alternative modes of interventionism. Apparently, such a procedure must necessarily be supra-economic, because the market process can only register individual choices rather than social ones. Social choices can instead be expressed only in the sphere of politics. This leads to another, equally important, conclusion. Neo-Austrians are justified in claiming that the view of the social whole as a uniform economic subject is problematic. They fail to take into account, however, that the choice of a mode of interventionism is necessarily a choice among alternative and, therefore, mutually exclusive such modes. Evidently, such a selection can be based on no other procedure than the principle of the majority.

Neo-Austrians could still put forward another counter-argument. If their proposal for the abolition of the state's role in the economy, encapsulated in the idea of the spontaneous order, can ensure both the efficiency of the economy as well as personal liberty, the ability of the social whole to select among alternative modes of interventionism becomes redundant, as it has been theoretically proven that only the spontaneous order can have positive effects on society. Such a view is, however, based on the Utopian belief that the demand for state interventionism does not derive from the market process itself. If the contrary holds, then the neo-Austrian proposal is tantamount to the demand that the state's involvement in the economy be dictated exclusively by the needs of the reproduction of capital, with society as a whole not even having the right to express an opinion. This is, after all, the underlying logic of Hayek's proposal for constitutional reform.

We thus conclude that the demand for the restriction of the state's role in the economy is actually equivalent to the demand for depriving society as a whole of any possibility to have any control over the effects of state interventionism. It does not, and cannot, mean the abolition of interventionism. If now, as Hayek supposes, the possibility of coercion is inherent in any state activity, then the abolition of social control can only increase this possibility. Thus, what actually increases the possibility of coercion is not state interventionism itself, but its independence from the political process.

Notes

1. See Mises (1920). The argument was expounded further in Mises (1922/1981). For a detailed analysis of the problem see Hoff (1949). Lavoie (1985) provides the most comprehensive recent reassessment of the debate.
2. See, for example, the view of Otto Neurath as presented in Hayek (1935a, p. 31).
3. We have already touched upon the notion of calculation in Chapter 7.
4. See Dickinson (1933), Lerner (1934–5; 1937), and Durbin (1936).
5. Thus, as Dickinson notes (1933, p. 240), the demand schedule in a socialist economy is not just a theoretical construct but a measurable element of reality.
6. They are equilibrium prices because all enterprises are operating on the basis of the simple rule that price must always equal cost.
7. Dickinson's view can be considered as the most extreme expression of the mathematical solution while, as we shall subsequently see, it constituted the main target of Hayek's criticism. Other supporters of the mathematical solution were seeking to establish alternative mathematical models, which would not simply be describing the functioning of the socialist economy but could also be used for its effective administration. According to Durbin (1936), the system's equilibrium could be secured by the central authority not only through the solution of a huge system of simultaneous equations but also by obliging each enterprise to use every means of production in a way that guarantees its highest possible yield. According to Lerner (1937, p. 257), the basic direction that should be followed by every socialist enterprise is the equation of the price with marginal production cost. However, regardless of its various versions, it is obvious that the mathematical solution is but an effort to model socialist society as the perfect embodiment of the principles of the neoclassical theory. As Dickinson (1933, p. 247) maintains, 'The beautiful systems of economic equilibrium described by Böhm Bawerk, Wieser, Marshall and Cassel are not descriptions of society as it is but prophetic visions of a socialist economy of the future'.
8. See Lange (1938). Lange's proposal is really an elaboration on the argument first put forth by Taylor (1928).
9. Mises's initial position in relation to the impossibility of price-calculation in the socialist economy is due, according to Lange, to a misunderstanding of the two meanings of the term 'price'. First, price means exchange ratio between two goods, a meaning which cannot be conceived independently of the possibility of exchange. Second, however, it expresses the 'terms on which alternatives are offered'. This second meaning does not require the possibility of exchange.
10. The central authority will be trying to equate supply with demand in every specific market. Thus, although from the technical point of view its role resembles the role of the Walrasian auctioneer, in reality, as Keizer (1989) points out, Lange's proposal is a partial equilibrium model.
11. According to Lavoie (1985), it is precisely the static outlook of neoclassical theory that prevented the socialists who participated in the debate – the 'neoclassical socialists' as they will later be described – from grasping the essence of the neo-Austrians' arguments.
12. Although the socialist calculation debate ends at the beginning of the 1940s, Hayek's subsequent economic, philosophical and political work can be considered as a continuation and further development of his arguments in the debate. His articles (1945; 1946a) on the role of knowledge in the market process and on competition as a discovery procedure, as Caldwell (1988, p. 535) points out, can actually be interpreted as elaborations of his conviction on the impossibility of central planning. Even *The Road to Serfdom*, which was published in the mid-1940s, can be considered as a detailed presentation of his political argument which, as we have seen, marked the conclusion of his critique of Lange's proposal.
13. A fact that is also recognized by modern neo-Austrians. See, for example, Rothbard (1976b), Murrell (1983) and Lavoie (1981; 1985, p. 13).
14. These considerations explain the interest of many contemporary intellectuals of the Left in a re-examination of the relation between the market and planning in a socialist

system. See Nove (1983), Hodgson (1984), Forbes (1986), Plant (1984) and Le Grand and Estrin (1989).

15. Tomlinson (1990, p. 118) has aptly described this idea as the 'slippery slope' argument, implying that, according to Hayek, state interventionism will inevitably lead to a fully centrally-planned system.
16. See Vaughn (1980) who also uses this term.
17. See Holloway and Picciotto (1977) for an analysis of the phenomenon of state interventionism from the point of view of Marxian theory. See Bleaney (1976) for an analysis of the theories of underconsumption. Karl Polanyi's views are expressed in his widely-read *The Great Transformation* (1957). For a historical account of the state's role in the economy see Clarke (1988).
18. See Hirsch (1977) who considers state interventionism in times of crisis as mobilizing the counter-tendencies to the falling rate of profit.
19. See Fine and Harris (1987, p. 369) for a similar conclusion contrary to neoliberal doctrines. For an interesting account of neoliberal policies in the US and Britain in the 1980s, see King (1987).

12 The market, competition and democracy

Our aim in this book was to establish three critical points against neo-Austrian theory. Contrary to the neo-Austrian rejection of the possibility of any objective knowledge of economic phenomena, our first aim was to show that the economist-observer is indeed in a position to discover the trends and the structures which the market process generates. Our second objective was to show that neo-Austrian theory is based on a view of the functioning of the economy, which is just as static as that of the orthodox neoclassical school. Our final point concerned the political implications of neo-Austrian theory, as we tried to show that the abolition of the state's role in the economy may actually lead to the increase of coercion, instead of ensuring the freedom of the individual as neo-Austrians believe.

This chapter will begin with a brief summary of the main critical arguments which have been put forward so far. We will then proceed with some further thoughts on neo-Austrian political ideas, especially with regard to democratic politics. Finally, we will attempt to assess the significance of the neo-Austrian school for the New Right movement of the 1980s.

On economic objectivity

The foundations of our conclusion on the possibility of objective knowledge of economic processes were laid in Chapter 3. We saw that it is the market process itself which constantly tends to objectify the knowledge circulating in the economy, by transforming it from tacit into conscious. It is again the market process that generates the trend toward ever larger enterprise size. The culmination of this process was analysed in Chapter 4. Contrary to the fundamental neo-Austrian claim that the economy consists of the simultaneous unfolding of countless processes which the economist-observer is not in a position to perceive, we concluded that these processes tend to generate a specific pyramid-like structure of the economic system. It is precisely this structure that can be perceived by the economist-observer, when he/she studies the trends set in motion by the market process.

For neo-Austrians, the theory of entrepreneurship constitutes the basis for the understanding of the subjective character of market activity. However, as argued in Chapter 5, the notion of entrepreneurship can only be salvaged if identified with the function of the objective category of capital. It is for this reason that neo-Austrians try to strip their notion of capital of any objective content, as argued in Chapter 7. However, their one-dimensional notion of capital renders impossible the methodological distinction between the categories of capital and private property. Moreover, it makes it impossible to sustain the concept of the cyclical reproduction of capital, as it is a concept which would again objectify the function of capital. The essence of this argument constitutes the basis for our critique of the neo-Austrian theory of money in Chapter 8. The absolute subjectivity of the neo-Austrian conception of money renders the distinction between a barter and a monetary economy impossible. Contrary to that view, we argued that such a distinction requires the objectification of the category of money – the establishment of its unique character.

Our arguments against the neo-Austrian denial of economic objectivity have evidently affirmed the possibility of objective knowledge of economic phenomena from two points of view. First, we have established the objectivity of some crucial methodological categories, such as capital, money and cyclical reproduction. The objective character of these categories does not stem from the fact that they are empirically observable but, rather, from the fact that the economist-observer is in a position to theoretically construct them from his/her experience of economic processes and thus study their function in the context of the market system. Therefore, the conception of objectivity we have established is very different from the positivist view of the orthodox neoclassical school.

The second point of view reaffirms the possibility of objective knowledge in another sense. We have shown that the economist-observer is not confronted with a system in ceaseless and, moreover, indeterminate motion, but with a system that tends to be reproduced constantly and to take on a specific structure. Again, this is a view radically different from the neoclassical concept of perfect knowledge. At the same time, however, it is also a view that allows the normative evaluation of the market system, not in the sense that the economist-observer can attain perfect knowledge of the effects of its operation on every single individual, but in the sense that he/she is in a position to recognize that the market process itself tends to have predictable effects on different social strata.

On economic dynamics

Our argument on the issue of dynamics is based on the conclusions reached in Chapter 6. We argued that the supposedly dynamic character of neo-Austrian theory may indeed explain the ceaseless motion within the economic system, but it cannot explain the direction of this motion. Moreover, the invocation of the concept of accident implies that the evolution of the economy as a whole lies beyond the scope of economic theory. Neo-Austrians thus end up with a static view of economic processes, which is almost identical to that of the neoclassical school. This conclusion was reinforced by the discussion in Chapter 9 on the theory of the trade cycle. We showed that neo-Austrian theory sees the market system as inherently stable. In other words, neo-Austrians believe that the only forces which may cause the phenomenon of the cycle are necessarily exogenous, since they are set in motion by the manipulation of the money supply by the monetary authorities. Thus, what the neo-Austrian theory of the trade cycle seems to lack is endogeneity, the most essential characteristic of a genuinely dynamic theory.

The static character of neo-Austrian theory was further examined in Chapter 7. We argued that the neo-Austrian theory of capital is not in a position to sustain the notion of a cyclically repeated process of production, because of its one-dimensional concentration on the category of capital goods. We argued, however, that it is only the notion of the cyclical reproduction which can constitute the basis for understanding the changes in the economy's capital structure. The consequences of this argument are evident in the conclusions in Chapter 9. The physical character of the category of capital goods inevitably limits the analysis to the sphere of exchange. However, the fluctuations of values in exchange lead the economy, by definition, toward equilibrium and, consequently, cannot possibly constitute the basis for the analysis of market dynamics. By contrast, we argued that this basis should be sought in the interaction between the value and the physical spheres of the economy, and we showed that neo-Austrians are not in a position to methodologically distinguish between these two spheres.

The political implications of neo-Austrian theory

We began to address the political essence of neo-Austrian theory in the last two chapters. In Chapter 10, we reached two conclusions. We argued, first, that the abolition of the state's role in the economy does not necessarily prevent the exercise of coercion in modern society. For instance, the denationalization of money would transfer the ability to exercise coercion from a public to a private institution. Consequently, the ability to coerce is not exclusively linked to the state but is, rather, inherent in those outcomes of the market process that tend to concentrate rather than diffuse the control of economic activity. Our second conclusion concerned the very conception of politics held by neo-Austrians. They believe that politics is par excellence the realm where the primordial sentiments of solidarity and altruism are expressed, in the form of demands for ever greater interventions in the market process. We argued that this view proclaims the market as the only institution that can guarantee social cohesion and, thus, creates the demand that political activity ought to be drastically restricted.

In Chapter 11 we first discussed the Utopian character of the neo-Austrian view of politics. We argued that the market process demands the intervention of a supra-economic subject which can secure the continuation of the process of capital accumulation. Consequently, the causes of state interventionism do not lie outside the sphere of the economy, as neo-Austrians believe, but spring, instead, from the market process itself. Therefore, the aim of restricting the sphere of politics amounts to the demand that state interventionism exclusively serve the reproduction of capital, unobstructed from any social control.

Liberalism and democracy

There is one further aspect of the neo-Austrians' view of politics which needs to be examined – their ideas toward the institutions that constitute the democratic polity. Neo-Austrians view democracy as no more than a technique for the selection of the administrators of public affairs. As a technique, democracy cannot be considered to have the character of an absolute and universal value but, rather, the character of a technical principle, the application of which should be subject to restrictions depending on whether it is seen as benefiting the development of personal liberty or as undermining it. This view underlies the whole of neo-Austrian reasoning.[1] For example, a fundamental element of Hayek's proposal for constitutional reform is the removal of the right to elect representatives to the governmental assembly from those who are directly dependent on state allowances, such as civil servants, pensioners and the unemployed.[2]

The reason neo-Austrians undervalue the issue of political democracy is because they consider the market as the only institution that guarantees social cohesion as well as the participation of the individual in the social process. In their view, the market provides the framework for the only truly democratic participation process, because in the market no individual is prevented from realizing the exchanges he/she wishes. Unlike political democracy where the minority is totally excluded from the exercise of power, the market has no majorities or minorities and, therefore, nobody is prevented from pursuing his/her interests. Evidently, neo-Austrian theory seems to justify the often-cited observation about the incompatibility of philosophical liberalism with the democratic ideal.[3] We must, therefore, delve deeper into this matter to see how this incompatibility is more specifically revealed in the context of neo-Austrian theory.

Capitalism and simple commodity production

The analysis of the neo-Austrian stance on the issue of political democracy should begin by addressing the form of society this stance actually presumes. In Chapter 10, we saw that the society neo-Austrians, and Hayek in particular, envisage is an organism consisting of countless family units, with the market being the only point of contact and communication amongst them. For this idea of society to be realistic, it must be assumed that all individuals are owners of exchangeable commodities. In that context, the outcomes of each individual's participation in the market process would indeed depend entirely on his/her skill and luck, as Hayek maintains, because in such a society there is no group which always tends to lose and another which by rule profits.

The major difference between this model of society and the modern capitalist system stems from the existence of capital. In the capitalist system, a person's success in the market process depends primarily on whether he/she is an owner of capital. Thus, the process which is of paramount importance for the understanding of social dynamics is the reproduction of capital, which in turn determines the reproduction of society itself. Of course, the main characteristic of the capitalist system which must be reproduced in order for the system to retain its character, is the unequal distribution of property – the pyramid-like structure of society, as argued in Chapter 4.

Evidently, the society envisaged by Hayek is closer to the Marxian idea of simple commodity production than to the modern capitalist system. The basic characteristic of capitalism is the unequal distribution of property. The major characteristic of a society of simple commodity production is, by contrast, that all its members are, and remain, owners of commodities. The importance of this assertion would be trivial, if it merely led us to note that the society Hayek describes bears no relation to the modern capitalist system. However, the essence of the matter lies deeper. The reforms proposed by Hayek at the economic, institutional and political level can be seen as aiming to transform capitalist society into a society of simple commodity production. It is precisely the fact that this is a Utopian task, which allows us to consider these reforms themselves as Utopian, as we have repeatedly argued.[4]

However, what interests us here is not the Utopian character of Hayek's view of society, but its political implications. If a fundamental characteristic of capitalist society is indeed the unequal distribution of property, then the constitutional reform he proposes is tantamount to depriving those members of society who do not possess means of production of any possibility to alter their social position. Since this position is constantly being reproduced through market exchange, it can never be altered through participation in the market process. Of course, this does not mean that a specific individual will always remain in a particular social position, as there is indeed the possibility of social mobility in capitalist society. However, this does not invalidate the basic truth that the very existence of the capitalist system demands the ceaseless reproduction of the unequal distribution of property. Thus, the main objective of Hayek's reform proposals is to prevent the non-owners from taking collective action – that is, political action – aiming at transforming society.

The authoritarian character of neo-Austrian theory

Hayek concedes (1982, vol. II, pp. 151–3) that in a free society individuals must indeed have the right to create 'voluntary associations' for the promotion of common interests. However, collective action is only permissible under the condition that associations will not be enjoying any institutional privileges allowing them to exercise coercion. Evidently, the main form of coercion Hayek is concerned with is coercion on the functioning of the market by the monopolistic behaviour of associations.[5] Therefore, the individuals of his ideal society are free to form associations provided that their collective actions do not distort the operation of the fundamental social institution, the market. Consequently, Hayek's objective is to ensure that each member of society will participate in the market process strictly as an individual.

Hayek's argument against collective action is not confined to collective action in the context of markets but encompasses political action as well. We have seen that Hayek considers the suppression of the sentiments of altruism and solidarity as a basic prerequisite for the preservation of the market order. In modern society, such sentiments constitute, according to him (1983, p. 41), the basis of socialist ideology. It logically follows that the suppression of the primordial sentiments of altruism and solidarity cannot but require the suppression of their modern political expression – socialist politics.[6] Admittedly, Hayek does not explicitly express this demand. It is, however, evident that the very logic of his proposals aims at depriving the socialist-oriented part of the political spectrum of every means to exercise a socialist policy.

Thus, the fundamental neo-Austrian conclusion is that the preservation of the market order requires the drastic restriction of political democracy. Hayek (1983, p. 40), for instance, claims that even though market ethics tended to oust the primordial instincts from the world of human sentiments for centuries, this process has been reversed during the last 100 or 150 years. The reason for this is that increasingly more members of society have ceased to be directly connected with the market process, as their social existence has come to depend on the operation of great organizations – private corporations or the state mechanism. The result of this development, as Hayek admits (1983, p. 43), is that 99 per cent of the globe's population are socialists. Therefore, Hayek's objective is to prevent this 99 per cent from transforming their instincts into a political programme, by depriving them of the ability to act collectively both at the market level as well as in the sphere of politics. In Hayek's thought, the market is thus transformed from a mere mechanism which ensures the compatibility of plans, into an institution demanding service and obedience.[7] Hence, to claim, as he does, that the unhindered operation of the market constitutes the indispensable prerequisite for human freedom, seems like a great illusion.

Neo-Austrians could counter this argument on the basis of their idea of freedom which, as seen in Chapter 6, is defined negatively as the absence of coercion upon the individual. The crucial point is, according to neo-Austrians, that coercion can be exercised only by an individual or collective will.[8] Thus, the spontaneous order of the market cannot possibly exercise coercion, as it is not associated with any such will. It is precisely for this reason that the market is considered to constitute the fundamental institution for the preservation of human liberty.

This conception of freedom is apparently very much dependent upon the type of society one has in mind. It is convincing in a system of simple commodity production, in which the status of individuals as owners of commodities is constantly reproduced through market exchange and the success of each individual depends on his/her skill and luck. However, seen in the light of our conclusions on the issues of objectivity and dynamics, such a conception cannot be accepted. If success in the market depends on a person's property, and if the market process ceaselessly tends to reproduce the unequal distribution of property, then it is precisely the market process that coerces those who lack the resources needed in order to alter their place in the social pyramid. Therefore, contrary to what neo-Austrians believe, the market tends to produce predictable results, which can be evaluated in terms of the freedom they allow to the members of society. It is precisely the possibility of this evaluation which, in our view, makes political democracy an indispensable requirement of human freedom.

Democracy and economic efficiency

One further argument against political democracy has to be confronted. Even if the absolute value of democracy for human freedom is accepted, it could be argued that the democratic process should stop where the freedom of the market begins. Based on the idea that political interventions in the economy reduce the entrepreneurial motivation of private agents, this argument is actually calling upon modern society to choose between the two poles of a trade-off: democratic participation or economic efficiency.

Contrary to Hayek's views which, as we have argued, have little bearing on the reality of capitalism, the argument we are now examining seems to pose a real political dilemma. The collapse of the command economies of eastern Europe and the submission of western governments to the pressures of sectional interests are indisputable facts, which seem to justify the view that political management of economic activity can only be achieved at the expense of economic efficiency.

Thus, the question as to the line separating the realm where the market should be allowed to operate freely from that where the will of the majority should be sovereign, constitutes a real problem of modern societies. As a dilemma of current politics, it can neither be ignored nor solved by assigning priority to either of its two poles. So far, our argument was turned against the neo-Austrian position which assigns absolute priority to the freedom of the market and considers the restriction of the democratic principle an indispensable prerequisite for economic efficiency. We have, however, already implicitly rejected an answer to the dilemma that would give absolute priority to the democratic pole. Such an answer could only be grounded on the conviction that economic processes are entirely objective – a view we have rejected in our criticism of the neoclassical socialists.

The neo-Austrian answer to the dilemma is based on the hypothesis that the sphere of the economy and the sphere of politics constitute two completely self-sufficient and self-regulating realms of social activity. It is precisely for this reason that neo-Austrians regard the political regulation of the market as an invasion of the economic by the political realm. Such a view is based on a conception of economic processes as fundamentally indeterminate. This conception does not merely imply that the economic and the political spheres are self-sufficient but, moreover, that they are hierarchically interrelated. It is the primacy of the economic sphere for human prosperity and freedom that demands restrictions in the sphere of politics, restrictions which will render any political intervention in the market process impossible.

We have already rejected this view of the interrelation between politics and economics on two counts. First, we have shown that state interventionism is a requirement of the market process itself. Therefore, the involvement of a supra-economic institution like the state in the economy is a *sine qua non* for economic efficiency. Second, our argument for economic objectivity obviously challenges this view in a further sense. If members of society can form an objective view of the general characteristics of modern society and of the tendencies it generates, they can also evaluate social reality. It is precisely these evaluations that furnish the basis for political action.[9]

Contrary to what neo-Austrians believe, we are thus led to the conclusion that the spheres of the economy and politics are not self-regulating but, rather, inter-regulating. Therefore, the solution to the dilemma 'democracy or efficiency' must not be sought in the insulation of the two spheres but should take the form of a selection amongst alternative 'modes of interventionism', as we have used this term in the preceding chapter. Therefore, the issue of the limit up to which the market should be freely functioning and of the limit up to which the will of the majority should be sovereign is a matter that is solved through the competition amongst alternative modes of interventionism in the political process. However, this line of reasoning sheds new light on the political implications of neo-Austrian theory. The institutional abolition of political choice, which neo-Austrians are aiming at, is a further confirmation of the anti-democratic and authoritarian character of their political stance.

The neo-Austrian school within the context of the politics of the New Right

This book concludes with some thoughts on the political contribution of the neo-Austrian school to the neoliberal movement of the 1970s and 1980s. Its most significant contribution stems from the fact that it enabled conservatism to reappear in a radical guise. This is precisely what was characterized in Chapter 10 as the political advantage of the neo-Austrian position: the coexistence of conservatism with radicalism. It is easy to comprehend the basis of this coexistence. The neo-Austrian conception of social phenomena as fundamentally indeterminate leads to the denial of the possibility of consciously redesigning social activity. This view demands the uncritical acceptance of tradition, as the knowledge deriving from tradition can never be conscious and cannot, therefore, be evaluated rationally. Evidently, this is a restatement of the essence of conservatism, which even Burke would have envied.

However, the distinction between phenomena which are spontaneous outcomes of social evolution and those which are products of conscious design, furnishes the basis for the expression of radical political proposals. The former type of phenomena includes all the institutions, social practices, rules of conduct and so on, which are compatible with the spontaneous market order. By contrast, the second type includes all phenomena which spring from violations of this spontaneity and, thus, the preservation of market society demands the suppression of the causes that create them. Therefore, the fact that the acceptance of tradition should be uncritical does not cancel the need for reformist policies aiming at the annihilation of those elements of tradition which are incompatible with the preservation of market society. This is exactly where the radical element of the neo-Austrian position lies.

During the initial stages of the rise of the New Right movements, it was the conservative aspect of neo-Austrian theory which was politically influential. The view of economic phenomena as fundamentally indeterminate was arming the supporters of market freedom with a powerful ideological weapon during a historical phase (the 1970s) in which state interventionism seemed increasingly incapable of leading western economies out of the recession. During the time in which the New Right movements were gaining their first electoral victories,[10] it was the slogan demanding the freedom of the individual from the state which rendered the acceptance of the austerity policies and of the explosive unemployment rates much easier. Finally, when neoliberal governments began the privatization of public corporations, the vision of a society where any person, regardless of the volume of his/her property, would have the opportunity to be an entrepreneur, was put forward as a major ideological argument under the title of popular capitalism.

In the beginning of the 1990s, however, the political climate seems to have changed. Although the New Right remains ideologically and politically strong, it is evident that it has lost its initial momentum. At this phase, its major political objective is not to persuade public opinion to accept, or at least to tolerate, the neoliberal political project but, rather, to protect its political achievements against a possible socialist backlash. What the New Right movement needs now is not ideological slogans but an institutional reform aiming to solidify the political framework it has formulated. It is in these circumstances that the supposedly radical aspect of neo-Austrian theory assumes political priority.

The question that ncw emerges is whether neo-Austrians can indeed provide the ideological and political basis for a policy aiming at reforming political institutions themselves. Chapter 10 referred to the fundamental inconsistency of neo-Austrian theory – the contradiction between the demand for the uncritical acceptance of tradition and the demand for such reforms of political institutions that would render any political intervention in the market process impossible. Even though we have argued that the coexistence of the conservative with the radical aspect of neo-Austrian theory constitutes a political advantage, it is obvious that when political priority demands that emphasis be placed upon the second of these aspects, this coexistence begins to be problematic. It is, therefore, natural that the ideological and political vanguard will shift to a position less equivocal on the necessity of reformist interventions at the level of the political system, interventions aiming at the restriction of the democratic principle. Such views are expressed with great consistency by the Public Choice school. If we consider international academic recognition as a safe indication of such theoretical shifts, our conclusion appears to be justified. In 1974 the Nobel Prize for Economics was awarded to Hayek, while in 1986 it was Buchanan's turn.

Are we on the eve of a new eclipse of the neo-Austrian school, following its brief revival? A definite answer to this question would perhaps be untimely. It is, however, certain that any such answer would not only depend on the internal theoretical consistency of the neo-Austrian paradigm but should also take into account political developments and, in particular, the new theoretical and ideological demands of the New Right movement.

Notes

1. In 1927, Mises (1927/1985, p. 51) declared that 'It cannot be denied that Fascism ... [is] full of the best intentions and ... has ... saved European civilization'. Obviously, what Mises thought that Fascism had 'saved', was nothing else but the institution of private property.
2. See Hayek (1982, vol. III, p. 119).
3. See Macpherson (1977, p. 43).

4. We have already analysed the Utopian element of such a task in Chapter 4, where we examined Hayek's proposals on the extension of property rights from material to non-material objects and his criticism of the extension of contract rights from individuals to limited companies. As argued, Hayek seems unable to comprehend that these developments are consequences of the market process itself rather than of political interventions in the operation of the market order. In other words, it is precisely the demands of the accumulation of capital that lead to the commodification and, thus, to the capitalization of increasingly larger sectors of social activity.
5. Hayek's argument mainly refers to the monopolistic behaviour of labour unions, as seen in Chapter 4. Hayek's views on this matter are convincingly criticized by Tomlinson (1990, pp. 87–99).
6. For a similar conclusion, see Belsey (1986, p. 187).
7. Ibid., p. 182
8. See Hayek (1960, p. 12).
9. If the character of social evolution were indeed accidental and indeterminate, then the opinions of the members of society on this character and the resulting collective actions would be unable to influence social evolution in any systematic way. However, this argument is contradicting the reasoning of Hayek (1952/1979, p. 130) himself who, in criticizing the tradition of positivism and socialism, claims that it is not merely an ideological fallacy but that it has also had momentous effects on social evolution.
10. We mainly refer to the electoral victories of Margaret Thatcher in Britain and of Ronald Reagan in the US.

Bibliography

Addleson, M. (1986), '"Radical Subjectivism" and the Language of Austrian Economics', in Kirzner (1986).

Armentano, D.T. (1978), 'A Critique of Neoclassical and Austrian Monopoly Theory', in Spadaro (1978).

Arrow, K.J. (1959), 'Toward a Theory of Price Adjustment', in M. Abramovitz *et al.* (eds), *The Allocation of Economic Resources*, Stanford: Stanford University Press.

Arrow, K.J. and Hahn, F.H. (1971), *General Competitive Analysis*, Amsterdam: North Holland.

Bain, J.S. (1956), *Barriers to New Competition*, Cambridge: Harvard University Press.

Barry, N.P. (1979), *Hayek's Social and Economic Philosophy*, London: Macmillan Press.

Barry, N.P. (1981), 'Restating the Liberal Order: Hayek's Philosophical Economics', in Shackleton and Locksley (1981).

Bell, D. and Kristol, I. (eds) (1981), *The Crisis in Economic Theory*, New York: Basic Books.

Belsey, A. (1986), 'The New Right, Social Order and Civil Liberties', in Levitas (1986).

Blaug, M. (1968), *Economic Theory in Retrospect*, London: Heinemann.

Bleaney, M. (1976), *Underconsumption Theories*, London: Lawrence and Wishart.

Boehm, S. (1986), 'Time and Equilibrium: Hayek's Notion of Intertemporal Equilibrium Reconsidered', in Kirzner (1986).

Bosanquet, N. (1983), *After The New Right*, London: Heinemann.

Caldwell, B.J. (1988), 'Hayek's Transformation', *History of Political Economy*, **20**, (4), 513–41.

Chamberlin, E.H. (1933/1962), *The Theory of Monopolistic Competition*, Cambridge: Harvard University Press.

Chamberlin, E.H. (ed.) (1954), *Monopoly and Competition and Their Regulation*, London: Oxford University Press.

Chisholm, R.M. (1986), 'Brentano on Preference, Desire and Intrinsic Value', in Grassl and Smith (1986).

Clarke, S. (1982), *Marx, Marginalism and Modern Sociology: From Adam Smith to Max Weber*, London: Macmillan Press.

Clarke, S. (1988), *Keynesianism, Monetarism and the Crisis of the State*, Aldershot: Edward Elgar.

Collison Black, R.D., Coats, A.W. and Goodwin, C.D.W. (eds) (1973), *The Marginal Revolution in Economics*, Durham: Duke University Press.

Cournot, A. (1929), *Researches into the Mathematical Principles of the Theory of Wealth*, New York: Macmillan.

Craver, E. (1986), 'The Emigration of the Austrian Economists', *History of Political Economy*, **18**, (1), 1–32.

Dahrendorf, R. (1990), *Reflections on the Revolution in Europe*, London: Chatto & Windus.

De Brunhoff, S. (1976), *Marx on Money*, New York: Urizen Books.

Dickinson, H.D. (1933), 'Price Formation in a Socialist Community', *Economic Journal*, **43**, June, 237–50.

Dolan, E.G. (ed.) (1976), *The Foundations of Modern Austrian Economics*, Kansas City: Sheed & Ward.

Durbin, E.F.M. (1936), 'Economic Calculus in a Planned Economy', *Economic Journal*, **46**, December, 676–90.

Fabian, R. and Simons, P.M. (1986), 'The Second Austrian School of Value Theory', in Grassl and Smith (1986).

Fine, B. and Harris, L. (1987), 'Ideology and Markets: Economic Theory and the "New Right"', in R. Milliband, L. Panitch and J. Saville (eds), *Socialist Register*, London: Merlin Press.

Forbes, I. (ed.) (1986), *Market Socialism: Whose Choice?*, London: Fabian Society Tract 516.

Friedman, D. (1973), *The Machinery of Freedom*, New York: Harper Colophon.

Friedman, M. (ed.) (1956), *Studies in the Quantity Theory of Money*, Chicago: University of Chicago Press.

Galbraith, J.K. (1967), *The New Industrial State*, New York: Houghton Mifflin.

Gamble, A. (1986), 'The Political Economy of Freedom', in Levitas (1986).

Garrison, R.W. (1985), 'A Subjectivist Theory of a Capital-using Economy', in O'Driscoll and Rizzo (1985).

Grassl, W. and Smith, B. (eds) (1986), *Austrian Economics: Historical and Philosophical Background*, London: Croom Helm.

Gray, J. (1986), *Hayek on Liberty*, Oxford: Blackwell.

Grossman, H. (1977), 'Marx, Classical Political Economy and the Problem of Dynamics, Part I', *Capital & Class*, (2), 32–55.

Grossman, H. (1977a), 'Marx, Classical Political Economy and the Problem of Dynamics, Part II', *Capital & Class*, (3), 67–99.

Gunning J.P. (1985), 'Causes of Unemployment: The Austrian Perspective', *History of Political Economy*, **17**, (2), 223–44.

Haberler, G. (1937), *Prosperity and Depression*, London: George Allen & Unwin.

Hayek, F.A. (1928/1933), *Monetary Theory and the Trade Cycle*, London: Jonathan Cape.

Hayek, F.A. (1931), 'Reflections on the Pure Theory of Money of Mr. J.M. Keynes', Part I, *Economica*, **11**, (33), August, 270–95.

Hayek, F.A. (1931/1935), *Prices and Production*, London: George Routledge & Sons.

Hayek, F.A. (1932), 'A Note on the Development of the Doctrine of "Forced Saving"', in Hayek (1939/1975).

Hayek, F.A. (1932a), 'Money and Capital: A Reply', *Economic Journal*, **42**, June, 237–49.

Hayek, F.A. (1932b), 'Reflections on the Pure Theory of Money of Mr. J.M. Keynes', Part II, *Economica*, **12**, (35), February, 22–44.

Hayek, F.A. (1933), 'The Trend of Economic Thinking', *Economica*, **13**, May, 121–37.

Hayek, F.A. (1934), 'Introduction', in Menger (1981).

Hayek, F.A. (ed.) (1935/1975), *Collectivist Economic Planning*, Clifton New Jersey: Augustus Kelly.

Hayek, F.A. (1935a), 'The Nature and History of the Problem', in Hayek (1935/1975).

Hayek, F.A. (1935b), 'The Present State of the Debate', in Hayek (1935/1975).

Hayek, F.A. (1937), 'Economics and Knowledge', in Hayek (1949).

Hayek, F.A. (1939/1975), *Profits, Interest and Investment*, Clifton New Jersey: Augustus Kelly.

Hayek, F.A. (1940), 'Socialist Calculation III: The Competitive "Solution"', in Hayek (1949).

Hayek, F.A. (1941), *The Pure Theory of Capital*, London: Macmillan and Co. Ltd.

Hayek, F.A. (1943), 'The Facts of the Social Sciences', in Hayek (1949).

Hayek, F.A. (1944/1979), *The Road to Serfdom*, London: Routledge & Kegan Paul.

Hayek, F.A. (1945), 'The Use of Knowledge in Society', in Hayek (1949).

Hayek, F.A. (1945a), 'Time-Preference and Productivity: A Reconsideration', *Economica*, (12), February.

Hayek, F.A. (1946), 'Individualism True and False', in Hayek (1949).

Hayek, F.A. (1946a), 'The Meaning of Competition', in Hayek (1949)

Hayek, F.A. (1947), 'Free Enterprise and Competitive Order', in Hayek (1949).

Hayek, F.A. (1949), *Individualism and Economic Order*, London: Routledge & Kegan Paul.

Hayek, F.A. (1949a), 'The Intellectuals and Socialism', in Hayek (1967).
Hayek, F.A. (1950), 'Full Employment, Planning and Inflation', in Hayek (1967).
Hayek, F.A. (1952/1979), *The Counter-Revolution of Science*, Indianapolis: Liberty Press.
Hayek, F.A. (1952a), *The Sensory Order: An Inquiry into the Foundations of Theoretical Psychology*, London: Routledge & Kegan Paul.
Hayek, F.A. (1955), 'Degrees of Explanation', in Hayek (1967).
Hayek, F.A. (1956), '*The Road to Serfdom* after Twelve Years', in Hayek (1967).
Hayek, F.A. (1958), 'Inflation Resulting from the Downward Inflexibility of Wages', in Hayek (1967).
Hayek, F.A. (1960), *The Constitution of Liberty*, London: Routledge & Kegan Paul.
Hayek, F.A. (1960a), 'The Corporation in a Democratic Society: In Whose Interest Ought it To and Will It Be Run?', in Hayek (1967).
Hayek, F.A. (1963), 'Rules, Perception and Intelligibility', in Hayek (1967).
Hayek, F.A. (1964), 'The Theory of Complex Phenomena', in Hayek (1967).
Hayek, F.A. (1966), 'The Principles of a Liberal Social Order', in Hayek (1967).
Hayek, F.A. (1967), *Studies in Philosophy, Politics and Economics*, London: Routledge & Kegan Paul.
Hayek, F.A. (1967a), 'Notes on the Evolution of Systems of Rules of Conduct', in Hayek (1967).
Hayek, F.A. (1968), 'Competition as a Discovery Procedure', in Hayek (1978).
Hayek, F.A. (1973), 'The Place of Menger's *Grundsätze* in the History of Economic Thought', in Hayek (1978).
Hayek, F.A. (1975), 'Inflation, the Misdirection of Labour, and Unemployment', in Hayek (1978).
Hayek, F.A. (1976), 'The Atavism of Social Justice', in Hayek (1978).
Hayek, F.A. (1976a), *Denationalisation of Money*, London: The Institute of Economic Affairs.
Hayek, F.A. (1978), *New Studies in Philosophy, Politics, Economics and the History of Ideas*, London: Routledge & Kegan Paul.
Hayek, F.A. (1978a), *A Tiger by the Tail*, London: Institute of Economic Affairs.
Hayek, F.A. (1978b), *Denationalisation of Money: The Argument Refined*, 2nd (extended) ed., London: Institute of Economic Affairs.
Hayek, F.A. (1982), *Law, Legislation and Liberty*, London: Routledge & Kegan Paul.

Hayek, F.A. (1983), *Knowledge, Evolution and Society*, London: Adam Smith Institute.

Hayek, F.A. (1986), 'Market Standards of Money', *Economic Affairs*, April–May, 8–10.

Hayek, F.A. (1988), *The Fatal Conceit: The Errors of Socialism*, London: Routledge.

High, J. (1986), 'Equilibration and Disequilibration in the Market Process', in Kirzner (1986).

Hirsch, J. (1977), 'The State Apparatus and Social Reproduction: Elements of a Theory of the Bourgeois State', in J. Holloway and S. Picciotto (eds), *The State and Capital: A Marxist Debate*, London: Edward Arnold.

Hodgson, G. (1984), *The Democratic Economy*, Harmondsworth: Penguin Books.

Hoff, T.J.B. (1949), *Economic Calculation in the Socialist Society*, Edinburgh: William Hodge.

Holloway, J. and Picciotto, S. (1977), 'Capital, Crisis and the State', *Capital and Class*, (2), 76–101.

Hutchison, T.W. (1962), *A Review of Economic Doctrines 1870–1929*, Oxford: Clarendon Press.

Hutchison, T.W. (1981), *The Politics and Philosophy of Economics*, Oxford: Basil Blackwell.

Hutchison, T.W. (1981a), 'Austrians on Philosophy and Method', in Hutchison (1981).

Hutchison, T.W. (1981b), 'Carl Menger on Philosophy and Method', in Hutchison (1981).

Jaffé, W. (1976), 'Menger, Jevons and Walras De-homogenized', *Economic Inquiry*, (14), December, 511–24.

Jevons, W.S. (1970), *The Theory of Political Economy*, Harmondsworth: Penguin Books.

Kaldor, N. (1949–50), 'The Economic Aspects of Advertising', *Review of Economic Studies*, (18), 1–27.

Kaldor, N. (1972), 'The Irrelevance of Equilibrium Economics', *Economic Journal*, **82**, December.

Kauder, E. (1965), *A History of Marginal Utility Theory*, Princeton: Princeton University Press.

Keizer, W. (1989), 'Recent Reinterpretations of the Socialist Calculation Debate', *Journal of Economic Studies*, **16**, (2), 63–83.

Keynes, J.M. (1931), 'A Reply to Dr. Hayek', *Economica*, **12**, November, 387–97.

Keynes, J.M. (1936/1973), *The General Theory of Employment, Interest and Money*, London: Macmillan.

King, D.S. (1987), *The New Right: Politics, Markets and Citizenship*, London: Macmillan.

Kirzner, I.M. (1963), *Market Theory and the Price System*, Princeton NJ: Van Nostrand.

Kirzner, I.M. (1969), 'Entrepreneurship and the Market Approach to Development', in Kirzner (1979).

Kirzner, I.M. (1973), *Competition and Entrepreneurship*, Chicago: University of Chicago Press.

Kirzner, I.M. (1973a), 'Producer, Entrepreneur, and the Right to Property', in Kirzner (1979).

Kirzner, I.M. (1974), 'Equilibrium versus Market Process', in Kirzner (1979).

Kirzner, I.M. (1974a), 'Capital, Competition, and Capitalism', in Kirzner (1979).

Kirzner, I.M. (1974b), 'Ludwig von Mises and the Theory of Capital and Interest', in Kirzner (1979).

Kirzner, I.M. (1975), 'Hayek, Knowledge, and Market Processes', in Kirzner (1979).

Kirzner, I.M. (1975a), 'Classical Economics and the Entrepreneurial Role', in Kirzner (1979).

Kirzner, I.M. (1976), 'On the Method of Austrian Economics', in Dolan (1976).

Kirzner, I.M. (1976a), 'Knowing about Knowledge: A Subjectivist View of the Role of Information', in Kirzner (1979)

Kirzner, I.M. (1976b), 'Economics and Error', in Kirzner (1979).

Kirzner, I.M. (1976c), 'The Theory of Capital', in Dolan (1976).

Kirzner, I.M. (1977), 'The Entrepreneurial Role in Menger's System', in Kirzner (1979).

Kirzner, I.M. (1978), 'Alertness, Luck, and Entrepreneurial Profit', in Kirzner (1979).

Kirzner, I.M. (1978a), 'Entrepreneurship, Entitlement and Economic Justice', in Kirzner (1979).

Kirzner, I.M. (1979), *Perception, Opportunity and Profit*, Chicago: University of Chicago Press.

Kirzner, I.M. (1980), 'The Primacy of Entrepreneurial Discovery', in *Prime Mover of Progress*, (Readings 23), London: Institute of Economic Affairs.

Kirzner, I.M. (1981), 'The "Austrian" Perspective on the Crisis', in D. Bell and I. Kristol (1981).

Kirzner, I.M. (ed.) (1982), *Method, Process, and Austrian Economics*, Lexington Massachusetts: Lexington Books.

Kirzner, I.M. (1982a), 'Uncertainty, Discovery, and Human Action: A Study of the Entrepreneurial Profile in the Misesian System', in Kirzner (1982).

Kirzner, I.M. (ed.) (1986), *Subjectivism, Intelligibiity and Economic Understanding*, London: Macmillan Press.

Knight, F.H. (1941), 'Professor Mises and the theory of capital', *Economica*, (8), November.

Kuhn, T.S. (1967), *The Structure of Scientific Revolutions*, Chicago: University of Chicago Press.

Lachmann, L.M. (1940), 'A Reconsideration of the Austrian Theory of Industrial Fluctuations', in Lachmann (1977).

Lachmann, L.M. (1947), 'Complementarity and Substitution in the Theory of Capital', in Lachmann (1977).

Lachmann, L.M. (1956/1978), *Capital and its Structure*, Kansas City: Sheed Andrews and McMeel.

Lachmann, L.M. (1966), 'Model Constructions and the Market Economy', in Lachmann (1977).

Lachmann, L.M. (1976), 'On the Central Concept of Austrian Economics: Market Process', in Dolan (1976).

Lachmann, L.M. (1976a), 'From Mises to Shackle: An Essay on Austrian Economics and the Kaleidic Society', *Journal of Economic Literature*, (14), March, 54–61.

Lachmann, L.M. (1977), *Capital, Expectations, and the Market Process*, Kansas City: Sheed Andrews and McMeel.

Lachmann, L.M. (1986), 'Austrian Economics under Fire: The Hayek-Sraffa Duel in Retrospect', in Grassl and Smith (1986).

Lange, O. (1938), 'On the Economic Theory of Socialism', in Lippincott (1938/1964).

Lavoie, D. (1981), 'A Critique of the Standard Account of the Socialist Calculation Debate', *The Journal of Libertarian Studies*, 41–87.

Lavoie, D. (1985), *Rivalry and Central Planning*, Cambridge: Cambridge University Press.

Le Grand, J. and Estrin, S. (eds) (1989), *Market Socialism*, Oxford: Clarendon Press.

Lerner, A.P. (1934–5), 'Economic Theory and Socialist Economy', *Review of Economic Studies*, **II**, 51–61.

Lerner, A.P. (1937), 'Statics and Dynamics in Socialist Economics', *Economic Journal*, **xlvii**, (186), June, 253–70.

Leube, K.R. and Zlabinger, A.H. (eds) (1984), *The Political Economy of Freedom: Essays in Honor of F.A. Hayek*, Munich: Philosophia Verlag.

Levitas, R. (ed.) (1986), *The Ideology of the New Right*, Cambridge: Polity Press.

Lippincott, B.E. (ed.) (1938/1964), *On the Economic Theory of Socialism*, New York: McGraw Hill.

Littlechild, S.C. (1982), 'Equilibrium and the Market Process', in Kirzner (1982).

Loasby, B.J. (1982), 'Economics of Dispersed and Incomplete Information', in Kirzner (1982).

Machlup, F. (1974), 'Hayek's Contribution to Economics', in Machlup (1977).

Machlup, F. (ed.) (1977), *Essays on Hayek*, London: Routledge & Kegan Paul.

McNulty, P.J. (1967), 'A Note on the History of Perfect Competition', *Journal of Political Economy*, **75**, August, 395–9.

McNulty, P.J. (1968), 'Economic Theory and the Meaning of Competition', *Quarterly Journal of Economics*, **82**, November, 639–56.

Macpherson, C.B. (1977), *The Life and Times of Liberal Democracy*, Oxford: Oxford University Press.

Marx, K. (1974), *Capital*, London: Lawrence and Wishart.

Mason, E.S. (1967), *Economic Concentration and the Monopoly Problem*, Cambridge: Harvard University Press.

Menger, C. (1981), *Principles of Economics*, New York: New York University Press.

Menger, C. (1985), *Investigations into the Method of the Social Sciences*, New York: New York University Press.

Mill, J.S. (1864), *Principles of Political Economy*, New York: D. Appleton.

Milne, S. (1987), 'The Crisis of the Dismal Science', *The Guardian*, 12, 13, 14 January.

Mises, L. von (1912/1934), *The Theory of Money and Credit*, London: Jonathan Cape.

Mises, L. von (1920), 'Economic Calculation in the Socialist Commonwealth', in Hayek (1935/1975).

Mises, L. von (1922/1981), *Socialism*, Indianapolis: Liberty Classics.

Mises, L. von (1927/1985), *Liberalism*, San Francisco: Cobden Press.

Mises, L. von (1928), 'Monetary Stabilization and Cyclical Policy', in Mises (1978).

Mises, L. von (1946), 'The Trade Cycle and Credit Expansion: The Economic Consequences of Cheap Money', in von Mises (1978).

Mises, L. von (1949), *Human Action: A Treatise on Economics*, New Haven: Yale University Press.

Mises, L. von (1976), *Epistemological Problems of Economics*, New York: New York University Press.

Mises, L. von (1978), *On the Manipulation of Money and Credit*, New York: Free Market Books.

Moss, L.S. (1976), 'The Monetary Economics of Ludwig von Mises', in Moss (1976a).

Moss, L.S. (ed.) (1976a), *The Economics of Ludwig von Mises: Toward a Critical Reappraisal*, Kansas City: Sheed and Ward Inc.

Murrell, P. (1983), 'Did the Theory of Market Socialism Answer the Challenge of Ludwig von Mises? A Reinterpretation of the Socialist Controversy', *History of Political Economy*, **15**, 92–105.

Muth, J.F. (1961), 'Rational Expectations and the Theory of Price Movements', *Econometrica*, (29), 315–35.

Niskanen, W.A. (1968), 'The Peculiar Economics of Bureaucracy', *American Economic Review*, **58**, 293–305.

Nove, A. (1983), *The Economics of Feasible Socialism*, London: George Allen & Unwin.

O'Driscoll, G.P. Jr (1977), *Economics as a Coordination Problem: The Contributions of F.A. Hayek*, Kansas City: Sheed Andrews and McMeel.

O'Driscoll, G.P. Jr (1978), 'Spontaneous Order and the Coordination of Economic Activities', in Spadaro (1978).

O'Driscoll, G.P. Jr (1982), 'Monopoly in Theory and Practice', in Kirzner (1982).

O'Driscoll, G.P. Jr and Rizzo, M.J. (1985), *The Economics of Time and Ignorance*, Oxford: Blackwell.

O'Driscoll, G.P. Jr and Shenoy, S.R. (1976), 'Inflation, Recession and Stagflation', in Dolan (1976).

Pasour, E.C. Jr (1982), 'Monopoly Theory and Practice – Some Subjectivist Implications', in Kirzner (1982).

Pigou, A.C. (1932), *The Economics of Welfare*, 4th ed., London: Macmillan.

Plant, R. (1984), *Equality, Markets and the State*, London Fabian Society Tract 494.

Polanyi, K. (1957), *The Great Transformation: The Political and Economic Origins of our Time*, Boston: Beacon Press.

Reekie, W.D. (1984), *Markets, Entrepreneurs and Liberty: An Austrian View of Capitalism*, Brighton: Wheatsheaf Books.

Robbins, L. (1962), *An Essay on the Nature and Significance of Economic Science*, London: Macmillan.

Robinson, J. (1933/1979), *The Economics of Imperfect Competition*, London: Macmillan.

Robinson, J. (1978), 'History Versus Equilibrium', in *Contributions to Modern Economics*, Oxford: Basil Blackwell.

Rothbard, M.N. (1962), *Man, Economy and State*, Princeton NJ: Van Nostrand.

Rothbard, M.N. (1976), 'Praxeology: The Methodology of Austrian Economics', in Dolan (1976).

Rothbard, M.N. (1976a), 'The Austrian Theory of Money', in Dolan (1976).

Rothbard, M.N. (1976b), 'Ludwig von Mises and Economic Calculation under Socialism', in Moss (1976).

Rothbard, M.N. (1978), 'Austrian Definitions of the Supply of Money', in Spadaro (1978).

Schumpeter, J.A. (1954), *History of Economic Analysis*, London: George Allen & Unwin.

Semmler, W. (1982), 'Theories of Competition and Monopoly', *Capital and Class*, (18), Winter, 91–116.

Semmler, W. (1983), 'Competition, Monopoly, and Differentials of Profit Rates: A Reply', *Review of Radical Political Economics*, **15**, (4), 92–9.

Shackleton, J.R. and Locksley, G. (eds) (1981), *Twelve Contemporary Economists*, London: Macmillan.

Shand, A.H. (1984), *The Capitalist Alternative: An Introduction to Neo-Austrian Economics*, Brighton: Wheatsheaf.

Simons, H.C. (1948), *Economic Policy for a Free Society*, Chicago: University of Chicago Press.

Smith, B. (1986), 'Austrian Economics and Austrian Philosophy', in Grassl and Smith (1986).

Spadaro, L.M. (ed.) (1978), *New Directions in Austrian Economics*, Kansas City: Sheed Andrews and McMeel.

Sraffa, P. (1932), 'Dr. Hayek on Money and Capital', *Economic Journal*, **42**, March, 42–53.

Sraffa, P. (1932a), 'A Rejoinder', *Economic Journal*, **42**, June, 249–51.

Stigler, G.J. (1941), *Production and Distribution Theories*, New York: Macmillan.

Stigler, G.J. (1957), 'Perfect Competition, Historically Contemplated', *Journal of Political Economy*, **lxv**, February.

Stigler, G.J. (1961), 'The Economics of Information', *Journal of Political Economy*, **lxix**, June, 213–25.

Streissler, E. (1973), 'To What Extent was the Austrian School Marginalist?', in Collison Black *et al.* (1973).

Taylor, F.M. (1928), 'The Guidance of Production in a Socialist State', in Lippincott (1938/1964).

Tomlinson, J. (1990), *Hayek and the Market*, London: Pluto Press.

Vaughn, K.I. (1980), 'Economic Calculation under Socialism: The Austrian Contribution', *Economic Inquiry*, **xviii**, October.

Walras, L. (1965), *Correspondence of Leon Walras and Related Papers, ed. W. Jaffe*, vol. II, Amsterdam: North Holland.

Walras, L. (1984), *Elements of Pure Economics*, Philadelphia: Orion Editions.

Wegehenkel, L. (1984), 'Property Rights and Entrepreneurial Motivation', in Leube and Zlabinger (1984).

White, L.H. (1986), 'A Subjectivist Perspective on the Definition and Identification of Money', in Kirzner (1986).

Index